KILLING THE LIEUTENANT

Killing the Lieutenant published by:
WILDBLUE PRESS
P.O. Box 102440
Denver, Colorado 80250

Publisher Disclaimer: Any opinions, statements of fact or fiction, descriptions, dialogue, and citations found in this book were provided by the author, and are solely those of the author. The publisher makes no claim as to their veracity or accuracy, and assumes no liability for the content.

Copyright 2026 by Raul J. Diaz and Sean Oliver

All rights reserved. No part of this book may be reproduced in any form or by any means without the prior written consent of the Publisher, excepting brief quotes used in reviews.

WILDBLUE PRESS is registered at the U.S. Patent and Trademark Offices.

ISBN 978-1-970361-23-0 Hardcover
ISBN 978-1-970361-24-7 Trade Paperback
ISBN 978-1-970361-22-3 eBook

Cover design © 2026 WildBlue Press. All rights reserved.

Interior Formatting and Book Cover Design by Elijah Toten
www.totencreative.com

KILLING THE LIEUTENANT

FIGHTING MIAMI'S COCAINE WARS, HUNTING GRISELDA BLANCO, AND MY FIGHT TO STAY ALIVE

LT. RAUL J. DIAZ AND SEAN OLIVER

WILDBLUE
PRESS

WildBluePress.com

ALSO BY SEAN OLIVER

Nonfiction

Monkey Morales

Insane Clown Posse: Unaccepted, Vol. I—The Wrestling

Tod is God

The Business of Kayfabe

Fathers' Blood

Kayfabe

Fiction

Transfer

The Consultant

Sophie's Journal

*For Miguel. Never has anyone made the world
a better place in a shorter amount of time.*

—RD

For Nicole. Everything.

—SO

CONTENTS

FOREWORD

When I came to Miami in 1976 to work as a television news reporter, I had a grandiose time-specific plan. I would stay in Miami for no more than five years and then seek a more "adult-level" job elsewhere in journalism. I dreamed of eventually covering the White House or Congress, or maybe working for big stations in New York or Los Angeles. But, in 1980, four years into my five-year plan, chaos and crime struck Miami so hard that everything around us seemed to either collapse or explode. The city's history was immediately rewritten, lives changed dramatically, and my own planned exodus went on permanent hold as Miami became the most dramatic news town in America.

On the scene, in the middle of it all, was a man I would soon meet and cover in the streets: Lieutenant Raul Diaz of the Miami-Dade County Police Department. Even before 1980 arrived, he could see that Miami was already on fire. In July of 1979, a lethal broad-daylight shootout erupted at the busy Dadeland Mall shopping center involving drug traffickers and a homemade armored truck dubbed the "war wagon." After seeing the victims and hundreds of shell casings, Diaz and other officials realized Miami was now in the throes of a vicious Colombian cocaine war.

By the next year, Miami had careened out of control as four cataclysmic events hit town at virtually the same time, drawing Diaz deeper into the maelstrom. The Cocaine

Cowboys, as they came to be known, were in full battle mode, flooding South Florida with tons of illegal drugs and killing each other in businesses and nice neighborhoods, and on highways and city streets without concern for innocent bystanders.

Also in 1980, the Mariel boatlift brought 125,000 Cuban refugees to South Florida, some of whom had come from Fidel Castro's prisons and mental institutions. Thousands of desperate Haitians were arriving, too, often in rickety sailboats with countless lives lost at sea. In the spring of that year, a bloody race riot broke out after a jury acquitted police officers of charges stemming from the beating death of a black motorcyclist, Arthur McDuffie. Eighteen people were killed during the horrific first day of violence.

Lt. Diaz was always known for being streetwise and charismatic, with an uncanny ability to develop informants and target suspects. He seemed to know everyone and preferred being on the scene rather than in the office, even after he formed and ran CENTAC-26, an effective multi-agency task force targeting the traffickers. Diaz took time to share his knowledge for our WPLG television news series called "Colombian Drug Wars," and put us in touch with his computer crime analyst and the rest of the team. He also took us on nighttime raids and, through our camera, tried to convince Miami—and Washington—to wake up and realize the skyrocketing murder rate was the result of a foreign criminal invasion that would only get worse if it wasn't tackled aggressively. He was also the first to tell us about his most dramatic nemesis: the flamboyant and murderous Colombian trafficker, Griselda Blanco.

What you are about to read in the pages ahead is different than the flood of newspaper articles, magazine features, books, movies, documentaries, crime series, and TV shows devoted to the "Paradise Lost" side of Miami in its most difficult time. Most of the authors of those stories were great reporters and writers, but few were actual participants in events they covered. *Killing The Lieutenant*, on the other hand, is told by a man who was right there, deeply involved, surrounded by the daily chaos—an integral part of the story himself.

Diaz's story is also different because it has a dark personal side that is by no means pretty or heroic. A life under pressure, hanging out in bars and clubs, sometimes with shady characters at all hours of the night, took a devastating toll on his life physically, emotionally, and in his marriage and family. Years later, Diaz now takes responsibility and talks about it openly. He was also the subject of several investigations which sidelined his work against the traffickers and eventually ended his career—in effect, killing the lieutenant—even though no charges were ever filed. Diaz reflects on that, too, and shares his thoughts on why it happened.

Since his arrival in Miami as a teenager in 1961 aboard a Pedro Pan refugee flight from Cuba after the revolution, Diaz has seen Miami as few others would ever experience it: from the anti-Castro exile bombers, to the CIA plotters, to the Watergate burglars, to the secretive Colombian assassins whose confusing cases he initially described not as "whodunnits", but as "who-is-its". His life has been complicated, with lots of angles. And it's quite a story!

Mark Potter

NBC News correspondent, former correspondent at CNN and ABC News

INTRODUCTION

If this son of a bitch gets away, it's gonna be my ass.

We finally had Rafael Leon Rodriguez stopped on the road, right across from the Burger King loaded with students from Coral Gables High School. It was broad daylight; the road was dense with midday traffic and businesses were full, with pedestrians obliviously strolling down LeJeune Rd. None of them had any idea that the car that came to a sudden stop in the middle of the street was carrying one of the most dangerous men in Miami, wanted for murders there, as well as in New York, Bolivia, and Colombia.

Rodriguez, known as Amilcar on the streets, was number one on the most-wanted list of my newly formed multi-agency task force, CENTAC-26. We'd just gone operational that month, December 1981, and within a couple of weeks our top draft pick was right in front of us, sitting in the car with his bodyguard. My team radioed me.

"What should we do?"

They were waiting on my call, and in truth, all eyes had been on me since I'd gotten the task force greenlit by our partners in the Drug Enforcement Administration (DEA). There's a fair amount of jealousy in law enforcement as it is, and now the most elite squad in any department—the homicide unit—had an even more elite squad within it. Imagine the New York Yankees creating a small faction of their players regarded as the Super Yankees, or something.

That would certainly piss off everyone else wearing the pinstripes.

Dead bodies had been piling up in Miami for a couple of years thanks to what had become known as the Cocaine Wars. A new breed of Cuban criminals had been unleashed by Fidel Castro, who was more than happy to open the doors of his prisons and mental asylums as the US pledged to welcome any refugees who could get there from Mariel Harbor. Couple that with the ruthlessness of the Colombian cartels who had taken a foothold in the coke trade, and you had a tinder box of violence in South Florida.

Miami wasn't the most violent city in the US, until it was. Once a vacation mainstay of the East Coast, the city was now spoken about in cautious tones. The style of carnage in broad daylight was media fodder, and the terror it elicited was constant. The headlines dripped crimson: the gunmen who entered the crowded Cozzoli's Pizza and opened fire on two men, killing one, as the restaurant full of kids looked on; the shooting victim's corpse that washed up on the shore off Rickenbacker Causeway; the man beaten to death at the produce market.

That was all on the same day.

Much of the chaos could be attributed to the directives of one woman named Griselda Blanco, in whose swamp of shit I'd been swimming since I first heard the name in July of 1979. She was responsible for countless murders in just those few years and had pumped a fortune in cocaine into the streets and nostrils of America. Information about the networks of these new smugglers and assassins needed to be corralled into a more centralized system, within which law enforcement across multiple cities and agencies could instantly have access to names, ballistics, and modus operandi of nomadic international offenders. In essence, I saw the CENTAC-26 task force as a way to shrink their networks, and inflate ours. This is how we'd get them, and Lord knows we needed to do something to get an edge.

Griselda Blanco and her kingpin compadres had us chasing our tails.

Amilcar and his driver remained in the car, parked amidst the Coral Gables citizens, while my team sat poised to act on my word. I couldn't take any chances; it was odd that Amilcar and his partner had stopped their car in the middle of traffic. I figured we'd been made. We'd been on him all day with ten cars and a plane, starting at the swanky Mutiny Hotel in Coconut Grove, and we'd already lost him once. Yeah—we had a fucking *plane* and we still lost this guy.

I wasn't going to let him get away again. CENTAC-26's first at-bat wasn't going to be a strikeout; I didn't hesitate when my team asked what they should do.

"Take him down," I replied.

We pulled up behind Amilcar's vehicle as another police car swung around the front, blocking them in.

This was it—CENTAC-26's first arrest, and the highest profile one we could make. A flood of invincibility infuses anyone who takes a risk that pays off, whether calling for that suicide squeeze at the plate, or the Hail Mary pass in the fourth quarter. That decision is sliding all your chips into the center of the table because you know you have the other guy beat.

But more than that—it's the kind of moxie needed for overcoming steep odds since being placed on an airplane as a kid and shipped off to a new land without parents. It's hitting the streets as the head of gang in high school, then hitting those same streets as a police officer and climbing the ranks of one of the most honorable professions in the world.

That profession itself presented its own share of challenges to overcome. I'd endured supervisors determined to keep me down and see me fail, and I watched officers I'd been close to fail themselves and become embroiled in illegal activities. I'd been questioned, doubted, targeted, and there I sat, ready to pull up on the scene that would undoubtedly slay those dragons and validate CENTAC-26, and vindicate *me*.

I felt all of that as I threw the car in park, ready to triumphantly slap cuffs on CENTAC-26's most wanted. That's when the suspects started firing on us, blasting right through the windshield of their car with reckless abandon.

I'm here recounting that story, so we obviously won that battle. But looking back at that day and others, I have to wonder if I was just lucky, or very hard to kill.

CHAPTER ONE

OUT OF CUBA

Miguel is going to crack.

I could see it in my kid brother's eyes; he was scared, and who wouldn't be while being interrogated by two Cuban military G2 agents? We knew the kinds of things they'd be asking as we tried to leave the country. We'd prepared for this, knew what to say, but the real game was different than practice.

Hang on, bro.

I could tell he was nervous. I knew him better than anyone in the world, and this was a hell of a lot to ask of a six-year-old. I was sure *twenty*-six-year-olds folded to Castro's goons all the time. And I doubted those people had contraband sewn into the seams of their jackets like we did.

The questions kept coming.

"How long will you be out of Cuba?"

Miguel was still clammed up.

I spoke. "We'll be with our aunt until the end of the summer."

"Where is she?"

"Florida."

This was the story our parents had told us to use. It seemed to work because the agents were quiet now. Then they looked over at my brother, a touch of concern on their faces—his nose was bleeding. Poor little guy was so freaked out he'd actually gotten a nosebleed from the stress. But he did his damn job; he didn't say a word to these pricks and let his big brother do the talking. I was thirteen, and the agents were directing most of the questions to me anyway. I told Miguel to tilt his head back and pinch the bridge of his nose.

And just like that, we were led out of that back room at Rancho Boyeros Airport in Havana, and returned to the holding area we'd been plucked from for interrogation. There, we were deposited in the glass enclosure called *la pecera*, the fishbowl, without their ever having found what was in our jackets—some cash and saints dangling from gold chains that my mom had sewn in.

I caught a glimpse of her with my dad as they stood on the outside, cordoned off from those that were heading out of Cuba. She looked relieved now that Miguel and I were returned to the fishbowl. Previously she'd been crying, my father consoling her as she watched the agents pulling travelers off the line.

Imagine the conflicted feelings as a parent, placing your two children on a plane to a new country, hoping and praying they'd arrive safely and fare well until you joined them, if you even could. That risk, taken by thousands of parents, was a commentary on Fidel Castro's destructive effect on the people of Cuba.

—

My brother and I landed at Miami International Airport on July 25, 1961 in the country that would serve as our refuge. We were granted entry under the country's 1960 government program Operation Pedro Pan, wherein children were granted passage on a special visa waiver. All they had to do was get there, which wasn't an easy task, hence the lies about our trip that Miguel and I told the agents. In the end, more than 14,000 children between the ages of four and sixteen would come to the United States in the operation's two years.

Our trip had been arranged by Jose Elias de la Torriente, a wealthy landowner in Cuba and close family friend. I would run into Torriente years later, in 1974, though under less auspicious circumstances.

The Catholic Archdiocese of Miami processed the Pedro Pan escapees and sought to place the unaccompanied children into foster care if they had nowhere to go. The only true part of my tale to Cuban agents was my having an aunt and uncle in Miami. My *Tía* Lala and *Tío* Jose lived in Westchester, and my brother and I joined them there, where we lived with their two children, my cousins Mayra and Jose Jr. A large population of early arrivals from Cuba landed in the Westchester section of Miami.

It turned out we had more family near us. My uncle's sister Martha was just three blocks away, having arrived here shortly before her husband Domingo Trueba's death in Cuba earlier that year. He was working as a CIA operative providing information to the US who would assist in the Bay of Pigs invasion. His role was uncovered when Castro's G2 secret police agents raided a meeting house, and he was put on the wall beside his fellow operatives and executed. This was the reality Cubans were facing back home.

Tío Jose dropped $2.50 and bought me a used bicycle that I would ride with my brother to fish at Maule Lake near the airport. We'd catch bream and, if we were lucky, an occasional bass. Unfortunately, proper fishing tackle was well outside my aunt and uncle's budget, so Miguel and I had to find creative ways to acquire it—namely, his watching as look-out while I ripped off the Woolworth's five and dime. I loved fishing, and I soon caught my first saltwater fish in the US—prophetically enough, a barracuda I snagged from Biscayne Bay in Matheson Hammock County Park.

I foolishly left my bike outside overnight, and you don't have to be Sherlock Holmes to figure out how that went in Miami. As heartbreaking as that was for me, I knew it would hurt Tío more when he learned of the theft. He and Lala were struggling as it was, and they'd added two mouths to their table by taking in me and my brother. My uncle saved money for that bike, and I basically gave it away.

"You're going to learn the value of a dollar now," he told me.

Tío operated a Red and White auto service station on NW 17th Ave. and 18th St., so I was soon off to work with him. He paid me a little money for my time each day, and I had my first job. I worked my ass off there. On my first two days I'd scaled the ladder a dozen times, repeatedly changing the numbers displaying the price of gas per gallon. It seemed stupid, but when I asked, he told me we were in the middle of a "gas war." I noticed he was being called to the phone several times a day where he'd be told what amount to adjust the price to.

A two-story house across from the gas station caught my attention. It seemed there was always traffic going in and out, mostly young and middle-aged Cuban men. I asked my uncle what was going on there.

"Don't ask about that," he said, so I dropped it for the time being.

My parents finally arrived from Cuba in November 1961 and a month later we moved from Lala and Jose's to our own apartment on 82nd St. in Miami Beach. My dad started working at Tío's gas station with us, and my curiosity about the house across the street was further piqued when the guys that hung out there began coming to the station to talk with my dad. It didn't seem like business; they were always laughing and hugging when greeting him. One day, I ignored Tío's dictate when he was out of eyesight.

"Papi, who are all those men?"

"My students from Cuba," he said. Many also played baseball for him when he coached in Cuba, he told me. That seemed logical to me, but why was Tío being so secretive? It seemed silly, until years later I learned what a CIA "safe house" was. Young Cuban men were being groomed to carry out clandestine missions against Castro for our government. The Bay of Pigs debacle hadn't ended our planned offensives against the communist threat just south of us. The US just needed to better shroud their missions in darkness.

One day, my father took all of us to Camp Matecumbe, where all the Pedro Pan kids stopped on their way to being placed in foster homes all over the country. We were going to visit Carlos Capote, a seven-year-old boy who had been my father's student in Cuba and had arrived in the US without any relatives here. Carlos was about to be sent somewhere in the country, to one of the many foster homes waiting for Pedro Pan kids. All of us felt badly about Carlito's fate when he told us, and I overheard my parents having a conversation about him. The only thing that really stuck out was my mother's final proclamation to my dad.

"Where there's food for four, five can eat," she said. And just like that, Miguel and I had another brother. Carlos was about the same age as Miguel, so they became very close.

It's hard to illustrate just how much fear the Castro regime had instilled in our people. Simply getting out of Cuba may have kept the refugees safe, but so many had been forever damaged as people. Shortly after arriving in the US, my mother took me and Miguel to Sears department store on Biscayne Blvd. downtown. We were messing around while my mom shopped and I was cracking Miguel up by pretending to shake a mannequin's outstretched hand. Pretty hilarious until the damn thing tipped off the base and crashed face-first onto the tile floor and its head rolled down the aisle. Miguel fell into outright hysterics, laughing until he couldn't breathe at the public decapitation.

My mother, though, was not at all amused. I expected she'd be pissed, but she began sobbing, nearly becoming hysterical. It wasn't that big of a deal to us, but my brother and I became more concerned as it seemed she might have a breakdown.

Through her tears she told us we might be arrested by agents of the state.

"It was an accident," I told her. "Nothing is going to happen."

Of course it didn't, and she eventually calmed down and realized this country was different than Cuba. But the degree to which Castro had broken citizens' spirits was significant and tragic. It has influenced how Cubans feel toward anything resembling communism even today. They fight like hell against it, even here, because it was a fight they lost at home. And so many had paid with their lives.

—

"What do you call *this*?"

I was kind of in shock looking at the Black lady staring down at me as she spoke. Don't get me wrong—the lunch ladies were all very nice, especially when they snuck us extra Jell-O if my friends and I asked.

I guess I just didn't expect this one to reach down and grab my crotch.

I was thirteen and it was rather shocking, but I came to find out this was nothing out of the ordinary at Nautilus Junior High. Apparently, this woman did it to all the Cuban boys there, and it had earned her the nickname *Pinga*, which meant dick. It didn't seem to be a secret; my friends would openly call out to her from down the lunch line.

"Hey *Pinga*, we need more milk here."

"Excuse me, *Pinga*, can I have a straw?"

She wasn't fazed; she just gave the frigging straw. I guess times were different.

Though I should've been in ninth grade, I was placed in eighth due to their determination that my English was subpar, despite my having studied it every year at school in Cuba. Though it was my best subject, the powers that be at Nautilus thought I was behind.

Besides my grammar class, I was also excelling at fucking off in my spare time. Our apartment had a beautiful mango tree in the courtyard that my brother and I used to grab fruit from. The building owner's ancient father would hobble around the thing throughout the day looking for ripe fruit to pick. One day, my brother and I took a rock-hard, unripened green mango and painted it bright yellow and red, then laid it back on a branch. It looked delicious up there, and my brother and I crowded at the bathroom window and waited. Sure enough, the old man came shuffling out and was stopped in his tracks by what seemed the most beautiful mango ever grown. He whacked the branch with his stick and caught mine and Miguel's artificially engineered treat. We laughed our asses off and went about the day, our important work for the afternoon having been completed.

We asked about the old man after not seeing him for a while.

"He died," my mother said.

Holy shit—the green mango! We were really screwed now. American cops might not give a shit about knocking off a mannequin's head, but poisoning an old man was surely different. My brother and I were scared shitless and spent many a sleepless night suspecting we were responsible for taking a life. We couldn't take it anymore and Miguel and I confessed to our parents. Our mother told us he'd died from heart failure—he was like a thousand, for Christ's sake— but Miguel and I still weren't convinced the mango hadn't exacerbated his condition.

My friends and I also made an exciting pastime of watching the apartment building across from mine. Well, not so much the building as the glass door belonging to the beautiful American woman who would undress with the shades open. We were very secretive about it at first, hiding and pretending not to look. But it soon became obvious that she was deliberately positioning herself in front of the door and opening the shades. It got to the point where as soon as we saw her come home, we'd grab folding chairs and set them up outside to watch. When our being even *that* obvious failed to make her cover up, we began to cheer during the undressing. The only one who got pissed was my father, who quickly shut it down when he discovered us.

Within a year of coming here, I met Juan "Pipo" Vila who'd go on to become my closest friend. Fortunately for him, and for me, Pipo wasn't above some of the shenanigans I found to be a fine pastime. One afternoon, me, Pipo, and another friend were walking along Crespi Blvd. where we saw a couple of kids fishing with their grandfather across the street. We hung back and watched them catch a few fish, and as the sun began to set, they wrapped up and headed home for dinner. Their grandpa leaned the rods against the fence and placed the tackle box beside them. Once he sauntered off, my crew and I all got the same idea.

We'd seen the house they entered across the street, and we crept over and watched through the window as they sat down to dinner. It was now fully dark outside; the time was perfect.

We rushed back across the street and our friend scaled the fence and passed the rods and tackle box to Pipo and me. I'd always heard that to be a successful thief you just need a good fence. Sorry; I couldn't resist. Anyhow, humor aside, those rods and that tackle box probably kept Pipo and me out of a lot of trouble over the years.

My career in larceny continued when we realized stores would pay for empty containers—as much as twenty cents for a large seltzer bottle. Luckily for my crew, we lived in Miami Beach, the seltzer consumption capital of the world due to the abundant, aging Jewish population. In no time, we'd done enough reconnaissance to know which houses put out the greatest number of bottles, and we went down the line at night, loading a suitcase with bottles. We snatched enough to make five bucks each per night. Considering the bus cost a nickel with a student ID, the double feature at the Cameo Theater was a quarter, and two hot dogs and a soda cost fifty cents, our haul was a fortune.

Man, we had fun. We really were good kids, never out to hurt anyone; we were just bored and craved some adventure. We messed with each other a lot too. A new arrival named Emilio started hanging with us and his English was the shits. One afternoon he needed a haircut and asked our friend Carlos Arguelles how to say it in English as they walked toward the barber. So Carlos, naturally, was very helpful.

"Say, 'crew cut,'" he told Emilio.

"Crew?"

"Listen…'crew cut.'"

Emilio sat in the chair and did as we'd instructed, then watched in abject horror as the barber sheared a channel through his mop.

"No!" Emilio exclaimed. "I say 'crew cut.'"

"Yes," the barber said, "crew cut," then went about shaving this poor bastard's head like a sheep.

The best part of my time at Nautilus was my finding a mentor in Coach Kouchalakos. He reminded me of my dad, not just because he was a Phys. Ed coach, but more in the way that he was always strict, but fair. If you went to Coach K. with a problem, he always made time to talk with you. He was a special guy, and I'd visit him a couple of times a year after I left school and into my adulthood. I ran into him in 1980 at Polo Park, where he was instructing his class at the pull-up bars. I wanted to let him know I'd just been promoted to lieutenant, so I approached, and he didn't miss a beat.

"Diaz," he said, "you've put on weight. Give me twenty." He pointed at the bar and I accepted the challenge, barely passing the test. We talked for a long time that afternoon.

—

On November 22, 1963, President John F. Kennedy and I, over a thousand miles apart, each had a rifle pointed at us. The result of his was fatal. Mine, not so much. Though, he was connected to my incident.

I'd just started at Miami Beach Senior High that year and the students were sent home early on the afternoon of Kennedy's assassination. I went with my friends Emilio (his hair fully grown back), his offender Carlos, Emilio's brother Jose, another kid named Jose, and Pipo to Crespi Park to shoot hoops that day and take advantage of the extended afternoon of free time. We were having fun, laughing and playing as usual, when a man darted out of a house across the street. He yelled, lambasting us from his porch for carrying on when the President of the United States had just been assassinated.

I need to pause here and relay the climate of 1963 in the Cuban community. Many Cubans felt abandoned by the Kennedy administration after the US's failure to support the Cuban exiles they'd sent to attack Castro's army at the Bay of Pigs. Jose and Carlos's dad had been on that mission and was captured and imprisoned by Castro, so Carlos felt compelled to answer the man on behalf of his dad.

"Fuck Kennedy, and fuck you!"

The man went back into the house and we went back to our game. Emilio took a long shot that we watched heading right for the hoop, only to have our attention broken by the sound of a round being racked in the chamber. We looked across the street at the angry patriot on his porch, aiming a rifle at us. We hauled ass and jumped the fence before Emilio's shot even hit the basket.

Many years later while walking our dog, I met that man at that same house and told him the story. He laughed and went into the house for a minute, then came back out with the rifle—a damn Daisy BB-gun. We should've finished the game.

My first job in the US, other than helping out Tío Miguel, was as a pool boy at the Casablanca and Delmonico hotels in Miami Beach. I would set up the pool area in the mornings, then clean up in the afternoons. My first bosses were Jack "Murph the Surf" Murphy and Roger Clark. I thought it curious that when the pools closed in the evening, they, along with a friend Allan Kuhn, would literally scale the walls of the Sherry Frontenac Hotel. They'd climb to the roof and then scale down again. I had no idea that they were training for their upcoming heist at New York City's Museum of Natural History, wherein they rappelled into the gem room and made off with the priceless Star of India sapphire. I wonder if the plan was hatched while I obliviously picked up towels around them.

In 1964, me and a group of friends founded "The Lords," a fraternity of sorts, though today it would more commonly be identified as a gang. There were small groups like ours being formed by young Cuban men all over Miami, many for protection from existing gangs in the neighborhoods where they lived. I was elected the first president of the Lords, the first group of its kind to accept Jewish and other non-Cuban kids.

High school wasn't going along as swimmingly. I was placed in a French language class without my request or approval, and my grades were shitty. I probably could've learned another language if I'd applied myself, but I had Pipo and the other guys in our crew in that class with me. We messed around so much we didn't have a prayer of passing Madame Rick's class. We were all in the same boat, and Pipo wasn't the type to sit back and let fate dictate.

After finishing our French final exam, Pipo stopped me as I was about to exit the class.

"Wait for everyone to leave," he said. I sat back with him until we were alone with the small, middle-aged Mme. Ricks. He took my test from my hand, walked to her, and stood at her podium. He smacked it, and she popped to attention.

He glared at her. "You live across the street from North Shore Park with your two children. You drive a brown Nash Rambler station wagon, and if you don't pass Raul and me, I will burn you and your children inside the car."

Mme. Ricks recoiled, breathing heavily as the blood rushed from her face. I was concerned, but knew I had to remain stoic beside the menacing Pipo. Too late to turn back now.

Our teacher began gagging, leaning over like she was about to vomit. She was full on hyperventilating now.

"Let's go," Pipo said and strolled from the room.

We are definitely going to jail, was all that ran through my head repeatedly as I walked beside him. How the hell was he so calm?

When we were alone in the hallway, our sweet French teacher choking behind us, Pipo turned to me.

"We're passing French class," he said with a smirk.

And we did.

Bobby Gonzalez was another Lord that I'd become close with. His family had come here before the Castro exiles, and he grew up in Miami. Though the Lords was mostly a Miami Beach crew, we did take a couple of guys from the mainland to grow our group, and he was one of them. He was always hanging around me; my mother cooked for him and even washed his damn clothes.

Did this motherfucker just say that?

That's what I was thinking minutes after my English teacher, Mr. Hageman, just told a kid in class that he was yapping as loud "as a Cuban woman." Inspired by some laughter in the back of the room, our teacher went on to mock some other characteristics he felt exclusive to Cuban ladies.

The three Cuban girls beside me in class were less than amused. They turned to me expectantly, and as the only Cuban male in the room I felt a responsibility to raise my hand. He called on me.

"Mr. Hageman, you owe an apology."

"To whom?"

"Your Cuban students."

He didn't flinch.

"I have no intention to apologize to anybody," he said, closing out the issue. For him, anyway.

I was infuriated, so I gathered my books and started out of the classroom but was stopped at the door by Hageman.

"Where are you going?" he asked.

"I'm going to speak with Principal Moore."

"Sit down," he growled and slid over to block more of the doorway.

I shoved him out of the way and bolted from the class. I trotted down the hall as the possible ramifications for hitting a teacher flooded my head. I had to get to Principal Moore before Hageman did; I wanted him to hear my version first. I got there and was told to wait outside his office, where I watched Hageman stomp in and get his audience with the principal before me.

The three Cuban girls from class came into the office next and were directed to sit next to me and wait for Moore to call us in. When Hageman left, it was our turn. I went in first and told the principal what had happened. He called the girls in next, and their version of events corroborated mine. However, Mr. Moore said he'd need to call my parents because I had to be suspended. Great. This was my senior year and I was just two months from graduation. Would that even happen now? Details aside, I had just decked a teacher.

My father stormed into the building with the face only a coach on the way into the locker room after a hellacious loss could pull off—there was both a scolding and a lesson waiting for me. I stopped him before he made it to the office.

"Wait…you need to listen to these three girls before you meet with the principal."

They came over and told him what happened, and when we got into the principal's office my father listened to what Mr. Moore had to say. The principal said despite my believing I had justification, I still couldn't hit a teacher. He wasn't wrong, and my father didn't think he was either. But my dad did have one concern.

"When my son returns to school will he be placed in that man's class again?"

Mr. Moore explained it was too late in the year to transfer me to another class and I already had two study halls in my schedule. I had to return to Hageman's class. My father was silent, considering it all. He looked at me, then turned to Mr. Moore.

"I was a teacher in Cuba," he began, "and I would never say what that man did. I'm not going to allow that poor excuse for a teacher to educate my son one minute more. We'll find another school."

I was as much shocked as I was proud of my father as we stood and marched out. I was enrolled at Drexel Private Academy next, having left Miami Beach High with both my dignity and status as a rock star to three cute Cuban girls.

I'd had a few girlfriends to that point, starting back in Nautilus Junior High. One of them, Fran Belous, went on to become Vice Mayor of West Hollywood years later, though

I don't think my time with her served as inspiration for the accomplishment. I remained friendly with all my girlfriends well into adulthood.

My most serious relationship in high school came when I went roller skating at a local middle school and met Thania Amengual. She was beautiful and very shy, but once we started talking I learned both she and her sister were Pedro Pan kids too, just like me and Miguel. They'd had it a little rougher than us, having been sent to an orphanage in Colorado upon arriving here. Eventually, her mother got into the country and moved them to Miami Beach.

We started dating pretty quickly, always going out in large groups or accompanied by a chaperone. An old Cuban tradition required that young ladies going out with their boyfriends must be accompanied by adults. It was designed to protect the girl's virtue, though they should've found a more foolproof system. School ended at three o'clock, and all of our parents worked past five. That gave every high school student a two-hour window alone with their partners. So, given that schedule, none of us minded a chaperone hanging out with us later that night.

Thania and I kept going strong, and she'd apparently had big plans in mind. Unbeknownst to me, when I entered her school to skate that night, she'd turned to her friend Marlene with a proclamation: "I'm going to marry him."

—

THANIA: He came to the gym because there was a party, you know, and I was in like eighth or ninth grade. I was roller skating and he just came in and I did not know him. But I looked at him and said to my friend, "I'm going to marry him." And she looked at me and said, "Right, okay, whatever." Because I was fourteen and looked like a ten-year old. I was very skinny, with long hair. And we just said hello and goodbye and went our own ways, you know.

Well, I started dating him later, when I was fifteen or sixteen years old. My mother was not too thrilled, so I sort of did not tell her that we were dating. I was a child and Raul was eighteen.

—

The Lords fraternity was also going strong. We were having success raising funds with our Open House dances, wherein we'd rent the Miami Beach Fraternal Order of Police Hall on Alton Rd. and book a local band, often comprised of some Lords members. We offered refreshments and consistently packed two or three hundred people in there.

The FOP required us to hire an off-duty police officer for security at each event, and we always seemed to be assigned the same sergeant. We knew him from the city and he was a total asshole. When my friends and I would all hang out at Lum's Restaurant on Lincoln Rd. in several cars, he'd always stop us and demand five dollars from each car, purportedly for a "parade permit" since we'd all driven there in a group. It was horseshit and we all knew it, but that didn't stop him from doing it every time he recognized one of our cars, which was easy since we all had "Lords" on our rear windshields. He eventually started shaking us down whenever he saw one of us, parade or not. We decided we had to do something about that guy.

One night at a Lords dance, some of our members got into a scuffle and Sgt. Shithead ran over to break it up. When he did, everyone descended on him and mauled him. We'd staged the fake fight to draw him in, then left him roughed up, shirt torn, and stole his hat and badge. We were gone by the time his backup arrived. The prick never collected parade permit fees from us again, nor did he ever pick up another Lords dance as an off-duty job.

As in any profession, law enforcement has both heroes and those whose capes are a little dirtier. Heroes and villains, singularly colored through and through, only exist in movies. The off-duty sergeant robbing us was a pretty clear-cut case of abuse of power, but, in reality, the lines are often blurry. I had no idea while I was running dances for the youth gang in which I'd been elected president, but I was about to plunge into murky and dangerous waters where everybody's motives had to be questioned, no matter what cape they wore.

CHAPTER TWO

SEEING BLUE

Math was always my strongest subject, so I chose accounting as my major when I registered at Miami Dade Junior College. I was still president of The Lords, and in August 1967 a couple of members and I planned a road trip up the East Coast to New York City—a little "surfari," if you will. Three of us loaded our surf boards onto my parents' car and set out to drink up as much of the summer beach action as we could. One thing we hadn't planned on was the northeast's water temperatures. Holy shit—we were used to the bathwater in Florida all year, so when we dropped our boards in the water in Atlantic City, NJ, we were out of the Atlantic Ocean as fast as we'd jumped into it. What the hell? It was August, and it was only New Jersey. Had we missed the exit and landed in Montreal?

We didn't want to waste the trip, so we decided to regroup and get better prepared before trying out the waves again. We grabbed our wetsuits from my car, paid an older guy on the boardwalk to buy us a bottle of Bacardi from the liquor store, and headed back to the beach. When we were suited up and sufficiently warmed by the beverage, we hit the surf again with much more success. We spent the whole day at the beach and caught a showing of *Endless Summer* in the theater at the Steel Pier.

Back home in Miami, the underworld had been experiencing a rash of bombings in what newspapers were calling the "bookie wars." Bombings in Miami's Cuban community were nothing new. When it was clear the US had moved on from its promise to cripple Castro with the use of more than a thousand CIA-trained Cuban mercenaries, many of those exiles formed bombing groups in Miami. They took out warehouses shipping to Cuba, freighters, travel agencies handling tourism there, embassies, consulates of nations deemed to be too friendly with Cuba, and more. So many rogue bombing groups had popped up in the mid-1960s that *The Miami Herald* even kept a running total in a feature they called the "Miami Bombing Box Score."

But this bookie war thing was different. Lefty Rosenthal, a Chicago-connected mobster, had come to Miami to establish a stronghold on illegal gambling for his boss up north. This resulted in explosions going off in rival and renegade operators' establishments, and when I called home from my surfing trip to check in, my mom dropped a bomb of her own.

My mother was a talented seamstress and designer. Years before in Cuba, she was highly sought after for her work, and even had the First Lady of Cuba, Martha Fernandez, as a client. She began getting work as a seamstress since arriving in the United States, and one of her clients in Miami was Marianne Cook, the attractive Playboy bunny wife of John Clarence Cook, a character far less attractive in every way. Cook was a notorious jewel thief, and was deeply connected to Lefty and the Chicago guys. My mother had just left the Cook home after dropping off a dress to Marianne when a bomb ripped apart the property. She was already gone and hadn't been injured, but she was shaken up upon hearing about it.

That was the first of two troubling phone calls that derailed my summer getaway. The second came when I checked in on my girlfriend Thania who told me Jose Mendez, the Lords' Vice President, needed to speak with me urgently. I called him right away and he told me he'd gotten word that one of the members I was with planned to hide several hundred hits of LSD in my parents' car and traffic it back down to Miami. Rather, he was planning on having *me* traffic it back down to Miami. If we got busted, I would've sounded like so many traffickers I'd come to hear over the years: "Officer, I have no idea how several thousand dollars' worth of drugs ended up here." No cop alive would've believed me, though in my case it would've been true.

The next morning, I didn't tell my friends what I'd learned. Instead of heading to Manhattan as planned for the final stretch of our trip, I turned the car around and got on I-95 South. I made up a story about having a family emergency back in Miami. We got home on Friday morning, and that night at our group meeting I announced I'd gotten word that there was excessive drug use in the gang. Right there on the spot, I kicked half my crew out of the Lords.

That was the hardest decision I'd made in my life to that point. Most of these guys had been my very best friends since I arrived in the US. After asking around for a few days, I learned that two local Anglos, both named Paul, had been selling the drugs to the guys in my gang. I didn't do anything about it just yet, but I committed their names to memory. I was about to meet some people that were more than happy to assist me in handling them.

My world would expand when I met those men who would shape the rest of my professional life. And I was just a few years away from forging a partnership with the man who'd almost blown my mother to smithereens.

—

I was back from that sojourn to New York for about a month when I began an internship with the Miami Beach Police Department. The college offered it as part of the Law Enforcement Assistance Program (LEAP) wherein students could earn credits and money along with their internship with a local police department.

One day while I was working at the station, I approached Lt. Bert Bernstein in the narcotics bureau. I told him about my fraternity—I didn't use the word "gang" in that building—and shared the issue I was having with my guys and their drug use. I told him I knew who the two dealers were, and his wheels started turning.

"Do you think you could make a controlled buy for us?" he asked.

"What's that?" I had no idea.

He explained that I would set up a deal with the two Pauls and make the purchase while being watched over by Bernstein's men, then I'd turn the drugs I bought over to them. Sounded simple enough. I didn't think I'd be made; no one would think I was a cop *and* president of a gang. Bernstein had hit a goldmine with me—I was under deep cover.

"I'll try it," I told him. But first I needed to do some work on my own to engender the trust of the Pauls.

I started playing pool at a billiards parlor across the street from the college on NW 27th St. where I knew they hung out. I knew them casually from high school, but I made sure to say a little something to them each time I saw them in the pool hall. In time, we were talking more and when I felt the time was right, I asked them where I could score some pot. They said they would hook me up and we set up a meeting for the coming Friday in the parking lot of the Prince Motel on Harding Ave. and 85th St.

When I got to my internship the next day, I told Lt. Bernstein that I'd finally set up a buy with the targets. With that, he got up and led me across the floor to Sgts. James

Kelly and Tom Hasley who would spearhead the next phase of the operation.

That Friday, I met with Kelly and Hasley who searched me to ensure I wasn't carrying any drugs to plant on these guys, then drove me a block from the motel. They were able to see the lot from their car and watched me buy a little marijuana from the guys. I walked home and the cops followed me, then took possession of the contraband. I was nervous, but more so excited. Maybe I was too young to know the danger I might've been in, but the adventure got my blood pumping. I was the star, standing center stage for these grown men who did this every day. It was exhilarating.

A couple of days later, Lt. Bernstein approached me at work.

"Your buy tested positive for marijuana," he said, "but it was all wet." He suggested I call them back to complain and light a fire under them by stating if they couldn't get good stuff for me, I'd need to find someone else to buy from.

I did that and left the Pauls hanging. About a week later they called me.

"Hey man, we got some dynamite grass—you won't be disappointed with this stuff."

Hardball had worked. I told the guys if it was as good as they said, I'd take two pounds. They were happy and we set up another buy, this time at a Paul's apartment which turned out to be just three blocks from the police station. Good thing he liked hanging in the pool room more than playing stickball in the streets, or he might've randomly seen me walking into the station for my internship one day.

Bernstein, Kelly, and Hasley met with me at the station to go over the plan. My job didn't end with just a purchase this time.

"Note the lay out of the apartment," Bernstein told me. "Make a mental note of how it's furnished and where all the rooms are." They'd prepared a search warrant and would hit the place once my part was done. Bernstein suggested my wearing a wire so they could monitor the buy, but Sgt. Kelly shot it down, saying I didn't know the targets well enough yet. They might pat me down.

It was obvious these officers really trusted me, and that felt good. There was a sense of purpose coming alive in me; something larger than the shit I was doing all day long in the Lords and at college, which was good because I'd changed my major to criminal justice.

Bernstein handed me $250 and told me they'd be in place when I got to the first Paul's house at the appointed time. I walked in and was immediately asked to raise my shirt.

Thank you, Sgt. Kelly.

I pulled off my shirt and even dropped my pants. Then I pointed to the Pauls.

"Okay, you next."

They did so and we moved on to business. One of the Pauls walked to a back bedroom and returned with a plastic package. I placed it on a scale they had on the table and saw they'd delivered the two pounds they promised. Like any good doper, I didn't leave without putting them on notice.

"If this stuff isn't better than the crap you gave me last time, I'm coming back for my money."

"I told you…this is *dynamite* grass," the first Paul reiterated. It certainly would be explosive, and the poor guy couldn't see the fuse.

I gave my team the takedown signal by opening my trunk and placing the package inside. A second later, I was swarmed by cops and cars with screeching tires.

"Get down! Get down!" There was shouting from all points around me. Bernstein took me to the ground while Hasley, Kelly, and their guys stormed the house. The cops hadn't told me about all this, but it made sense when I thought about it later. They wanted me to be scared just like the Pauls, for authenticity's sake.

The Pauls and I were all cuffed and placed in three separate squad cars and taken to the police department for booking. I was put in the same holding cell as one of the Pauls, who turned to me when the cops were out of earshot.

"You set us up."

"Bullshit," I barked. "I should've never trusted you two, and when we get out of here I'm gonna find you and beat the shit out of you both."

He denied it, but I kept my pilot light burning.

"Who sold you that grass? Because if it wasn't you two, then *that's* the motherfucker who set us up." It would've been nice to feed the cops the name of their source, but Paul shut down and didn't talk anymore.

Once the Pauls were gone, Sgt. Kelly let me out of the cell and shook my hand.

"You made your bones," he said. The cops took me for a celebratory round at Ronnie's Lounge at the Sea Isle Hotel. No one seemed to mind that I was only twenty years old, though a year later when I celebrated my twenty-first birthday there, Ronnie glanced at me with a you-son-of-a-gun look on his face, realizing I'd been underage drinking with cops in his bar for a year. The place would become my home away from home for a long time to come.

My time learning from Sgt. Kelly during that internship would serve me well. He imparted the tough things a cop has to glean if they ever expect to be highly effective. I was taught how to act while undercover, the value of good informants, and the importance of maintaining contacts in other agencies. Every one of those skills would be necessary in propelling me to the top of my field. I might've figured them out on my own while working, but to have these instilled in me as a college kid allowed me to hit the ground running when I got called up to the majors.

But that was still in the future. I was still a member of another fraternity that would probably become a conflict as I considered the next phase of my life.

In addition to my internship with Miami Beach PD, I was working a second part-time job at Surf Drugs on Collins Ave. while still in school. One morning while at the drugstore, I recognized Capt. Schemp from MBPD talking with the owner. I knew he worked Internal Affairs—the cops of other cops—and I couldn't think of another link between Surf and the department except me. I became nervous, and sure enough, when they were done talking, Schemp asked me to join him outside. Shit. Was it the Lords stuff finally catching up with me? Maybe it was the fight we staged to rough up the sergeant that worked our dances. Hey, he was fucking with *us*.

When we were on the sidewalk outside the store, Schemp began.

"Listen kid, I don't want anyone in the department knowing I was here today. Surf was burglarized last night and a Canadian tourist saw two uniform cops carrying shit out of the store and loading it into two squad cars."

I couldn't believe it. That seemed so brazen, even stupid. I told him I'd keep my mouth shut and was impressed that he'd trusted me enough to tell me that. My reputation among the cops in the department had obviously been elevated by my undercover work.

These two cops in question didn't stop with Surf Drugs. Next, they burglarized another business on Lincoln Rd., F & F Sundry Supplies, which was a very big mistake. Thania's mother worked there, so I was privy to a tidbit of information they obviously weren't—the owner, Eli Quain, was an associate of gangster Meyer Lansky. But Quain was also a good friend of MBPD Chief Rocky Pomerance, which was probably the only thing that kept the two officers from a tragic fate.

At the next roll call, the captain on duty simply asked that whichever cops in the room stole the merchandise please return it before the store opened. Remarkably, all the stolen goods were stacked neatly at the store's front doors by sunrise. I asked Sgt. Kelly about it and he told me everyone in the department knew the two guys were thieves, but they had a "good rabbi" above them in the chain of command that made them untouchable.

This entire episode made me rethink actually going to work for MBPD after graduation, if the opportunity presented itself. I wasn't naive—I knew there were good cops and bad ones, the extortionist at the Lords dances being a fine example of the latter. But I didn't expect this kind of blatant behavior to be so widely known in the department and go unpunished.

I was working at Surf's one afternoon when my Lords guy Pipo came in, covered in blood. He looked like he'd been machine gunned to pieces, and women started screaming and scrambling out of the store. It turned out to be more blood than injury, though he'd been beaten up pretty badly by some guys across the street. They started by calling him a "narc" and began roughing him up before tossing him through a doctor's office glass door, the shards of which explained the amount of blood. Someone had erroneously identified him as working with the cops, which was likely a case of mistaken identity. They probably wanted me.

This was on my mind all day, so after work I took Pipo to the Southwind Bar on Alton Rd., which I knew to be a hangout for the MB cops. Owner Bob Gallup had to reinforce the walls with steel because of the spontaneous target practice sessions that would erupt when drunk officers thought it a fine time to engage in such behavior. In one of Miami's endless conundrums, the front half of the bar was the cops' hangout and shooting range, and the back room was a gay bar.

In the front room, I ran into Sgt. Kelly and the massively built Dick Izzo, who was a great guy but could scare the shit out of anyone who didn't know that. Izzo worked in the Miami Beach Task Force, which was basically charged with harassing jewel thieves and other undesirables in the city. This was a good pair to hear Pipo's story.

"Show us where they live," Kelly said as they both led us out the door. Pipo had recognized two of the guys and a girl in the group as siblings that lived in an apartment at the corner of Harding Ave. and 83rd. So that's where we took them.

We parked a block away from the building and Kelly and Izzo got out of the car.

"Wait for us," Kelly said, and they headed toward the place and went in. After ten minutes, gunshots rang out and the two cops bolted out the back laughing and ran to us, then jumped in the car.

"Those guys aren't going to mess with you anymore," Izzo said as we drove off. He wasn't wrong, but I was terrified that the cops had shot them to death. Eventually I saw a couple of them on 84th St. and was actually relieved. But man, did cops do things differently than I expected in Miami Beach.

In June 1968, I decided to retire from the Lords. I'd served as its only president for four years, and I was becoming more involved with policing. I'd be graduating next year and would likely be interviewing for jobs in law enforcement. It was easier to leave the Lords now than have to explain my role there later.

I was assigned to the Juvenile Bureau in the latter part of my internship, and one night I was visited by Hugh Page, one of my professors at Miami-Dade College and a retired FBI agent. Apparently, he wasn't as retired as I thought.

"Raul, would you be willing to help out the FBI?"

Me? Is no one around here more qualified? I wondered.

He explained the operation and it all made sense. Their target was the Iranian Students Association (ISA) and Students for a Democratic Society (SDS) on my college campus, and who better to infiltrate and collect information than a verifiable, actual student at the college. The SDS had turned increasingly more violent, and some members were suspected of larger scale terrorist acts.

Mr. Page explained I was expected to start monitoring the organizations, their meetings, and their members. I was furnished with recording equipment and set off to devise a way to collect the info. Being left in the wind like that was a great opportunity to hone my planning and management skills, as I had to find some damn way to get all this intel and remain clandestine while still working at MBPD.

I began carrying a camera around campus and snapping pictures of the members and positioned myself near rallies and meetings to get more shots of them in action. I was also recording what they said when I could get close enough to them.

Initially, I turned over all my evidence and reported all findings to my suddenly very *not* retired professor. Page would collect it all and hand it over to the case agents at the Bureau. I eventually got to meet the agents when they came to thank me in person for my service. As crazy as Miami Beach was proving to be, I was afforded some amazing opportunities while there. I seized upon every one and none of the lessons learned were taken for granted. It was later reported that some of the visiting SDS members I'd identified were proven to be members of the Weather Underground, a domestic left-wing terrorist group.

In May of 1969, just before my graduation from Miami-Dade, I attended my first seminar given by the Bureau of Narcotics and Dangerous Drugs (BNDD), which was the precursor to today's Drug Enforcement Administration (DEA). The agents came to our station, and we were given some important information and then viewed a short film with Sonny and Cher discussing the evils of marijuana. Talk about driving the point home.

Sgt. Kelly pulled me aside after the workshop and introduced me to a BNDD agent named Gus Kritikos, who encouraged me to get into narcotics enforcement once I was hired by a department. He clearly saw a future there, and that discussion would prove to be a foreshadowing.

I continued working with Miami Beach PD until my graduation from Miami-Dade in 1969. I returned the FBI equipment to Mr. Page and realized I had some big decisions ahead of me. In preparation, I swapped gold chains with my brother, giving him my Saint John Bosco and taking his Saint Michael Archangel. It was more fitting for me to travel with the patron saint of cops.

—

I sat across from Sgt. Kelly at Ronnie's Lounge, discussing my future. It was early 1970, I was a college graduate, and I'd clearly made an impression on the MBPD during my tenure interning there. Kelly told me as much and said I should apply there right away. The fact that I wasn't yet a US citizen didn't matter. I could file a Declaration of Intention, take the police test, and be hired as a civilian until I got my citizenship.

I was still uncertain about Miami Beach and how they did things there. On a local law enforcement level, my options were Miami Beach, Miami PD, or the Dade County Public Safety Department (PSD), which would eventually become Metro-Dade Police. I had strong ties to Miami Beach since I'd been working with them, but I listened to my second thoughts and told Kelly I would wait a while before committing.

Not long after that, I was at the Dream Bar in the Johnina Hotel with my two friends from the Lords, Carlos

De Armendi and Sal Behar, celebrating Sal's having been exempted from the Vietnam War draft. It was after 3 a.m. when I told the guys to wrap it up; I was exhausted. I seemed the most sober so I offered to drive everyone home, but Sal got offended and got in his Volkswagen and took off. Carlos and I got in my car to follow him home, just in case. I lost him somewhere on 26th by Indian Creek. I slowed down and continued along Indian Creek, looking around to see where he might've gone, and spotted the red VW Beetle bobbing in a saltwater lake. I pulled over and we jumped out of my car.

I figured Sal's VW could float there while one of us went for help. I yelled across the lake.

"Sal, stay in the car!"

With that, he opened the door and dropped his 195-pound frame into the lake.

"Swim! Swim!" Carlos started shouting, but Sal had gone down out of sight. I dove into the lake and swam to him. He outweighed me by about forty pounds, and I fought like hell to keep hold of him while I swam to shore, but I started to lose it, and Sal. My muscles were numb, and I could barely move my limbs. I knew there were palm fronds lying about the shoreline, having fallen from the trees above. I called to Carlos to find a long one and reach out—I needed to be pulled in. He found a massive one long enough to reach me and, in his nervousness, he threw it to me. Some help he was.

I kept chugging, towing Sal, until I felt ground below me. Carlos ran out to meet me and we dragged Sal, totally unconscious, to the shoreline. Once we laid him down, I had to decide whether to try and help Sal or beat the shit out of Carlos for throwing the palm branch into the water. A passerby must've called 911 because fire rescue came before Sal died and Carlos was assaulted. The paramedics revived Sal and sat him in the front seat.

The sun was up by the time emergency vehicles had vacated the scene, and Carlos pointed into the water, right where I'd dove in. There were two thick dock posts cut off right below the surface of the water; how I'd missed smashing my head is anyone's guess. Between that and the rescue effort, I knew my guardian angel was flying around me somewhere.

This escapade resulted in my receiving a commendation from the City of Miami Beach and my first appearance in a newspaper when a reporter named Edna Buchanan wrote about it in the *Miami Beach Sun Reporter*. Edna would go on to cover me much more frequently in years to come as she became the face of Miami crime reporting.

I still had to decide which municipality I'd apply to, since I'd just been granted my US citizenship. I got some good advice when my Lords friend Bobby Gonzalez introduced me to a motor cop he knew named Kenny Harms. Bobby wanted to become a cop too, so he talked up the officers who frequented the gas station at which he worked. When I met Kenny, an officer for Miami PD, I asked him where he thought I should go.

"If I was starting my career now, I would go to Dade PSD," he said. He thought there was more opportunity there than Miami Beach or Miami PD. He explained that hiring would soon explode at the county level and there would be much more opportunity for advancement. I went back to Sgt. Kelly at Miami Beach and told him what I'd learned.

"Apply here anyway," he said. "You're already family." I did apply, mainly to appease Kelly, figuring I could take the police test both there and also at PSD. I planned to purposely tank the test for MBPD and pass the one at PSD, thereby having a built-in excuse to avoid Miami Beach and not offend the officers that had looked out for me while I was interning there. I took the test and intentionally answered incorrectly, or left answers blank altogether. There was no way I was passing that test and might've even gotten some proclamation for having the worst score in history. Next up was the Public Safety Dept. exam, for which I studied and focused intently. I'd played the hand perfectly and awaited my results. It was perfect.

Enter Eli Quain. You remember him—the owner of F & F Sundry Supplies where Thania's mom worked and good friend to both gangster Meyer Lansky and MBPD Chief Rocky Pomerance. Eli was a fixture in Miami Beach and was connected to the mayor, the Justice of the Peace, and any other person of influence in the city. When my results came and I told Thania how poorly I'd done, she must've shared her disappointment with her mom, who must've been wearing the disappointment on her face when going to work at Eli's store.

Two nights after getting those shitty test scores in the mail from MBPD, I got a call from Eli Quain himself.

"Congratulations on passing the Miami Beach police test!" he exclaimed.

"Mr. Quain, there must be some mistake," I said. "I failed it."

"Nah, that's why I'm calling. I talked with Rocky Pomerance today and he said there was some mistake. You actually passed with a 93!"

"Um, you sure about that?"

"Rocky is the Chief of Police, for Pete's sake. He would know."

I'd almost forgotten I was dealing with Miami Beach—the shenanigans capital of the world. That call only reinforced my instinct never to work there. I thanked Eli for the call but lied and told him I'd accepted a job with PSD after receiving the low scores from MBPD. That was taking a big chance, as I'd not even gotten the PSD scores back yet.

The next part of my foolproof plan relied on prayer, and a lot of it. I prayed every day until my scores came in from PSD—89%. I was in.

With my professional future somewhat set and looking promising, it was time to lock another thing down—Thania and I got engaged.

—

Things were going well for me at the police academy, or so I felt, until Sgt. Arnie DeLuca plucked me from training and brought me into his office. His face indicated I was not about to receive a Cadet of the Decade award.

He closed the door and stood across from me. "Why would the Department of Justice have an interest in you?"

I had no idea what he was talking about and told him as much. He thought I was lying, and wasn't really up for much discussion about it.

"Diaz, it's better to resign than get expelled."

"Why would I resign? I didn't do anything wrong."

He kept pushing, but I wasn't going to drop out after all I had done to secure a spot with PSD. I told him there must've been some mistake, but I wasn't going anywhere.

"That's your choice," DeLuca said. "But if you mess up just one time, I'm expelling you. Understand?"

I left on eggshells, uncertain as to how that had all come about, but careful not to step off the straight and narrow.

A couple of days later I was over at Thania's house and her stepdad came in the room.

"Congratulations, Raul," he said.

I assumed he was talking about the engagement.

"No, no," he said. "I mean the academy. I hear you're doing very well, nearly the top of the class."

I was confused. "Thank you, but how do you know?"

And here is where my soon-to-be in-laws, trying to be helpful, almost got me fucked.

Thania's stepfather, Eugenio Rolando Martinez, alias *Musculito*, meaning little muscle, was quite a character. He'd been a Cuban-born CIA operative since 1959, and when his daughter became engaged to me, he wanted to know a little more about me. Most fathers would, but unlike all those other dads, this guy had the means to find out just about anything he wanted. That culminated in his asking legendary CIA officer, E. Howard Hunt, to find out how I was doing. Hunt went as far as visiting the academy in-person and producing his DOJ credentials for Sgt. DeLuca. Hunt asked for a run-down on my performance, and anything else they knew. That was the red flag that sent DeLuca into a tizzy.

Musculito told me he'd only asked a friend to make a discreet inquiry.

"Well, that discreet inquiry almost got me indiscreetly expelled," I said.

"Oh. Well, I'll fix it."

Jesus Christ, no.

He went on. "I'm going to send my friend back there to make it right."

"No, please…it's better to just let it go."

Can you imagine E. Howard Hunt going back and trying to explain something that had absolutely no justification for involving the Central Intelligence Agency? Thank God Musculito dropped it at my request. Unbeknownst to anyone, my soon-to-be father-in-law and his pal Hunt were planning another clandestine project together that would soon take place in Washington D.C. on a larger scale.

My well-meaning but meddlesome in-laws stayed out of my business for the rest of my tenure at the academy, but they weren't the only family members that almost cost me a career.

One Saturday afternoon, I was in the house studying when my brother stormed in, red-faced and watery-eyed, and grabbed a baseball bat from his room and headed back out.

"Whoa, where are you going with that?" I asked.

Miguel told me he was playing basketball at Stillwater Park a couple of blocks from our house with his girlfriend and another friend. These two Jewish kids came up and started messing with them. My brother and his friend were speaking to each other in Spanish, so one of the kids said

Stillwater wasn't a place for spics and took the ball and wouldn't give it back.

"Listen," I said, "I'll go with you and talk to these guys and get your ball back." He led me out the door and I saw the two teenagers still in the park—one short kid and one big kid with glasses. Really big. I was hoping he wasn't the one who called them the name. I asked Miguel which one it was as we got closer.

"The big one."

Of course.

I recognized them from the neighborhood, but we were never really friends. We were familiar enough that I could comfortably walk up and start talking, which I did. I told them what my brother told me and asked if they'd called him a name.

"Yeah," the big guy said. "I called him a spic."

I explained he was embarrassed in front of his girlfriend and if they just apologized we could all move on. I asked him how it would feel if someone called them "kikes." The big guy threw the ball at me.

"I ain't apologizing to him, any spic, their girlfriend, or their brother."

I took a breath and told him the only reason I hadn't hit him yet was because he was wearing glasses. I knew what would happen when I said that—he turned and handed them to his friend, exposing the side of his face to me. I belted him. He landed on the court with a thud and his friend stood frozen. I grabbed my brother's ball and we headed home.

Three hours later I got a call from MBPD Capt. Von Eiff, who I'd gotten to know well during my internship there. He told me they had a warrant for my arrest. There I was, six weeks away from graduating from the academy and these two assholes at the park had gone to the cops and charged me with assault and battery. I thought about Sgt. DeLuca and what he'd told me when Hunt visited the academy. I saw my future going to hell and decided to go talk with the two guys, who turned out to be brothers. If I couldn't convince them to withdraw the charges, I'd be arrested and expelled from the academy.

They lived only a couple of blocks from us, so I walked over and knocked on the door. They were hesitant to come out, but when they finally did, we sat on the steps and talked for three hours about what happened, why it happened, and our situations as ethnic young people in Miami. In the end, they said they'd drop the charges.

I couldn't sleep that night because I kept thinking they might still change their minds. Sunday afternoon, Sgt. Von called me and said he didn't know what I had done, but he didn't want to know. The charges had been withdrawn. That night, I slept like a baby with a good right hook.

I graduated from the academy in the summer of 1971. I was proud of myself and chomping at the bit to make use of all I'd learned in MBPD's internship and the police academy. My gruff Field Training Officer, Wayne Abernathy, probably prepared me better than anyone else. Upon graduation, the only thing I had to do, according to Wayne, was forget all the bullshit I'd learned at the academy—my real education would begin now, on the streets of Liberty City.

How right he was.

CHAPTER THREE

ON-THE-JOB TRAINING

I was paired with FTO Abernathy after first working beside an old timer named Bob Caputo, who was very obviously ready for retirement. My main function riding in the patrol car beside him was to parrot what the dispatcher had just said over the radio because he was almost deaf. I promised myself I'd get out of the job before I got to that point and missed a call for an officer in danger or something. The guy moved like a paraplegic sloth.

I was placed in the Central District, which included Liberty City—one of the lowest-income areas in Miami. To say Central District was busy was an understatement; the common mantra in the department was that one year in Central was equivalent to three years in any other district in the city.

I had action from my first night on the job. Bob and I were dispatched to a person in distress call, and upon arriving we found a young Colombian woman doubled over, screaming. She was in such pain I was certain she'd been assaulted or shot. Then she stood upright and I saw the belly—she was about to give birth.

Yeah. Night One.

Bob, ever dutiful and prepared to be the shining example for his young acolyte, patted me on the shoulder.

"You handle this, I'll go back to the car and call for assistance."

"It's my first night," I said.

"Listen kid, in all my years in the department I've never handled childbirth and I'm not about to start now." He was gone before I could object.

Instinct and training kicked in and took control of my hands as they rummaged around to find something to put below the woman, whom I'd laid down. I grabbed some strewn newspaper and readied myself as she did all the hard work. In a matter of minutes, I had a newborn boy in my hands, who I wrapped in newspaper and placed with his mother. Paramedics rushed to the scene and took over the medical end of it, and I stood to give them room. The woman grabbed my arm.

"*Cómo te llamas?*" she asked.

"Raul."

She smiled through her exhaustion and said that would be the baby's name. It was one of those moments that remains etched in my soul forever. So Raul, if you were born on June 1, 1971 and you're reading this, nice to meet you.

Another moment that remains etched was watching Bob Caputo get congratulations from all the officers at the station when we returned from our shift. Apparently, he'd told everyone how *we* had delivered a baby that night.

My next FTO was Wayne Abernathy, the native Georgian Marine who'd served in Vietnam and told me to forget the academy and learn on the street. He was the streetwise guy I needed to ride with in those formative weeks. He roomed with a Cuban-American police officer, so I considered him "Cuban-broken." He'd only been on the force less than a year, but I credit his savvy as one of the main reasons I adapted so quickly and became a real producer for the squad. His Southern sensibility had a racist slant to it, though in his dealings with the public I'd never seen him as less than professional.

The guys I met in my first weeks ran the gamut. There were great cops like Wayne, and those less deserving of that designation, like Danny Benitez, whose brother I'd known from my internship at MBPD. Danny was obese, sloppy, quick to criticize others, and loud. If normal conversation is usually held at 60 decibels and a lawn mower measures at around 90, Danny could drown out the lawn mower. If he was excited you couldn't even stand near him. While driving, his average patrol speed was about 60 mph. We were civil to each other, but I quickly identified him as someone I didn't want to be around.

On the other end of that spectrum sat James Alfred Corbett III, with a Southern twang and the attitude to match. He was a straight up hillbilly from Jasper, Florida who weighed about 140 pounds soaking wet and had wispy, thinning hair. You couldn't find two people more opposite than us, but he and I struck up an unlikely friendship.

Our sergeant was Tommy Dunn, an easygoing guy who, like most supervisors, was focused on statistics, like arrests and traffic tickets. Jimmy Corbett liked writing tickets and I hated it, so I figured we'd make the perfect team. He could issue citations to his heart's content, and I could focus on the narcotics and prostitution arrests, thereby racking up double the numbers. We went to Sgt. Dunn and asked to be partnered up, as it would give him the results he craved.

One of the things I learned in those first months was that arrests lead to informants, which lead to more arrests. Our first informant was a streetwalker named Joanne who was nineteen but looked at least thirty. We grabbed her on a marijuana charge, and she flipped to avoid having the narcotics felony on her record. She gave us information on the pimps and dealers that hung out at Eddie's Dive Inn at NW 79th St. and 17th Ave. I was learning how to develop and work informants, and that would become the name of my game for years. It's a skill all cops should adopt early.

Shortly after I got placed in Central District, Bobby Gonzalez, my friend from the Lords who'd spent more time at my house than his own, graduated from the academy and landed at the airport. That was a detail reserved for graduates that didn't do as well in the academy, and Bobby didn't want to work there. I went to Capt. James Ross on his behalf and told him Bobby was my very good friend and would be an asset to our district. My captain requested him, and Bobby and I were together yet again, this time working Liberty City in uniform.

—

Eddie's Dive Inn at 17th Ave. and 79th St. lived up to its name and served as the corporate headquarters for the dozens of streetwalkers plying a trade for the CEOs standing in the shadows ready to collect their cut. The owner, Eddie Pittman, was a real character. He was outwardly friendly to police and dressed professionally, purporting to run a legitimate bar and grill free from illegalities. He acted completely oblivious to the women in miniskirts and heels who traversed the establishment all night long, handing money to the men in colorful suits and hats shooting pool. It was an act he'd put on for years, and only he believed it.

One night I was stopped at the traffic light at 79th St. across from Eddie's, when a pimp pulled a girl out of his large tricked-out Cadillac and struck her, dropping her to the ground. He began kicking her and I put my flashers on, called for backup, and pulled in front of his car.

"Face your car," I directed. "You're under arrest."

His reply was less than polite, and he squared up to me.

"Put your hands on the car," I said. He didn't comply, so I drew my baton and when he stepped toward me, I whacked his leg, which brought him to his knees. Backup arrived as I finally got him down and placed handcuffs on him.

"Hey you!" It came from the road. A black woman had stopped her car and was walking over to me, yelling. "I saw you hit him for no reason!"

As is too often the case, the last part of my exchange with the pimp was all that she saw. This woman, I would soon come to learn, was named Ms. Georgia Jones-Ayers—a prominent black activist in the community. In the moment, however, she was just an angry pedestrian about to interfere in a police investigation, and truthfully, it wouldn't have mattered if she was the Pope. Not having control of a scene can get you killed, and people coming at you on the street is dangerous.

"He's under arrest for assault and battery," I told her.

"He didn't assault anyone."

"He struck and kicked that woman."

"I don't believe you."

Things got very tricky when she tried to take the man from my grip demanding he be released. I yelled that she was about to be arrested herself and should get lost. She stopped, but told me I didn't know who she was and she'd have my job. It's a song that's sung to us a lot. I placed the prisoner in my car and started for the county jail when the dispatcher radioed me and directed to see my sergeant upon arriving at the lockup, which was behind our headquarters.

Sgt. Willie Morrison was a fair guy, and he asked me about the altercation. Ms. Jones-Ayers had obstructed our investigation and I was by all means justified in taking control of the scene, but the issue at hand was my style. On the scene, Ms. Jones-Ayers perceived me as disrespectful and, intention aside, maybe I did come across that way. It's hard to remember as it had happened during a tense and chaotic moment, so I agreed to meet with Ms. Jones-Ayers, who'd officially become the first person to file a complaint against me.

I met with her the following afternoon, and Sgt. Morrison stayed around to be the referee, if needed. We sat in his office and went at it; initially, at least.

There was clearly a misunderstanding at hand—she didn't know about the assault, and I didn't know all of the good she'd been doing for her community. I apologized, and she graciously accepted, dropping the complaint. She went as far as to say I could call her Georgia.

"If you ever need to talk about anything going on in the community," she said, "you're welcome in my home, day or night."

She left and Morrison said he'd overlook the incident because I'd made an "honest mistake." I would repeat those very words to Sgt. Morrison eleven years later.

—

I was on my way to Ronnie's Lounge for a Christmas party on December 14, 1971, after my shift. I encountered a Volkswagen driving without its headlights and didn't feel like pulling the guy over. It was after 9 p.m. and I wanted to hit the party before it wrapped up, so I just pulled behind him and flashed my headlights. He didn't get the hint, so I pulled beside him and waved to get his attention, which also didn't work. I called out to him on the PA, telling him to put on his lights, and he swerved toward me and nearly ran me off the road.

Now I was pissed and forgot all about the holiday tidings being shared at Ronnie's; I hit my lights and siren, and the guy sped off as fast as a VW Bug would allow. I floored it, and like that, I was in my first solo chase.

There are few things like the adrenaline rush of a pursuit, and if you're not careful that energy can overtake you. I started yelling into my radio that I was involved in a chase southbound on I-95 from NW 54th St. I barked the tag number and car description at the dispatcher, who didn't respond. What the hell was I doing wrong? I held the button more firmly and repeated everything, and again got no response. I did it again and again, yelling more loudly each time while speeding to keep up with the fleeing vehicle. I yelled so loudly I thought I heard my voice echoing outside my car.

That's because it was—I'd left my radio on PA mode after calling out to the guy. For the past four miles I'd been calling the chase into the air, so I took a long breath, then calmly told the dispatcher the details.

Meanwhile, this asshole exited 95 and got on US-1 in the oncoming lane. I had no choice but to follow, and he ran a police roadblock we'd set up at LeJeune Rd. The radio blared that he'd tried to run over one of the officers. Bad move; I knew what was coming next.

I saw flashes ahead as we neared the next intersection, and officers began firing on the approaching car—with me right behind it! I radioed the dispatcher and asked her to tell the officers to hold their fire. They did, and the pursuit continued past them.

Finally, the VW crashed into some trees at the University of Miami, and the driver bailed on foot. I'm sure he thought he was hauling ass, but it looked like a slow-motion replay of a Larry Csonka draw play. What didn't look like slow motion was the airborne officer tackling this fucker who'd tried to kill us.

The guy looked more normal than I'd imagined he would, even professorial, with a long beard and mustache. Turned out he was a history teacher at a local school, and he was high as the sky. We found an ounce of grass in the car, plus five roaches. Some other officers transported him back to the station while I helped at the crash site. When I got to the station I found him in the squad room, cuffed behind his back, with a paper bag over his head. I slid it off and saw he'd mysteriously lost the right side of his mustache and beard somewhere between the crash site and the station. When I brought him to the jail, the corrections officer turned to me.

"What happened to his face?" he asked.

"It was like that when we stopped him. Don't shave stoned."

Another lesson learned on my first solo chase—since that night I always transported my own prisoners.

Two days later, I received a commendation by one of the dispatchers for the "concise, calm, and professional manner" in which I handled a high-speed chase. No one had to know that half of Dade County heard the opposite performance blaring out of my PA before that.

—

My uncle Johnny was part-owner of a restaurant on SW 8th St. where Sgt. Vince Oller and Officer Bill Fernandez from the Organized Crime Bureau (OCB) used to dine with their wives frequently. Johnny took care of the bill for them most times, and when they were chatting on one such occasion, my uncle mentioned my assignment at Metro. Shortly after that, Oller called me in to meet me and we just had a casual chat, talked about my internship at MBPD, and hit it off. He seemed like a good sergeant and OCB was certainly an intriguing department; I was still just chasing Volkswagens and busting pimps.

One afternoon shortly after meeting Oller, he rang me.

"Raul, I have a temporary assignment I think you'd be good for," he said. "Are you interested?"

He went on to explain that US Customs was working with OCB on a special investigation into a major heroin operation that had tentacles in Miami.

"I'd love to," I said and was told to report to him on Monday.

I walked into OCB in the Terrorist and Security unit, from which four of us would be detached to US Customs. We were assigned to assist their efforts to disrupt a decades-old heroin distribution route that extended from Asia, to Turkey, to France, to Spain, and finally into the US for the operation famously known as the French Connection case. Specifically, Customs had OCB assisting their investigation of Mario Lobo and his group.

The Cuban-born Lobo led a group of smugglers out of New York City and brought them to Miami to receive a shipment of heroin from France, via Spain. Customs was monitoring a wiretap installed in New York, and our job was to surveil Lobo and his crew. I had never done extensive surveillance, and I found myself thrown into the task headlong when I was assigned to keep eyes on two cousins—Roberto and Aurelio Martinez-Martinez— by myself. Whenever Lobo joined either of them, I was expected to tail him also; I needed to clone myself. Twice.

These guys were young and bounced around all over the place. They had me going from Miami to Coral Gables, to Miami Beach, and back. They got dressed up and went to nice clubs at night, so I had to elevate my wardrobe a bit to get into those places and watch them. They were always trying to shake tails; they'd just come from New York where they were always followed by five guys, so they knew what to look for. When they'd head out all dressed up at night, I assumed they'd be heading into Miami Beach to party. I'd haul ass ahead of them, up MacArthur Causeway which led into Miami Beach, and just wait. By that time, they would have already been driving for twelve miles and shaken any tails, so their guards would be down when they passed me. I'd latch onto them as they entered Miami Beach.

One afternoon I followed Roberto to lunch at Esquina de Tejas on Flagler. He mustn't have been particularly concerned with remaining inconspicuous when he pulled the white linen suit out of his closet that afternoon and got dressed. Though he would've been easy to keep my eye on all day, he seemed to be waiting for someone and after their business was concluded I wouldn't be able to follow them both. I called Ofc. Bill Fernandez, assigned to the night surveillance team, and asked him for help.

"It's going to take me a little while to get to you," he said. "You have to hold them there."

Really? There was no time to slip into a waiter uniform and delay his order, so I resorted to the first thing that came to my mind. I pulled my switchblade out and casually strolled with the pedestrian foot traffic to his car, knelt to tie my shoe, and cut his rear tire. It was fun watching him curse his head off while blackening his suit changing the tire on the street. Needless to say, Bill made it down to me before Martinez-Martinez left.

Roberto was in receipt of a large container which he placed behind his house, where two Doberman Pinschers kept guard. I called Bill and reported this.

"You gotta get in there and see what it is," he advised. I don't know if Bill enjoyed giving me impossible game show tasks to complete, but he was sure full of them during my surveillance assignment. Bill was a great cop and went on to work for the DEA, so I guess this could be considered good training.

I sat on the house for a few days waiting for some divine intervention and a goddamn clue as to how I'd evade the attack dogs. Then one night it got cold and Roberto let the dogs in the house. Bingo.

I walked to his lawn, grabbed one of the large, white, concrete stones decorating the walkway, and somehow it flew through his front window, shattering it completely. I ran to my car and watched the two dutiful guard dogs leap outside and pursue an invisible perpetrator down the block. I walked around to the backyard and opened the box filled with kitchen tile, imported from Spain. We had intel that these guys were here to handle a shipment from Spain, and it obviously wasn't going to be tile. The box I'd opened was a trial run to see what the process would be for picking up a parcel from the port. They wanted to know what to expect when the real shit came over.

I wound up arresting Roberto's cousin, Aurelio, on a gun charge as he was a felon carrying a concealed firearm at a traffic stop. He was convicted and sentenced to five years, no probation. A couple of days later, I was at the *cafecito* window on NW 47th and Flagler when ringleader Mario Lobo approached me with an update on his guy's case.

"I'm going to have my lawyer appeal his case," he said. "But in the meantime, how would you like fifty thousand dollars?"

He was as subtle as a grenade, but I rolled with it. I looked around.

"Uh, Mario I can't really talk out here. Let me think about it and we can meet here tomorrow."

He agreed and the next day I got wired up at the station, ready to get our big target on tape offering a bribe. I headed back down to the restaurant and he was waiting, as agreed. I approached.

"Hey, Mario."

"Oh, Raul."

"Listen, I thought about it, and I'll do it."

He furrowed his brow. "Do what?"

"What we talked about yesterday."

"I didn't see you yesterday."

I saw where this was going. This crew was too savvy for something as easy as this, as evidenced by taking the time and care to do practice runs with tile while studying the actions of Customs agents at the port.

Two weeks later, Roberto's case was called before Judge Ellen Morphonios, our favorite judge. People in law enforcement called her the "hanging judge" because she gave maximum sentences on most of the cases we brought. She had a firm reputation of supporting law enforcement.

But occasionally, without any rhyme or reason that we could detect, she would recall a case and mitigate her previous sentence, often knocking it down to probation only, with no jail time. Two weeks after giving Roberto five years, she mitigated it down to probation only.

The next time I ran into Mario, he was all smiles. "Hey, Raul."

"Mario, I heard your boy is out," I said.

"Yeah," he sighed. "I'm out fifty grand, but it worked."

I don't know how many people in the police department or the courts got the offer after I declined it, but someone obviously took the deal.

The whole thing came tumbling down on all the bad guys when the French Connection was severed by federal authorities in early 1972. The arteries of this bust extended to the New York mafia and even into the NYPD, where tens of millions of dollars' worth of heroin disappeared from their very secure evidence room.

—

My temporary detachment ended and I went back to uniform, but only for three months. That summer, Sgt. Oller called me and offered me a permanent spot in OCB, and I grabbed it with both hands. That Friday night, June 16, 1972, I headed to Ronnie's to celebrate with some of the guys in my department, then a nightcap with Thania.

The next morning, I was roused from bed by a phone call from Thania's mom. She said Thania's stepdad had been in an accident in Washington D.C. and was being held by law enforcement. That was awfully vague, but I just assumed she was short on details. Then she told me I was getting a visitor.

"Someone will be coming to your place," she said. "They're going to drop off some boxes for you to give to the FBI."

It was odd, but I knew of Musculito's ties to the federal government, so this wasn't entirely unexpected. I got a knock on my door that afternoon and Thania's uncle dropped off two boxes and left. Inside were maps, paperwork, machine guns, and a particularly impressive .22 high standard HD military gun with a 1912 Maxime silencer, which was just too perfect to simply give away. I took that one out of Musculito's box. You know, for safe keeping.

Soon after, Agent Robert Dwyer of the FBI came by. Years later we would become very good friends working together, but that afternoon I didn't know him at all.

"I need to find your father-in-law's car," he said. "Do you know where it is?"

I didn't. Like my former French teacher Madame Ricks, he was driving a Rambler station wagon, but with a CIA-assigned tag that had been given to him by the FBI field office in Miami. They needed that car back ASAP, lest its tag draw a connection between the Bureau and the Watergate break-in.

The what?

I got in Agent Dwyer's car and we drove around Miami Airport's lots for three hours before finally finding the Rambler parked in a remote employee area outside the designated parking spaces.

By then, it was all over the national media. Rolando, along with four others, had been arrested for the break-in at the Democratic National Headquarters in the Watergate complex. Thania and her mom were freaking out and I had to get over there to help out. State Attorney Richard Gerstein and his investigator Martin Dardis were knocking on their door, along with media and everyone else wanting to talk to Thania's mom. We retained high-profile attorney Ellis Rubin for the family, and he finally got everyone off her back.

Meantime, I returned to OCB and started working narcotics cases with my new partner Sean Eagan. I did a lot of undercover work in Little Havana, doing buys and busting establishments where they were dealing drugs. In just a few months, my cases had closed five or six bars and lounges. It was a prolific time, but by November I was "burnt" in Miami. That's the term we used when an undercover cop got too exposed and could no longer work the detail. After a few cases in a short period of time, considering all the public court appearances, everyone in that world knows your face. From June to November of '72, I'd been burnt to a crisp in the city and was moved from OCB's Narcotics Squad to their Counter Terrorist unit.

One afternoon at the station, my sergeant called me to the third-floor cafeteria. Sgt. Oller gestured to an initially unimpressive man of average build standing about 5'8", but with the coldest, deadest eyes I'd ever seen.

"Raul, I'd like you to meet Ricardo Morales, the most important informant for us and the FBI."

CHAPTER FOUR

MONKEYING AROUND MIAMI

Ricardo "Monkey" Morales was only thirty-three when I met him, but his life was already worthy of a spy film. Actually, no—you couldn't get it all into a two-hour movie.

He was born in Cuba and was a former G2 agent for Fidel Castro but fled and became a CIA operative. He'd served in the elite Operation 40 unit, which was organized to effect covert strikes against Cuba after the Bay of Pigs invasion. More than a thousand Cuban exile men were used in an effort to achieve the US's goal of eliminating Castro while America's hands remained clean. After working Operation 40, Morales returned to Miami and carried out political bombings for the anti-Castro Cuban groups in the city. He knew the entire network and was enlisted by our department at the suggestion of the FBI to help local law enforcement understand the complex world of freelance Cuban bombers in our city.

The Monkey was a controversial figure to have working with cops. He'd been arrested for bombings and shooting a man seventeen times in broad daylight, though no charges ever seemed to stick to the former CIA operative and current paid FBI informant. He was a demolition expert, trained by the US government, and a reliable informant who seemingly had access to every influential Cuban on both sides of the law. But his real skill was his ability to play all those elements off each other to ensure his own freedom.

I shook Morales's hand as Sgt. Oller explained I would be working with him. He began riding with me and pointing out people but, more importantly for me, regaling me with stories—the guy was full of them. His resume could spin anyone's head. He talked about his CIA training in Homestead, Florida and deployments to Cuba to take down Fidel for the US. From there, the Agency sent him to the Belgian Congo where he fought the Russian-supported rebels and freed Western hostages.

Chicago mobster Frank "Lefty" Rosenthal employed Morales once the mercenary returned to the States and entered his bomber-for-hire stage in Miami. Lefty was engaged in the "bookie war" in Miami Beach and soon caught wind of Morales's reputation. His first job for him was blowing up Alfie's Newsstand, a gathering place for competing bookies, but also the place I played pinball that same summer.

Once the Monkey started talking, I realized how connected I was to him, besides his bombing one of my favorite hangouts. When we talked about Havana, we learned my dad was his physical education coach in grammar school. Then Morales told me about another job he did for Lefty wherein he detonated a bomb at a jewel thief's house with the assistance of a Dade County Sheriff's detective. The thief was John Clarence Cook, the man whose wife employed my mom as her seamstress. I told Morales his bomb had just missed her.

"You could have killed her," I said.

He looked at me with his cold, dead eyes.

"But I didn't."

I left it there. I dropped him off and said I'd pick him up the next day.

My training with Miami's most prolific bomber lasted a week. He truly knew every nook and cranny of the city, and after my short time riding with him, I did too. In a week, I knew every player in Miami, big and small. Though our prescribed time together was over, I was no fool. I knew keeping Ricardo Morales in my stead would help my career immensely. Plus, I kind of got a kick out of him. He had a sardonic sense of humor that, when not about my mother's near end, was amusing. He began coming over to my place on weekends and having breakfast with Thania and me.

It was impossible to work with Morales on any one single aspect of Miami's underworld—the man was tied into so many people, groups, and agencies that one case always bled into another. Such was the case with German Lamazares, an informant of mine from my OCB narcotics cases after I got burnt. We initially picked him up for his failure to register as a convicted felon, found cocaine on him, and charged him with possession. This was also a violation of his parole, so he was facing some real time. I was able to flip him and he started informing about his cocaine operation.

The DEA was also after Lamazares and when we picked him up, they got their claws into him. He was soon informing for both me and Agent Ruben Monzon for the DEA. But not every officer of the law operates the same way, and a critical difference in our two processes had a butterfly effect in Miami's underworld. When Lamazares gave me intel, I always recorded him and gave the tapes to my office for transcription. He never wrote anything down for me, nor did I sit and write notes myself. The tape recorder did all my work. Conversely, Agent Monzon had Lamazares write his own statements and turn them in periodically.

Lamazares's partner in crime as well as at a Hialeah car dealership was Eladio Armando Ruiz. He was delivering the coke for Lamazares and was no stranger to us. He'd been arrested for narcotics as well as being implicated in a string of supermarket robberies with Lamazares. Unbeknownst to Ruiz, his partner had been spilling the beans to me and Monzon about their narcotics operation. One day in February 1973, Ruiz borrowed German's Continental to run an errand, then returned and asked Lamazares to lunch. It would be his last.

German Lamazares was reported missing and would remain so for two months. I asked Monkey Morales if he'd heard anything. He said he knew Lamazares and his wife Nancy from around the city, and it just so happened he'd recently spoken about him with Eladio Ruiz, who Morales knew from their days fighting in the Congo. Ruiz told him when he'd borrowed Lamazares's car, he'd gone into the glove box for something. Lamazares had just used the car prior and left some of his crap in there, namely a bunch of handwritten pages on yellow lined paper. Ruiz paused when he saw his own name written on them. He'd just discovered the next batch of statements about their criminal activity that was to be turned in to Monzon at the DEA.

"So he got rid of him," Morales told me. I was excited to have gotten the hot lead, but very pissed that I'd lost an informant because of a careless DEA investigative procedure.

Though I had this major piece of intel, we still didn't have a body—that is until German's widow Nancy Lamazares contacted me and offered to take me to it. This was too damn good to be true, but I jumped all over it. I told her I'd meet her right away and she could tell me all about it, and as promised, she and another of her husband's partners were waiting for me at the Marriott.

"How do you know where your husband's body is?" I asked.

"My girlfriend Silvia told me."

"How does *she* know?"

"Because her boyfriend Eladio Ruiz killed him."

I took a second and put all the wacky, Miami ducks in a row: German's bisexual wife Nancy had a girlfriend named Silvia who had a boyfriend named Eladio who killed Nancy's husband, German. Okay, I had it.

"Take me to it," I said. She called Silvia, I called homicide, and we all converged in the marsh behind the Doral Country Club. Silvia wasn't lying. Homicide took over and began processing the scene surrounding German's remains.

I had Monkey Morales sign a formal affidavit recounting Ruiz's confession to him. That, coupled with Silvia and Nancy's information, would build the case against Ruiz. It was all compiled for the State Attorney's office and we got a warrant for Eladio Ruiz's arrest for murder. Next, we just had to find him.

One afternoon, I was having coffee with another informant across the street from a Chevrolet dealership when I saw Ruiz walking the lot looking at Corvettes. I excused myself from the table, radioed for backup, and strolled across the street while sliding my gun from the holster and keeping my hand down at my side. I weaved between cars on the lot and when Ruiz leaned into the front window of a 'Vette, I walked behind him and pressed the muzzle of my gun to the back of his head.

"You're under arrest, and if you move, I'm going to blow your fucking brains all over this beautiful car." This guy was a dangerous fucker, so I kept my gun at his head until backup arrived and he was placed under arrest. Disappointingly, he quickly paid the $5,000 bond—a pittance for first degree murder—and was out. This was now a particularly dangerous predicament because Morales, Nancy, and Silvia were all listed in the discovery evidence that was turned over to Ruiz's notorious defense attorney, Paul Pollack. Now, the murderer was walking the streets with those three names in his pocket.

On the night of May 25, 1973, I got a call from George Davis of the FBI. His informant, and mine, Monkey Morales, was just shot in the head and transported to Jackson

Memorial Hospital. I had to laugh as the myth of the Monkey grew when Davis told me Morales was still alive and had removed the bullet himself while waiting for the ambulance. It was wedged just below the surface of the skin, which was annoying him, so he pushed it out the entrance hole.

Earlier that night, Morales was parking when another car pulled beside him and fired a bullet through his window. He managed to crawl out of the car, draw his Browning automatic, and return fire at the driver—Eladio Ruiz in a wig.

Morales was released to me at the hospital, and I drove him to the Holiday Inn on Biscayne Boulevard. I gradually became Morales's de facto handler on the streets. Federal agencies like DEA, FBI, and Customs were always calling me to get in touch with him or deliver him to a location. He was instructed to lay low at the hotel until the FBI could procure an actual safe house before the trial.

—

I didn't see Nancy Lamazares for a while after her husband's murder. Then I ran into her one night at The Forge, one of Miami Beach's upscale restaurant-lounges. We were both there alone, so we sat for a drink or two, then headed to Sonny's Lounge, a well-known watering hole frequented by cops and mobsters alike. From there, we went to my apartment, and the rest kind of writes itself.

I saw her a few more times at my place, but we both soon tended to our other partners. Thania and I married in July of that year, and Nancy would end up meeting a young man named Juan Cid, a clean-cut professional type. She introduced us and he casually mentioned that his father was a doctor. My father told me that he went to medical school with his father, Juan Cid, MD, before my dad decided to teach. I mentioned it to Juan Jr., and we hit it off. He was a bright, good-looking kid who'd gone to med school in his father's footsteps. Though, that path would diverge significantly in the near future.

I'm not proud of my marital indiscretions over the years. Though I was not married when I had my fling with Nancy, Thania and I were engaged. It was the betrayal of a vow we'd not yet voiced publicly; not being married yet was not really a justification. Flings and short-term relationships would continue like this into my marriage as well, all of which I can only attribute to the selfishness that comes with an insatiable ego. I was simply unwilling to turn away from opportunity when it presented itself. I was reckless, and that would eventually come home to roost.

—

One of OCB's areas of investigation was police corruption. Whereas individual police officers were investigated by the Internal Affairs Department, larger scale corruption was handled by either the FBI, Florida Department of Law Enforcement (FDLE), the Organized Crime Bureau, or a combination thereof.

George Murphy was my Boston Irish partner, whose balls I loved to bust. He was an older irritable crank, and I was a wild-eyed young asshole. Perfect fit.

One day, he swung by my place to pick me up for an important meeting at the station, and from my window I saw he was wearing gray pants, a blue shirt, and a blue coat. I stalled my exit until we had almost no time to make it back, then finally came out.

Dressed in gray pants, a blue shirt, and blue coat.

"No," he barked when he saw me.

"What's wrong, Georgie?"

"Get the fuck in there and change your clothes!"

"I can't—we're late. Don't worry, no one is ever going to notice."

We jumped in the car and sped to the office. Though Georgie didn't know it, I'd called the office from my apartment in preparation for our arrival. We rushed into the building where the entire hallway was lined with cops waiting for us, applauding our coordinated outfits. Georgie immediately turned to me.

"You're a real asshole, kid!" he yelled.

His wife called me later that night and thanked me. "He told me what you did today," she said. "I haven't heard George laugh like that in a long time." That was nice to hear, and despite our Odd Couple pairing, we became a great team.

We were soon assigned to investigate possible corruption in the Hialeah PD Narcotics Section. We began poking around and it became clear to us that the guy in charge of the Narcotics Unit was the bad apple behind much of what was going on there. One afternoon George and I were sitting around the office strategizing how to get to him. We agreed that we had to flip someone in his Narcotics Unit; we just needed to find a cop who was involved in some shady shit. Another OCB investigator overheard us and walked over.

"I know a guy," he said. He went on to tell us about an officer in Hialeah Narcotics who'd come to a gathering at his home with a young lady companion that looked to be well underage. We took the info and began looking into twenty-four-year-old William Lee Smith.

We got Smith's roommate, another officer, to cooperate with us and confirmed the girl was indeed a fifteen-year-old runaway. In May 1973, we put cuffs on Smith and charged him with contributing to the delinquency of a minor. Georgie and I went to work on him, trying to pry information from him about the corruption in the department and the supervisor specifically. The kid wouldn't crack no matter what we tried, and our whole investigation into Hialeah died there.

Cases involving children always stayed with me the longest. We see a lot of shit on this job and eventually when you witness enough of man's inhumanity to man, you have to laugh about it; either that or go insane. Gallows humor for everyone else is called "cop humor" for us and it may seem insensitive at times. But how can you continue to swim in death and violence so often without building some kind of emotional life raft? You must disengage from the humanity of those situations.

But not with kids. Ever.

Years later this would hit me hardest when I was working homicide. We got an accidental death call where a little five-year-old boy named Elvis was crushed by a toppled refrigerator. Det. Steve Roadruck processed the scene and interviewed the father who told him the fridge had fallen forward, away from the wall it sat against, and killed his son. The dad said he'd picked the appliance back up into its place and tended to the child. Roadruck called me from the scene.

"Boss, we have a problem."

He related the details, and I asked what was wrong with the story.

"Spiderwebs," Roadruck said.

When he'd shined his flashlight behind the refrigerator, there were webs spun between the wall and the back of the fridge. That thing hadn't moved from the wall for quite some time, lest having landed on the child that day.

We kept that in mind and went to the medical examiner's the next day to observe the autopsy. I walked in to find this beautiful little boy—blonde hair, blue eyes—laying on the slab. I was fucking overcome, flushed with the worst feeling I'd ever had on the job. He looked like an angel laying there looking up and I couldn't stay in the room. I left the postmortem and let Roadruck handle it.

The medical findings proved him right, and eventually the father confessed. He was painting a wall and the boy put his hand in the wet paint. The father swung his arm to knock him away and ended up puncturing the kid's heart with the thin end of the paintbrush handle.

—

Besides "Irish" Georgie Murphy, I also loved working with Harry Crenshaw and Jerry Rudoff in OCB. We were another mismatched team—Jerry was Jewish, Harry was black, and obviously I'm very Cuban. You should've seen the three of us trying to work undercover at a KKK rally in South Dade. We would've been made even if we wore hoods and sheets. But it was great working with them, and we became very close. I was happy when Harry was promoted to sergeant in narcotics, but I was selfishly sad to see him go.

In May 1973, Harry was working a wiretap on a suspect named Charles Vassar, a longtime criminal with a rap sheet that included three prison stays for larceny and theft. Vassar was out on bond when Harry drove by and saw Vassar's car parked outside Harry's ex-wife and children's home. Harry sat on him to see what he was up to and intervene if he tried anything. Eventually, Vassar drove off and Harry pulled him over about six blocks down the road. Harry approached the car and was met by Vassar holding a handgun. The two wrestled and Vassar fired five shots during the struggle, with three hitting Harry, one fatally. I got the call while eating dinner with Thania, and I rushed out.

Officers swarmed the neighborhood and a few days later they caught Vassar from the description of his car. The shithead hung himself in his cell a couple of weeks later while awaiting trial. His family was outraged that the conditions in the jail were so subpar that he resorted to that. I was more outraged that my partner, a brilliant and dedicated public servant, died like a dog on the side of the road. Today his name is inscribed on the wall at the National

Law Enforcement Memorial—East Wall, Panel 34, Line 8—in Washington, D.C.

I was still dealing with that tragedy when I got the next earthshaking phone call. Monkey Morales had just killed his would-be assassin, Eladio Ruiz, shooting him to death on his doorstep. Morales was being sought by Miami Police. With this and the murder of German Lamazares, it seemed I was about to lose yet another damn informant, this time to prison.

I had to sit back and take a breath; I was really in the thick of it now. The action in the city was rising to meet my own ambitions and I was invigorated by the challenge. I couldn't tell how banged up I might get in the process, or when my guardian angel might quit on me. It was all moving too fast to consider playing it safe. Miami was rocking, and the tremors would only get more intense.

CHAPTER FIVE

POLITICAL HITS

If it hadn't been for Jose de la Torriente I might not have ever come to the US. He was the family friend who'd arranged for two visas for me and my brother by petitioning the archdiocese when Operation Pedro Pan went into effect. He'd come here in 1959 and dedicated part of his time to helping Cuban kids get into the US.

Torriente then became involved in the anti-Castro movement like so many exiled men. He had the money to finance such activities, and in 1969 produced a doctrine titled "The Working Plan for the Liberation of Cuba," commonly referred to as "Plan Torriente." His followers handled the anti-Castro efforts while his real estate firm, TVM Land Development, began work on housing developments in South Dade.

But the hardcore nationalists became wary of Torriente. They saw his real estate business pursuits as a distraction from his pledged crusade against Castro. They were troubled by an unexpected diversion of funds previously earmarked for the fight, and in 1973 the housing development was bombed to send a message.

A year later, we got a call from Coral Gables police. They had a shooting centered around the politics of the Cuban exiles, and therefore felt that Metro-Dade Homicide and OCB's Terrorist and Security Unit should be involved. We responded to the location, and I walked past the yellow tape into the living room to find Mr. de la Torriente dead on the couch. He'd sat down to watch *Ben Hur*, his back to the front windows, when at 8:45 p.m., four shots were fired into the living room, one striking him in the head and killing him. I told Coral Gables I knew him, and they were right to call us; this no doubt involved the Cuban thing.

Lloyd Hough, a homicide investigator and good ol' boy from Virginia, called me over and excitedly pointed out a 3x5 index card lying on the porch.

"Look what I found," he said, shining his flashlight on it.

The card had a zero drawn on it with "J.E.T." written above. At the bottom there was an equation, of sorts: "1x100h."

"We have to find out what it means," the homicide cop said. I knew exactly what it meant.

"Nothing," I told him.

"It's a clue."

It wasn't, unless a fingerprint could be lifted off the paper. The symbolism drawn on it was insignificant. The "J.E.T." represented Jose Elias de la Torriente's initials, but the rest was nonsense. The old Cuban assassins used diversionary shit like this all the time.

"Don't you think it means something?" the Virginia detective asked.

"It means you're going to spend the next five or six days trying to figure it out and forget all about this dead man here." And that's exactly what happened. They worked this "clue" for days as the case began to go cold.

We assisted their investigation and I knew this case would be solved on the streets, in the network of informants in the Cuban bombing groups. I contacted the Monkey first, though he was short on information for a change. Fortunately, a guy in prison in New York provided us the intel we needed to get the ball rolling. He contacted the FBI and said he knew that the 9mm weapon that was used in the murder had been transported from Cuban nationalists in New Jersey down to Miami by a guy nicknamed *Pototo*. I headed up north with homicide detective Fabio Alonso to meet the inmate with the loose lips who'd been in the Cuban Nationalist Organization with a man named Carlos Rivero.

Rivero was the editor of a Cuban newspaper and son of former Prime Minister of Cuba, Andres Rivero Agüero. Those little newspapers, often duplicated in small runs in editors' garages, were popular in areas where pockets of Cuban exiles lived. Unlike traditional news outlets, the Cuban papers openly took a political stance and carried stories that furthered their cause.

I'd been researching those papers hoping I'd find some careless "editor" tipping their hand about having knowledge of Torriente's murder. Rivero's rag, *Fé*, translated as "Faith," created a major lead for us when we discovered that two weeks before Torriente's murder, Rivero's newspaper ran a parody called "El Sepelio de El Viejito Chichi," or "The Funeral of Old Man Chichi," which mocked Torriente. The last page had a caricature of an old man in a casket with "J.E.T." written on his forehead. We definitely had some questions for Rivero, and we started investigating him.

He looked like a great suspect from the beginning, taunting newspaper cartoons notwithstanding. Rivero and his uncle Felipe ran an anti-communist terror group that switched between names Omega, Zero, and *Pragmatistas* in order to spread out responsibility for criminal actions into three separate police files. This is another example of the diversionary tactics employed by the Cuban operatives that were easily identifiable to me, but likely not to the American investigators and government agencies.

We learned Rivero had already fled their group's base in New Jersey and landed in Spain. We tracked him through Europe, with stops in England and France, then to Haiti and eventually back down to Cuba where he penned a book called *Los Sobrinos del Tío Sam*, or *Uncle Sam's Nephews*. While his return there may have seemed shocking on the surface, given he'd run anti-Cuba bombing groups, it made sense to me. With US agencies turning up the heat on his and Felipe's groups, he needed to escape to someplace with a barrier to US cooperation in case an extradition order was dropped when charges were brought against him for his group's actions. Cuba would seem a great option, but how does one acquire safe landing there after publicly railing against their politics and blowing up their interests across the world?

Cuban authorities no doubt wanted the high-profile Torriente removed from the landscape and his Plan Torriente forgotten. They would've needed a competent operative to carry out such a deed, and perhaps offered safe haven in Cuba in exchange for it. Writing a book critical of the US like *Uncle Sam's Nephews* would probably also be a good insurance policy to ensure Cuba's protection from American authorities.

I was vigorously pursuing Carlos Rivero until I learned he'd landed back in Cuba. That was it—now we'd never be able to touch him. I knew he wasn't the triggerman; I highly suspected it was another guy from New Jersey named Jesus Gonzalez Cartas, who they called *El Extraño*, "The Strange One." But everything in our investigation pointed to Rivero and his group of Pragmatistas as having been responsible for orchestrating the hit. It was all for naught. Rivero laid low in Cuba before eventually disappearing and landing in Colombia, where our intelligence indicated he remained.

The chaos of my culture had seemingly followed me to Miami and began coming for me, in a professional sense. From the day of Castro's seizure of power, through the Bay of Pigs, to the violence in Miami, Cuban blood was being spilled everywhere. It had become such a part of my life it didn't even feel abnormal.

Anyone of influence perceived as having an attitude lenient toward Cuba was instantly an enemy to the exile groups. And if those persons of influence were Cuban, they might as well have painted targets on their own backs. The logic behind whatever caused them to adopt that position was moot—they were seen as practically agents for Fidel Castro, and there were so many Cuban exile political gangs operating there that their days were surely numbered.

Luciano Nieves had been a *guajiro*, a guy connected to the old country, but seen as a part of the new Cuban mindset. He'd been a captain in Castro's revolution, and he was now in Miami working as an activist for a renewal of the relationship between Cuba and the US. He wasn't a bad guy—he just supported lifting the embargo against Cuba and moving toward working together. But the paranoia of the exile groups, understandably rooted in the betrayal and brutality of the Castro regime back home, contributed to the rumor on the streets that Nieves was a Cuban agent operating here.

On February 21, 1975, Nieves visited his young son at Variety Children's Hospital in Miami where he was being treated. Nieves left, stepped outside into the parking lot, and was brazenly shot to death in broad daylight. My phone rang and I knew what was going to be on the other end. I'm not psychic, but it was a Friday afternoon.

See, I don't know why this is, but I've found during my career that most political homicides and bombings happened on Fridays. I'm not sure if there was any forethought behind this, but we were indeed shorter-staffed on Friday afternoons and response time was therefore slower. Saturdays were not a regular shift, and the specialized units were off. If I didn't know better, I would say someone with inside knowledge of the inner workings of law enforcement helped plan all the bombings and assassinations I worked.

There was an informant named Willie Salon working with the Homicide Department. He was an unhappy member of the Pragmatistas and would provide information about the goings on inside the organization. Salon said the Pragmatistas had targeted Nieves and as a result of Salon's information, nine indictments were handed down for Nieves's murder. Seven of those charged were for conspiracy to commit the crime or accessory after the fact. Two charged, though, were hit with first degree murder—Jesus Lazo and Valentin Hernandez. Hernandez would eventually be caught and Lazo escaped to Colombia where he became a bombmaker for the drug cartels.

I'd just had my own run-in with the Pragmatistas. An informant of mine told me a friend of his named Rafik was being extorted by Pragmatistas. I met the man—a *bolita* operator, or numbers runner—who said two Pragmatistas were demanding money from him. It was a common fundraising tactic for the anti-Castro groups in Little Havana. He gave me the names of the accused—Paz and Valdes— and I told him not to pay them anything yet. We would try and get them first.

I knew both to be hardcore Pragmatistas. They were responsible for raising a lot of money for the group and were an important part of the operation, so I knew they meant business. We had to act fast, so I partnered with Art Castro, an officer I knew from the City of Miami PD, because this fell in their jurisdiction as well. We began talking to as many people as we could find to verify the information.

I came home on a Saturday afternoon after working day and night on the case and collapsed. I called Thania into the bedroom before I fell asleep.

"If anyone calls don't wake me up," I instructed. "And if it's a guy named Rafik, only get me if his house is burning down." I think I was unconscious before I finished the sentence.

It felt like I was asleep for ten seconds when Thania stood above me, shaking my arm.

"Raul, get up." I pried an eye open. She was holding the phone. "It's Rafik."

"I told you—"

"His house is burning down."

Sure enough, someone Molotov-cocktailed his house and the fire department was there trying to get him to leave. He told them he had to make a quick call first, to me. We arrested Eduardo Paz and Rafael Valdes the next day.

When they went to trial and I took the stand, prosecutor Jimmy Woodard had me demonstrate the huge .50 caliber rifle we seized from our search in Valdes's house. He asked me to show the jury how it worked, so I pulled back the lever and released it. It slammed so loudly the entire jury flinched.

When both sides rested, only an hour passed before we were notified the jury had reached a verdict. To our surprise, it was not guilty.

One of the jurors asked to speak with Woodard, so we took him up to the office and asked why they'd voted as they did.

"The gun," the juror said. When I'd cocked the weapon, it sounded so thunderously that it sent a message to the jury—bad people use guns like that, and those guns are fucking scary. They feared for their lives. Acquittal, across the board. And a lesson learned for this investigator for future courtroom testimony.

—

It was a challenge understanding the complexities of the Cuban exile world in Miami at any given time. There were so many personalities with ever-evolving perspectives on the politics of the US and Cuba, so when I needed guidance, one of the people I went to was Rolando Masferrer. He was one of the political heavies operating in Miami with quite a history. He was a newspaper publisher and had been a member of Congress in Cuba who eventually came to the US after Castro came to power. He won prestigious awards at the University of Havana, and was just overall brilliant.

Masferrer spent a great deal of time and energy plotting to get rid of the dictator. The radical activist did so by cavorting with and pleading his case to American mafia members and even President Kennedy himself. He didn't get any takers, obviously. But if I was dealing with some political operative whose motives I needed to sort out, I called Masferrer.

On a Thursday morning in October 1975, I got a call from a jittery Masferrer who invited me to his office on SW 1st St. When I got there, he closed the door and looked me dead in the eyes.

"I made a mistake that is going to cost me my life," he said.

He went on to explain that he'd published something in his weekly Cuban newspaper, *Libertad*, that he felt would come back to hurt him.

Masferrer had recently run a piece that reported the Novo brothers—a pair of active and dangerous anti-Castro mercenaries—had violated their parole by leaving US soil and traveling to the Dominican Republic to meet with a cadre of anti-Cuba terrorists to plan their next actions against the country.

On the morning he called me, Masferrer ran the following day's edition to the printer. When he came out, he saw Ignacio Novo in the parking lot with his hand in a paper bag. Masferrer drew his .45.

"I said, 'Freeze, Novo,'" Masferrer told me. "'Put that bag on top of the car.'"

Masferrer stopped his story and reached down into his desk, then placed that very paper bag atop it. He slid out a 9mm Beretta. I raised my eyebrows, nodding.

"He gave it to you?"

"*Sí.*"

"Then what did you do?" I asked.

"We talked. Philosophized."

"About what?"

"Why he shouldn't kill me."

He said Novo left without his gun, walking away with no more resolution than when they'd first begun talking. I told Masferrer I'd report that to the department and we should meet the following day for lunch.

Friday.

The next morning me and my partner Eddie Mederos swung by the station and grabbed our paychecks before heading to the bank. The plan was to cash them, pick up Masferrer at eleven, and then bring him to his favorite restaurant—Burger King. We'd strategize and get to the bottom of this whole Novo thing.

We were headed out of the station, my keys in hand, when a detective called out to us.

"Hang on," he said. "A call just came in for a bombing with a victim. Location is 6775 SW 27th St."

Shit.

Eddie sighed at the change of plans. "I'll call Masferrer and tell him we can't come."

"You won't need to," I told him. "That's his address."

It was a horrific scene. His 1968 blue Torino was a disjointed mess, sitting in the driveway with each section of the car reaching out in a different direction. Parts of Masferrer's body had been blown as far as fifty feet from the car. Worse still, the blast and dismemberment hadn't killed him. He actually died from smoke inhalation as whatever parts of him that remained on his body couldn't carry him from the burning car despite being conscious. It was brutal.

When I arrived, I was greeted by a homicide detective who I'd heard was a problem. He waved me off upon seeing me.

"This is our scene," he said.

"Yes," I replied. "As well as mine." Though it was indeed a homicide, OCB had jurisdiction over all bombings. When a bomb killed someone, both bureaus shared joint jurisdiction, as was the case with Masferrer. In addition to that, this goof wasn't even a supervisor. He had no right to dismiss me from a scene under my jurisdiction.

He didn't care. He was kicking me out, and very publicly. Other detectives and police officers were now watching the confrontation. The murder scene was bad enough; I wasn't going to make a further spectacle by arguing with this dick.

"Okay," I relented, "I'll leave. But this is your last fucking day in homicide. On Monday you'll be working in the Property Bureau."

The detective laughed with his cronies and went back to the scene. But come Monday, he wasn't laughing. He was transferred to Property. I'd love to say I had the sway to make such a judgment on someone, but the reality is less impressive.

Earlier in the week, I was in the office late with the cleaning crew. It was protocol that two investigators stay while the cleaning staff serviced OCB and the Director's office due to the sensitive files that were accessible. While killing time, I found some used carbon paper sheets in the garbage can in the Director's office. After using a sheet to duplicate something written on a form, you could hold it up to the light and see the impression of what had been written. That night I was looking at a carbon used for a transfer form. On that carbon, I saw that this asshole homicide detective was scheduled to be transferred to the Property Bureau. So, when he tried to kick me off the Masferrer crime scene I was happy to use this newfound intel. After his transfer, homicide detectives parted like the Red Sea when I walked into an elevator. I happily enjoyed my share of free coffees for a while.

I knew the murder of Masferrer or Novo at the other one's hand was inevitable after their confrontation. Neither one would've let the other live while they were still breathing. Only a week before his murder, Masferrer had written the following in *Libertad*:

> "You do not beg for freedom; you conquer it with the sharp edge of the machete. But today's weapon is not the machete. The enemy is not close enough so that he can be hit with the cold and sharpened edge of steel. That time will come. In the meantime, dynamite can speak in a uniquely eloquent manner…"

I was sitting on the knowledge of the parking lot confrontation between Novo and Masferrer the day before, though in Cuban exile circles that alone is not the smoking gun it might appear to be. Someone espousing the opinions on Cuba that Masferrer had would have enemies all over Miami. Thursday morning might've just been Ignacio Novo's turn at bat. A new hitter might've stepped into the box on Friday, and if he had failed there was likely someone else on deck. Such was the sport of the exiles' Miami. Nevertheless, I gave homicide that info for their investigation.

A year later, on September 21, 1976, Chilean ambassador Orlando Letelier was executed in a car bomb that killed both him and his aide Ronni Moffitt. The shocking assassination happened brazenly, right on the street in Washington D.C., and after the mechanics of the bomb were examined, some of my friends at ATF told me the device was identical to the one used on Masferrer. In 1978, federal indictments were brought against seven conspirators for the murder of Letelier, and one of the people charged was Novo. He was convicted and sentenced to life, then subsequently acquitted after being granted a new trial in 1981.

When the connection between the Masferrer bomb and the Letelier bomb was discovered, that was the end of the Rolando Masferrer investigation. As shitty as it seems, I don't think the feds wanted to close my case once that link was discovered. It wasn't some grand conspiracy—they were keeping a government witness named Townley under wraps.

When I got that information regarding the similarities in the bombs, I reached out to my source, Monkey Morales. He told me that the Letelier bomb was brought into the US from Chile by Michael Townley, an American-born agent of Chile's intelligence unit called DINA. After his arrest for participating in the Letelier murder, Townley provided the feds information about the bombing and was placed in the Witness Protection Program.

When I heard this, I contacted the FBI and requested an interview with Townley. He'd just provided the details of Letelier's murder at the hands of Novo and the others, so I wanted to bring him into the Masferrer case, but the feds denied me access to their witness. Given the identical nature of the explosives, he would've likely been the key to my closing the Masferrer case.

Townley was a valuable source of international information for the government, and they knew I had the scoop on everything going on in the exile circles in Miami. I believe they suspected Townley might've also been involved in far more than they knew about, and if he was involved in one of my cases it might've messed up something they were working on. They built a fence around their witness, and to date, no one has been charged for the murder of Rolando Masferrer.

——

I got a call from the manager of Versailles Restaurant, the venerable Cuban mainstay on the *Calle Ocho*. He told me that a well-known local exile named Aton Costanzo had come by looking for me and Monkey Morales, and it wasn't on cordial terms. He showed the manager a hand grenade with a pulled pin sitting tightly in a drinking glass, which he kept in his pocket. He let it be known that if he were tossed to the ground, against a wall, or handled in any manner that might break the glass, anyone in its vicinity would be blown apart, himself included. That was the mentality we were dealing with.

I assumed the grudge stemmed from his having been shot seventeen times by the Monkey back in 1968, when Morales learned Costanzo had picked up a contract on his life. This was before Morales started working with me and Miami Dade Police, but he was a valuable asset to the CIA and the FBI in their attempts to understand the Cuban anti-Castro bombing networks that he was never charged with Costanzo's shooting, and both men's mythological statuses rose in the city. Surviving the assassination attempt earned Costanzo the nickname *Atomico*, meaning Atomic.

Art Castro, Bobby Gonzalez, and I got in the car and headed out. I sat in the backseat with my 12-gauge shotgun beside me as we looked for Atomico and his hand grenade. We passed by his house, and, by chance, he was coming out with another man. They got in the car and we followed; I radioed the plate to dispatch and it came back with a charge attached to the registered owner.

"Thirty-one," dispatch said—a homicide.

We followed them along SW 8th Ave. where our two cars were the only ones on that stretch. There was no way to avoid being made. They slowed at 6th St. so we turned into an apartment parking lot nearby to give some space and see what they were up to. They turned around and pulled across the exit, blocking us in the lot.

We flew into action. Art and Bobby leapt from the front seats, hollering.

"Police!"

Atomico threw open the passenger door, which was facing our car. He pointed a .45 at us and I blasted their car with my shotgun from the backseat, which fucked up my hearing forever. The driver took his foot off the brake and their car rolled forward, causing my entire load to hit the side panel between the front and back windows.

Atomico's door slammed shut and they peeled out. We pursued them around the corner, back to Atomico's house. They bailed and ran inside, up to the second floor. We held our position outside, and Art Castro radioed his Miami PD dispatcher for uniform backup.

Atomico was yelling out the window, telling us not to shoot because there were children inside. A backup unit arrived and started a dialogue with the barricaded suspects.

"If there's a family in there, you better come out," I called to them. "Don't put them in danger and make us come in there."

Atomico replied that he wanted to talk to another cop. He didn't want to deal with me.

"Why not?" I yelled. "What's wrong with me?"

"You are friends with the Monkey."

It was hard to argue with that. If someone shot me seventeen times I wouldn't trust anyone they worked with either. Another officer talked them into surrendering and they came out with their hands raised. A woman and child followed; thank God we hadn't stormed the place. It's hard to keep a cool head when the adrenaline is lighting you up from the inside, but Art and I were seasoned enough to know better.

We searched the house and recovered blasting caps, wire, detonators, and other bomb making components. We charged them with everything and they got fifteen years.

Atomico's nemesis, Monkey Morales, was facing some music of his own.

—

Morales had been sought for questioning the minute police scooped Eladio Ruiz's dead body from Morales's doorstep. He wasn't in his apartment at the time, but Det. Gil Zamora reported to the scene and subsequently took a statement from a witness living in a unit across a parking lot from Morales who said he'd seen a man running from the complex.

Morales came into the station with his attorneys, turned over his gun, and gave a statement to Homicide Sgt. McCracken. He initially denied involvement in the shooting and was released that same night. The sole witness's bathroom window faced Morales's door across the lot, and he told officers he was showering and happened to glance out the window and saw a man fleeing. He was shown a line-up and supposedly identified Morales. That was enough to secure a warrant for his arrest.

As was always the case when something went down with the Monkey, all agencies poked their noses in. Everyone seemed to have some stake in his information. Agent George Davis of the FBI called me and asked if I could check out the witness whose information led to Morales's arrest.

I went and spoke to the man who'd seen Morales from the shower. He recounted basically what he'd told investigators initially, though I noticed something they obviously hadn't. There wasn't so much a problem with his story as with his face—he was wearing eyeglasses. Though I wasn't in the bathroom with him that day, I thought it safe to assume he wasn't showering with them on. I passed this finding onto Agent Davis and Morales's attorney, and this witness failed to identify Morales in the court room despite his sitting five feet from him. The charges against Morales were dropped, and prosecutor Doug Williams became my least fervent fan at that moment.

Shortly after this, Art Castro, Morales, and I went target shooting. All three of us carried 9mm Browning pistols, and when Ricardo tried to shoot, he had a misfire. He tried a couple of more times, with the same result. Morales stripped down his weapon and we noticed that its firing pin had been cut to where it wouldn't reach the primer. Unbeknownst to him, his gun had been rendered useless if needed. Morales told us that he hadn't checked his gun after it was returned to him by the Miami Police Department after his arrest for the Eladio Ruiz killing. Someone in the department was trying to hurt him.

My key informant had dodged a bullet with that murder charge, but the series of chaotic events he seemed to invite didn't end there. Morales was soon tapped to move to Venezuela where he was installed as a *comisario* in their intelligence agency DISIP (*Dirección de Inteligencia y Prevención*, or Directorate of Intelligence and Prevention, translated). No one rises in the ranks of an intelligence agency without a very high authority pulling those strings. In what would be impossible to consider a coincidence, by 1974, three of the top officials in DISIP—Orlando Garcia Vasquez, Luis Posada, and Morales—had all been Cuban-born CIA assets in the US.

As was his innate gift, Morales managed to tilt my universe off its axis even while serving the government of another country on another continent. Before I knew it, I was on a damn plane to Caracas to make sure the Monkey didn't completely fuck a case I'd made against an international terrorist.

CHAPTER SIX

A CONDOR SHITS ON THE FBI'S HEAD

Federal agencies in this country have never been able to get a handle on Cuba. Although South Florida local law enforcement was getting better at navigating the waters, they still had a long way to go. My time entrenched in the world of the Cuban exiles and knowledge of their politics created a unique niche for me in my career, but often prevented me from branching out.

In 1975, I was asked to leave the Counter Terrorist Unit to work a special airport and seaport security project that had been part of a federal grant we'd acquired. A small group of us would be there specifically to investigate the infiltration of organized crime into the seaport unions. My old Lords buddy Bobby Gonzalez heard about it too, and started singing a familiar song.

"Come on," he said. "Take me with you!" So I dragged him along. Actually, it wasn't that easy.

Before Bobby came on board, I was saddled with Danny Benitez, and very much by accident. I went to Maj. Bertucelli and requested Bobby Gonzalez be hired, then within a few months we had Benitez in OCB with us. He was the loud-talking, fast-driving guy that I'd worked with in Central District, and I was definitely dismayed to see that I was expected to do so again. He was obese, a sloppy dresser, and quick to criticize others. He and I were always civil to one another, but he was never my idea of a good representative for our job.

I went to Bertucelli about it.

"Why is this guy here?" I asked.

The Major stopped in his tracks. "Because you asked for him!"

"What?" How could that have happened? I told him I asked for Bobby Gonzalez.

Bertucelli threw up his hands. "Gonzalez…Benitez…I can't keep track."

I was annoyed that Benitez was here by my having been misunderstood by the Major, and I let Benitez know he was in my presence by error entirely.

Bobby Gonzalez had to wait a bit, but eventually he was brought on board and paired with me. Our first case was a massive theft of liquor from the railroad. I didn't think it fell under airport or seaport jurisdiction, but the general investigation guys made it our business. Bobby and I started working the case, and one afternoon I told him we should swing by some places around Hialeah I knew to be dumping grounds for abandoned cars and trailers. We had our best shot at finding the trailer dumped somewhere. We started patrolling and after a while Bobby spoke up.

"Raul, pull the car over." We'd been driving a while so it stood to reason he might have to use the bathroom or grab a soda. So, I pulled over and put the car in park, and realized nature was calling in a very different way. This nut got out, went into the backseat, and went to sleep. I could only shake my head. That was Bobby.

I drove while my partner snored, and finally I came across the trailer.

"Bobby, get up," I called. "I found it."

With that, he rubbed his eyes, grabbed the radio, and advised Lt. Lyons that *we'd* found the load. I couldn't believe it.

I'd put word out to my growing network of informants and eventually one of them gave up the load. We recovered every drop of liquor from the theft, and our little three-man operation instantly became the talk of department. It was a coup for Lt. Tommy Lyons, who quickly lavished in the credit for the seizure. He wrote a paper about cracking the case and it became part of his public speaking engagements for years.

I was eager to get rolling on the next case for the airport and seaport project since my work on the liquor case had made me a rockstar to the FBI and Customs. Steve Csukas of Customs asked me to get involved in what would become one of the largest national investigations into labor corruption in the country. But at that point, it just involved a guy named Joey Teitelbaum and a grudge.

Csukas had an informant named Wilfredo. He was our connection to Teitelbaum, a top executive of a major international shipping company based in Miami. Teitelbaum was owed money by someone out of the country for some time, and he decided to settle the matter, even at the expense of the debt. Teitelbaum put word out on the street that he was looking for a hitman. Enter me.

Csukas briefed me in his office, then Wilfredo and I went to meet Teitelbaum. It turned out that Teitelbaum needed someone to go to Venezuela and whack the debtor. So I got into character as a Cuban exile who could get dangerous things done and we went to the meeting. I needed to establish my credibility in the Cuban underworld in case Teitelbaum started asking around about me, so I turned to The Monkey. I brought Morales into the operation, which proved to be a good thing because I'd soon be off the case entirely.

Our director, E. Wilson Purdy, contacted my old Counter Terrorist Unit at that time. He asked them to prepare a summary of the Cuban terrorist organizations operating in Miami for a presentation he had to make to federal agencies. When the unit replied that it would take them a week, I was called by my sergeant and asked to prepare the report. I wrote ten pages from memory and handed it in overnight. I didn't realize it, but I'd just errantly proven myself indispensable to my old unit.

That was it—the end of my assignment with the airport and seaport project. I was pulled right back into the Counter Terrorist Unit without ever having the satisfaction of using my undercover role to yield a conviction on Teitelbaum. Morales ended up playing the hitman role and Teitelbaum was arrested and flipped, wearing a wire and providing the FBI enough ammunition to yield 129 indictments and 110 convictions. Although I was on the front lines for the genesis of the whole investigation, I wasn't there to share in the spoils of the bust. Though Lt. Lyons wasted no time in taking his bows once again.

Then on December 3, 1975, at 8:18 p.m., a pipe bomb exploded outside Miami's FBI building. At 8:45 p.m., another pipe bomb blew up at the US Post Office on Flagler. Eighteen minutes later, still another pipe bomb blew the windows out of the Post Office building at SW 8th St. and 68th Ave. At 9:40 p.m., a bomb detonated at the Social Security building on NW 14th St., just feet from Sgt. Tom Brodie of the bomb squad, who was there to investigate what was previously reported to be an undetonated device.

—

Two days of chaos erupted in Miami, sending our unit into a tailspin. Between December third and fourth, eight explosive devices had been planted in or around government buildings, including inside both the Miami Police station and the State Attorney's office in the Metro Justice building. This was too much to be coincidence, and it looked like we were under attack.

I contacted all my informants and they all agreed on one thing—those pipe bombs were as Cuban as royal palms. Though the bomber in this case was definitely Cuban, the targets didn't have any political meaning to me. I started believing it was someone with a more personal grudge.

Then we got a quick break. One of Miami's Cuban radio stations, WRHC, got a phone call from someone claiming to be the bomber. The caller, who identified himself as *El Condor*, said there was a letter for police in a phone booth on SW 8th St., placed inside the Yellow Pages at page 1,043. We responded and sure enough, there was an envelope in there that contained a typed note. Translated, it read:

> My name is El Condor. I am a member of JIN. The last activities we were forced to carry out because of the negative attitude of the traitorous system. We can increase our military strength and do great damage on a national level. This is only a demonstration.
>
> The main reasons which justify our position are:
>
> 1. To welcome the members of the Gestapo (FBI) who recently arrived
>
> 2. Constant lack of respect for Latins, especially the Cubans
>
> 3. The murder of Mr. Rolando Masferrer by the FBI because of the position he took in his last article which appeared in the weekly *Libertad.*
>
> 4. The kidnapping of Humberto Lopez from Santo Domingo

5. The repression and jailing of Cubans in this country. We demand that the US (sic) government immediately free all Cubans who were imprisoned for political reasons.

If this demand is not satisfied within 48 hours, we will attack military objectives, and

a. There will be no warning.

b. The danger to innocent people will increase.

c. We will demand fifty million dollars to be given to minorities in this country.

- El Condor

The note contained one additional thing—a fingerprint. But with no one to compare it to, it would just sit. This was before computers could scan databases in a millisecond. If we were going to find a match, we'd need to compare this print to a suspect's. Although, this print did match one taken off the latch of a locker after an explosion at Miami International Airport earlier in the year.

Monkey Morales called and asked about the case.

"You have any prints of value on the Condor?"

I told him we had a couple with no one to match them to, and I mentioned the match to the airport bombing.

"Try Rolando Otero Hernandez," he said.

Shit. I knew him.

Otero was one of the Brigade 2506 veterans on the Golden Falcons skydiving team. I'd talked with him at some of their demonstrations and found him to be a mellow guy. I knew he was involved with some sideways stuff, like marijuana and running *bolita*, the illegal Cuban lottery, but never would have figured him a bomber. He never came across as violent.

But not only did I know Otero from the Golden Falcons, I'd just seen him over Christmas. Some of the investigators and I were invited to Monkey Morales's place for a holiday party. I was there with my co-workers from Dade as well as some FBI agents, and I bumped into Otero. We made brief small talk while the drinks flowed and Morales spun records. Well, one in particular—Simon and Garfunkel's "El Condor Pasa," or in English, "The Condor Passes." He played the song twenty times that night and now I knew why. That prick had Otero milling with police all night. I couldn't help but laugh. They didn't call him The Monkey for nothing. Man, he loved stirring the shit.

The fingerprint was going to be an issue though. Otero hadn't been arrested by us and wasn't in our records. Then I remembered him once telling me he'd been driving a cab. I bolted out of my seat and sprinted to the taxi licensing office. All applicants for that job are printed, and I retrieved his fingerprint card and brought it up to Jimmy Hines in the crime lab on the fifth floor of our building. I told him to compare it to the prints from the case. Before I even got down to my desk on the third floor my phone was ringing.

"We got him," Jimmy said.

The Monkey had come through after his little prank at the holiday party, and he wasn't done yet. The FBI had muscled their way into the lead investigator's role and took over surveillance of Otero once I identified him as the bomber. My experience from that time was that the Bureau didn't so much assist in our local investigations as operate independently, unconcerned with the chaos that their taking and not giving had created. Monkey Morales had given *me* the tip that *they* were building the case upon. So, the FBI slid into place, took over, and followed Otero around while everyone waited for an indictment to be handed down.

Then Monkey called them with a tip.

"The Condor is about to fly," he said.

And fly he did. Remarkably, while the feds watched, Otero somehow headed to K-Mart, bought suitcases, new clothes, travel kits, and boarded a plane to the Dominican Republic on a ticket purchased for him by Ricardo "Monkey" Morales. The frigging Simon and Garfunkel record was our official notification that my prized informant and friend was orchestrating a three-ring circus for his own amusement.

The indictment finally came down on January 22, 1976, and Rolando Otero was now officially a fugitive. Morales, using his current position as a ranking official in Venezuela's intelligence unit called DISIP, moved him around, from the Dominican Republic to Venezuela and ultimately Chile, before Otero was extradited back to Miami.

I didn't go to the airport for the big return. Seeing the FBI holding Otero by the arm and leading him through the TV and newspaper cameras, strutting like peacocks past the throng, would've made me sick. I didn't have to suffer any more indignities at their hand.

Getting Otero back was one thing, but convicting him would be another. The Condor's federal trial was slated to take place in Jacksonville, FL, and Det. Eddie Mederos and I were there to testify. Someone who wasn't there was Monkey Morales. He was on deck to testify to having heard Otero's confession before giving it to me. Now, given his no-show, the prosecution had one big missing piece of the puzzle. My mind was racing as I realized the extent to which Morales had compromised the trial. Sure enough, Otero was acquitted.

I got on the phone with Asst. State Attorneys Hank Adorno and George Yoss. Otero simply could not walk on these charges. Adorno told me and Mederos to slap cuffs on him. Though the federal indictment was in the trash, Adorno would charge him at the State level. We arrested him and flew him down to Miami to face the music yet again, this time in Ft. Walton Beach. The State wanted to strengthen their case by getting Otero out of Miami, away from other exiles who might have landed on the jury and been sympathetic to his cause. Ft. Walton Beach is up in the Florida panhandle and closer to Alabama in every sense. "Them there" people didn't care for no foreigners settin' off bombs.

I sat beside Otero for the flight back after the Jacksonville acquittal. He was very cordial despite my having just arrested him. He was an incredible photographer and we talked cameras the entire trip. I enjoyed it—I actually learned a lot.

If the State was going to win a conviction, it was clear they needed to ensure Monkey Morales's participation. Adorno and his deputy Yoss wanted to go down to Caracas where Morales was stationed in Venezuela's DISIP agency. They needed some assurance that he would show up for this new trial—or else, why bother? It was Morales that had provided the information that was the entire basis for the print match and subsequent arrest.

My friendship with him came in handy. I more than made myself available to accompany the prosecutors down to sunny Caracas and act as their bodyguard. I grabbed my friend Art Castro from Miami PD and told him we were headed on an extended weekend vacation—I mean, an official assignment.

—

Venezuela was heating up. The political thermometer was rising due to the bombing of Cubana Airlines Flight 455—a political act by an alliance of Cuban anti-Castro bombers where seventy-three people died. It seemed the country's DISIP agency might've had some culpability in the terrorist act, which put Monkey Morales in the spotlight. As an expert bomber, it was impossible to fathom that their top commander didn't have some role in this. DISIP's being run by three Cuban CIA assets made it all the more suspect.

After the plane was blown up, I received a phone call from one of those Cubans—Orlando Garcia Vasquez, head of DISIP and Morales's boss. Orlando had been my father's schoolmate at the University of Havana and had gotten my number from Morales. He told me who he was and asked that I give my father an *abrazo*, a hug.

He said that he was under a great deal of pressure from Venezuelan President Carlos Andres Perez, who, in turn, was under a lot of pressure from Washington. The US wanted permission to send FBI, ATF, and any available hands from other agencies there to investigate the bombing. DISIP's leader Orlando wasn't amenable to that, for reasons that became more obvious as we learned more about the organization's role in the bombing.

"Raulito," he began, "how'd you feel about coming down here for a week? We'll get drunk and tell stories and lies every night." I told him I was all for it.

He told me that he would tell the FBI that he would allow me and just one other member of our Joint Terrorist Task Force to go to Venezuela and handle the investigation of the bombing. He called back a couple of days later and told me he had a green light, and I should just let him know when we wanted to go.

I told him that two state prosecutors needed to interview Morales in regard to his testimony against bombing suspect Rolando Otero, and they would like to travel with me. He approved that too, and I told Hank Adorno and George Yoss to pack a bag.

My trip down there was now two-fold—securing Morales for the upcoming Otero trial, and also interviewing him about the bombing of Flight 455.

I noticed some other familiar faces on the same flight as us, clearly on their way down to Caracas for the same issues. Prominent writers Taylor Branch, John Rothchild, and Latin American investigative reporter for *The Miami*

News, Hilda Inclan, went to probe Morales and DISIP about their possible role in the Flight 455 crime. We saw each other and all realized at once how prominent the country at the northern tip of South America was becoming in our part of the world.

The two prosecutors, Art Castro, and I were greeted warmly by Morales at the airport, where he was stationed. Unfortunately, the same couldn't be said for the meddlesome reporters when they disembarked. Hilda made the critical error of addressing Morales more casually than a commander in the intelligence agency probably should be.

"Aren't you The Monkey?" she asked.

After that, the contingent of reporters were followed by DISIP the entire day, and eventually rounded up by Morales at 6 a.m. the next morning and escorted to a waiting plane.

Art and I were escorted by Morales as well, though, after some cursory time in DISIP offices, mostly to beaches, pools, restaurants, and lounges. When Monkey told us, "Get some rest because we are starting early tomorrow," I didn't realize he meant drinking. We started at eleven in the morning and went hard until nine at night. A few restaurant visits were scattered throughout the day as well, and that schedule went on for the entire trip, minus the last two days because George Yoss fucked up.

The lawyers didn't receive the grand treatment the cops did. Yoss and Adorno had a conference call from their hotel room with State Attorney Richard Gerstein and Marty Dardis, chief investigator for the State Attorney's office. Gerstein was repeatedly warning them about trusting Morales, telling them to be careful while in his company. Monkey was their most crucial witness for the case, but they clearly weren't confident in him. Dardis chimed in, slamming Morales as well.

The moment they hung up on the conference call, their phone rang. It was Morales.

"Do you talk shit about all of your witnesses?" he barked. They realized he'd tapped their hotel room phone. Man, they should've known better. I knew what that meant for their case and I left Venezuela having accomplished nothing but a good time.

Later that year, Art and I headed up to the Florida panhandle for the Otero trial. It was a far cry from the waterfront resorts we'd just left in Caracas. We were placed in charge of security for the trial, and as such we'd need to be sworn in as deputy sheriffs by Sheriff Frankie Mills himself. We raised our hands and took some solemn oath to enforce this and that, and bam, we were deputy sheriffs. Art and I stepped out of the police station and thought the same thing.

"I need a drink."

We drove aimlessly and found a local spot—read "redneck bar"—pretty quickly. I hoped they wouldn't mind a couple of Cubans hangin with them for the afternoon. We walked in and, sure enough, the place stopped. All eyes were on us.

Well, on our purses, anyway.

In Venezuela, we'd bought these little bags with shoulder straps to put our guns in. Today, guys carrying bags might be seen as stylish in some circles, though not then, and not in the South.

"Wrong place for these things," I muttered to Art.

We sauntered to the bar, and I lifted my bag and dropped it on the bar, hard—could only be one thing inside that heavy. Art did the same and we looked at the bartender knowingly. He nodded back in kind. We grabbed a couple of scotches and were eventually joined by some guys we'd met at the sheriff's office. Everything was okay from that point forward. File that one under "how to survive in a redneck bar as a man with a purse." Bet you didn't count on getting that today.

In addition to the Otero trial, we had one more order of business while up there. E. Howard Hunt, the legendary CIA officer who'd been sent by my father-in-law to check up on me at the police academy years ago, had been convicted for his role in the Watergate scandal. He was serving time in Pensacola, not far from Ft. Walton Beach, so we were tasked with serving him a subpoena to appear at the trial and speak to Otero's time working for the CIA. The two new deputy sheriffs left their purses behind and headed to Eglin Federal Prison.

We identified ourselves and were led to a private cell where Hunt sat reading a book. I stepped toward him.

"Hi, Eduardo," I said, as that had been his *nom de guerre* during the Bay of Pigs days. "I'm Musculito's son-in-law."

"Oh my God," he said as he stood and embraced me. I introduced him to Art, whose father E. Howard Hunt had also known from his tenure with the CIA. He got a big hug as well.

The face of the prison official who'd escorted us was souring with each hug and back slap. He said something into his radio, and before I knew it we were joined by two more prison officials, then by two massive uniformed guards. He clearly hadn't expected the greeting we received; most subpoena servings didn't go that way, I suppose. They clearly thought we were up to something.

We left without incident, but once returning to Ft. Walton, the sheriff summoned me.

"What is your connection to E. Howard Hunt?" he asked.

I told him who Musculito was to me, what he had done with the CIA, and his connection to Hunt and Watergate.

"My Lord!" the sheriff said in reverence. "You're the son-in-law of a patriot." Well, from that moment on, this patriot could do no wrong in Fort Walton County. The story must've reached Judge Clyde B. Wells, who presided over the Otero trial, because he treated Art and I very well.

I wasn't wrong about my prediction regarding Morales in the Otero trial. After hearing the State Attorneys talking shit about him, he shut down completely. He didn't cooperate with them and no-showed the Condor's second trial, where he was acquitted on eight of the nine bombings he was charged with. The only one that stuck was the Miami airport bombing that left his fingerprint on the locker, for which he was sentenced to thirty years. Bless Judge Wells.

—

As smart as we think we are here in the US, we've consistently been played by Cuba. Forget the Bay of Pigs, the Cuban missile crisis, and all the other failures from the 60s. For years afterward, Cuba successfully infiltrated our government for its own purposes.

Right around the time of the El Condor escapades, I had an informant named Oscar Angulo, to whom I was introduced by FBI agents George Davis and Robert Dwyer. He'd been providing the FBI a warehouse of information, literally. They'd stored boxes and boxes of reports over the years, and they thought I'd be able to make use of much of his intel in the Dade County Organized Crime Bureau. So, I began working with Angulo.

I ran his name by Monkey Morales, who knew him from Cuba where they both worked for Castro's G2 secret police. They were friends, but truthfully, the more I got to know Angulo, the more I didn't like him. He was an ass-kisser and a worm.

My father-in-law, who'd been released from his fifteen-month prison stint for the Watergate break-in, and his associate Jose Aleman came to me with some information and an odd request.

"There is going to be a meeting," he told me. He and a group of anti-Cuba exiles were going to be hosting a Chilean journalist named Hector Duran in one of their homes. "Can you wire the place beforehand?" Aleman asked.

"What's so special about this meeting that you want it recorded?"

"Oscar Angulo is going to be there," Aleman said. "And we want you to hear him because we think he's a Cuban agent, working for Castro."

The implications certainly piqued my interest, so I contacted our IT people and we went into the apartment in Miami Springs and wired the whole place. Six men convened—Duran the Chilean, Musculito, Aleman, Ramiro De La Fe, Rafael Valdes, and Angulo. The subject of the meeting was the formation of a joint anti-communist league between Cubans in Miami and the Chilean government under dictator Augusto Pinochet. Everyone was expressing agreement with the proposal and exploring non-violent options their alliance could facilitate, when Angulo spoke up.

"No!" he exclaimed, bringing the meeting to a halt. "If there is no violence, there is no change." He proposed the bombing of a Bahamian ship in the Richard Bertram shipyard on the Miami River rather than the more subtle forms of influence on the table. The group discussed it and parted with a plan to get their hands on a cannon and carry out the terrorist act. I figured this was an impressive effort on Angulo the informant's part to record the other participants planning this for the FBI. The suspected double agent just didn't know we were recording his recording.

The following day, I met with Angulo and asked if he was ready to tell us everything that happened at the meeting, which he had no idea we were listening in on. Angulo asked for his customary typewriter—he was a newspaper writer and would only type his own reports—and began hammering out his account of the meeting before signing and handing it to us.

It was a fine work of fiction, and he apologized for what he'd written about my father-in-law.

Angulo reported that Musculito brought up the bombing and was trying to entice the reluctant members of the group to bomb the ship in Miami, rather than himself. I knew right there we had an issue. I went to Lt. Lyons.

"We have a problem with this Angulo guy," I said. I probed a little more, and it only got worse. Angulo had written four reports of that meeting—one for us in OCB, another for the FBI, still another for the City of Miami's Special Investigations Unit (SIU), and finally one for US Customs. And each report was different.

Had all the agencies not known what he'd written to each one—and if I hadn't been listening in on the meeting, no one would have—the participants in the non-violent alliance in the house that night would've now been targeted and possibly neutralized. Law enforcement would've gone after them and brought an end to their plans. This would have benefitted no one except Cuba. It was obvious to me that Musculito and Pepe were right about Angulo.

I immediately blackballed Angulo from being used by OCB. I no longer considered his information credible, and more so, it was deliberately misleading and dangerous. I called Agent Davis at the FBI and told him the issue I had with Angulo. I wanted them to know the danger he was potentially putting the Bureau in. He and Dwyer came to my office that day.

"Raul," Davis began, "we can't blackball him on our end. We will have to deal with him a little differently, but we can't lose him." Davis explained they had warehouses of information he'd provided over the years and their discrediting him would invalidate all information that had been used in the past and in the future on FBI investigations.

I was crestfallen. I had proof positive that this guy's information was bullshit and more than likely fabricated to serve a country with whom we had endless conflict and an embargo in place. Why didn't they just put the fucking Ayatollah on the stand for them?

This was the FBI—the highest federal law enforcement agency in the land—and the message they'd just given me was "our numbers are more important than truth."

Yes, discounting Angulo from investigations would have jeopardized investigations and maybe even overturned convictions for cases in which his information was used. But wouldn't those results have been warranted, given the circumstances?

Years later, I was reminded of the FBI's treatment of Angulo when the Brothers to the Rescue organization lost four pilots trying to lend humanitarian assistance to those looking to flee Cuba. The organization was founded by pilots and exiles from Cuba who learned people were dying while trying to get to the US on makeshift rafts and floats. They would fly overhead looking for people in trouble.

One of the pilots in the organization was a former Cuban Air Force pilot named Juan Roque. He'd come here in 1992 and began working with the Brothers to the Rescue group before surreptitiously returning to Cuba in February of 1996.

Two days later, on February 23, 1996, two Brothers to the Rescue aircrafts were shot down by Cuban Air Force planes, killing all four men on board. It was no wonder how they ascertained the information on the pilots' mission.

Roque was working for another group during his tenure with the Brothers—the FBI. They put this secret agent of Cuba on the payroll to spy on the group of pilots and provide information on their activities. Apparently, in the case of their Cuban informants, the Bureau just recruited and started paying a salary with no vetting or background checking. It wasn't like Cuba would have been cooperative anyway, but I was always skeptical of informants the FBI gave me, or any sources that I didn't develop myself.

Emilio Milian was probably the most popular Cuban radio personality in the Miami exile community. He started his talk radio show, *Habla el Pueblo* (The People Speak), in 1971 which became a place for callers in the Cuban community to be heard. Milian himself was a controversial figure since he'd taken a stance against bombings and political violence in the US as a way to further the cause for the citizens of Cuba and the US to exist in peace. That was a position, as I'd mentioned, that displeased the more radical groups in the city. If you weren't calling for Fidel's head, you were bowing to him.

I'd become close to Milian. I personally admired his strength in going public with denouncing violence in the cause of our motherland. He was the one voice in the exile community who criticized every act of violence; such actions made people fear our community and mimicked the behavior of the thugs we'd abandoned back home.

He said, "How could we, as freedom-loving Cubans, who denounce the atrocities perpetrated by the Castro regime, now sit idly by as bombs explode and people are executed in our adopted city?"

In addition to his outstanding character, Milian was professionally helpful to me. He provided me with information over the years about activities in the community he'd become privy to. He was the most popular host on the three Cuban radio stations in Miami and his ear was to the ground on everything. Beyond that, I just liked Emilio. He was very intelligent and spending time with him was stimulating. I learned a thing or two, which was not always the case with all my sources, to put it mildly.

One Tuesday night in April 1976, Milian was at home watching TV. He saw a car stop at the curb in front of his house, and a man got out and walked near Milian's car, then disappeared. A few minutes later, the same car returned, picked up the man who was now standing by Milian's car again, and left. Milian didn't see the guy do anything, but the scene raised a big red flag.

My phone rang the following morning. It was Milian asking if I could meet him at his house in NW Miami.

"Something strange happened last night," he began, "and I need your opinion."

I called my friend Art Castro in Miami's SIU and had him meet me there since Milian lived in their jurisdiction. He told us about the car dropping the guy off for a minute, and a curious observation he'd made: the car's headlights were off the entire time, there were no brake lights when it slowed and stopped, and when the door opened there was no dome light inside. The car was deliberately modified and rendered nearly invisible in the darkness.

"Was your car broken into?" I asked.

It wasn't.

"I fear someone is going to hurt me or my family. Can you get the police department to watch over us for a few days?"

I said we'd talk with the supervisors, and I advised him to get his brakes checked to ensure no one had messed with them. Art and I went back to our respective offices, and I went to Lt. Lyons and requested overtime to keep watch over Milian's house.

"That's within the City of Miami's boundaries," he said. "It should be MPD handling this."

"I understand that, but Emilio Milian has been extremely helpful to our department in the past. We owe him this much." It wasn't an outlandish request; it wouldn't have been the first time OCB protected someone outside our jurisdiction.

But I was denied. It was a shitty way to handle someone who'd been so valuable, and it planted seeds of discontent toward Lyons, who'd already shown himself to be a snake by hogging credit for others' accomplishments. I didn't argue my case any further; it was clear he wasn't giving my opinion any credence.

I called Art Castro and told him his department would have to take it, but he had already been denied by his bosses. I was forced to call Milian and tell him this shit. I told him to be very careful of his surroundings at all times and to call me if he saw anything suspicious. Although I wouldn't be compensated for my time, I would drop everything and head to him if he called, and I knew Art would do the same.

On the afternoon of Friday, April 30, Emilio Milian left the radio station and walked behind the building to his station wagon. He was approached by a woman named Rosa Delgado and some friends from a local college who reported they'd found a lost little boy. They asked if Milian could help, and he said to go into the radio station and someone would make sure it was broadcast.

Fortunately, she and her friends turned and began to walk toward the radio station when Milian turned the ignition. They were only about ten feet away when the car exploded.

Miss Delgado turned and, remarkably, ran toward the car to help Milian, who was still alive. She tried to open door to the smoking, fiery car, but burned her hand on the door handle. Milian was looking at her helplessly, shaking.

"Get out!" she yelled. "Open your door—I will help you!"

Milian lifted his thighs for her to see—there was nothing below his knees as his legs had been severed by the blast. Miraculously, he survived. If he had been driving a smaller car, as in Masferrer's case, he would've died instantly.

He was recovering in Jackson Memorial Hospital, and I headed there as soon as I got word that he was conscious. I slunk into his room where he lay alone, with the horrors he'd undergone playing repeatedly in his mind. I got to his bedside and looked down at him as he turned his face to me. Whatever dignity remained was visible in his eyes as he processed the fact that nearly half his body was taken from him.

I nodded to him, searching for something to say. His lips parted just below his trademark mustache. He beat me to the punch.

"This is your fault," he said quietly. His eyes never left mine.

What could I say? I certainly never intended for this to happen and would've done absolutely anything to help him. I had petitioned Lt. Lyons and Art Castro had done the same with his superior, but we were blocked from working any preventative detail. The slew of cases on my desk was eating my already scarce time, and I needed help from either of our departments to keep an eye on Milian. For whatever reason, they couldn't.

Despite that reality, a true warrior and voice for all of us in the respectable Cuban community had reached out for help. He could've called anyone—but he'd reached out to me. And this is what he got.

I replied to him with the only truth that I could find.

"You're right."

He turned from me, toward the window in the room he'd never be able to walk out of, and just gazed beyond the glass. My head sank, as did my heart, and I strode from his room unable to raise either for a long while. I wept the entire drive back from the hospital.

My anger toward Lt. Lyons didn't subside with time. While I was initially pissed he wouldn't make an accommodation for Milian, that began to simmer even more after the bombing. Beyond Milian's value to me as a source, Lyons knew we'd become close personally. I'd often meet him for lunch and spend time with him even when I didn't need information. So, after the attempted murder of my friend, Lyons offered exactly what I expected him to.

Nothing. Not a word.

Typical. I never told anyone outside of my department about what had happened, but it chewed at my soul every day.

The initial outcry following the bombing was fast and fierce. The FBI and ATF collaborated with us and the Miami Police Department. We all assigned as many investigators as possible to the case which, unfortunately, dragged on for years. Finally, on April 30, 1981, just hours shy of the expiration of the five-year statute of limitations, US Attorney Atlee Wampler indicted three men for the crime. Incredibly, the charges would soon be dropped when Wampler's replacement deemed one of the witnesses unreliable. All of it seemed sketchy, and very "70s Miami."

—

One afternoon, the receptionist at the front door to OCB rang me.

"You have two agents from the IRS here for you."

I wasn't expecting anyone, so I headed to the front where an old high school mate named Steve was waiting for me in reception. I knew he'd become an agent but hadn't seen him in a while, so I greeted him warmly. I couldn't help but notice another hulking agent who'd accompanied him. I said hello to him as well, all the while staring at his face as I tried to figure out how I knew him. He was familiar in a distant way, and I was pretty sure he wasn't anyone I'd dealt with on the job. Had he gone to school with me and Steve?

When he returned my greeting and looked at me through his thick glasses, it came to me in an instant.

"Sorry I hit you," I said. This was the huge prick who'd called my brother and his friend "spics" and told them to not play basketball at Stillwater Park. I reminded him of that, and we shared a good laugh. He filled in Steve, recounting how I'd come to his house, hat in hand, asking them to drop the charges against me.

"Steve, I never heard anyone beg so much in my life."

Did I mention he was as full of shit as he was big?

He asked about my brother Miguel, and I was happy to share how well he was doing. I'd always admired my brother—he was everything I was not. I didn't consider myself introverted, but no one could compare to Miguel. He was magnetic; people were drawn to him and the fact that he was very good looking didn't hurt. He was also a star baseball player in high school and had gone to Palm Beach Junior College for two years on a full scholarship, then played at Florida International University. My father was elated because he finally had an athlete in the family. Then, Miguel blew out his knee and couldn't play his final year at FIU.

I began studying for the sergeant's exam around this time, as is the rite of passage for young officers. I was the epitome of burning the candle at both ends, and I think I found some wick in the center to start burning as well. I was already working ungodly hours on these investigations of anything going *boom* in Miami, and there were plenty of them. Any hours outside of that were spent studying for the exam. Bobby Gonzalez was supposed to be studying with me, but I was so busy at work that he'd punked out and began studying with another guy and never told me.

Poor Thania got so little of me. Even when I was physically present, I wasn't mentally. I'd fall asleep thinking about a question from the study materials, and literally awaken in the middle of the night pondering the same thing, many times without an answer. The two or three hours my brain got to sleep was *still* occupied by procedural bullshit for the test.

There were times I'd walk into the house and crash without being able to say anything but hello. This came to a head one night when I got home and went into the bedroom to change and when I didn't come out, Thania went in to check on me. I'd fallen face-first onto the bed, fully clothed, and fallen asleep. That was not unusual for me at the time, but the fact that I was still clutching my two-inch .38 Smith and Wesson was. Thania wouldn't touch it and was scared to startle me if she woke me, so she called my friend, psychiatrist Dr. Pedro Rodriguez, to come over and disarm the sleeping corpse.

Pedro, who later went onto prominence as the Vice President of NORC, the psychiatric research organization, began treating me as a patient and not as a friend. He put me on something called Sinequan that began helping me, and also taught me some breathing exercises to get back to normal when I needed it.

It got so intense that some months later I was patrolling one night and got lost in the district, which is basically an impossibility. I knew every artery of that area and I couldn't understand why I was so foggy. My breaths were rapid-fire and my body shook. Nothing I was seeing looked familiar.

Where had I driven? Did I black out or something and end up in Georgia?

The more I thought about it, fought with my mind to straighten up, the more scarce oxygen became. It was a classic panic attack, but I'd never experienced one. I pulled over and got out of the car. I started Pedro's breathing exercises and stabilized my body and mind. I was still in Miami. It was scary, but there was really no time to consider it the warning sign that it was. There were more cases coming at me every day, and I was determined to ace the sergeants' exam and advance. There wasn't time to consider how it was affecting my health, or what that bottle of liquid stability I'd become friendly with was really doing.

CHAPTER SEVEN

SHIT SQUAD SERGEANT

When several boxes of dynamite were reported stolen by Maule Industries, a concrete company, my department was contacted because, well, Miami and explosives go together. I put word out to my informants in the Cuban community, figuring one of the anti-Castro bombing groups was involved. I told them to let me know if they heard about some new dynamite surfacing on the black market.

I got a call from a surprising source—an American guy I'd done a favor for years before. This guy was a member of the Outlaws motorcycle gang and the son of an older lady who worked as a cleaning woman for some of my friends. The kid was an asshole, but his mom reached out and begged me to help him, as she had no money for bail. I drove to the Dade County jail, got some basic information from him about the Outlaws, and officially registered him as an informant. That meant I could go see the prosecutor, and as a result he was let go with a slap on the wrist. Well, one hand washes the other and you might say I forced that wrist under water. Now, he owed *me*.

"I heard you're looking for some missing dynamite," he said to me one day, and I told him I was. He said he didn't have it, but he could take me to the person who did—a real heavy in the biker world.

My heritage helped me as I went undercover as a Cuban bomber in Miami. It was a perfect cover, and I didn't have to do a thing. I might've leaned a little more heavily on the accent. I got wired for sound and was brought to a second-floor apartment on Coral Way where I was introduced to the heavy—300-plus pound Janet Barnes, the "Motorcycle Mama." She was short but looked as strong as bull, and just like with narcotics, I asked for a sample to make sure the stuff she was peddling was the real deal.

"Whatcha need it for?" she asked.

"I'm Alpha 66," I said, referencing the well-known anti-Castro bombing group. "We need to make some bombs." I don't know if that was how they talked business, but she didn't bat an eyelash.

I handed her some money and was given a sweaty stick of dynamite rolled in a towel. That moisture covering the stick was not a good thing. When poorly made dynamite is not stored properly, the nitroglycerin can seep out and coat the stick with a combustible condensation. I put it in the trunk of my car, gently, and drove off already getting an awful headache from the nitro fumes. I met up with Tom Brodie of the bomb squad at around ten o'clock that night in the empty parking lot of a shopping center. He popped the trunk and looked inside.

"You're lucky, kid," he said with a chuckle. Brodie always laughed when the danger quotient was ratcheted up. He moved my parcel to the bomb truck, and it was carted away. They didn't even have to test it—the smell of the nitro confirmed this was legit. I moved forward with the operation and met up with Janet a couple of days later. I was again wired with a recording device.

"How was it?" she asked.

"Good. I blew it up in the Everglades. How much more can you get me?"

"How about a case?"

I agreed. Before I left, I wanted to see just how diabolical this woman was and get it on tape.

"Janet," I began, "I'm going to blow the shit out of Miami with this load. A lot of people are going to die—men, women, and children."

This bitch just shrugged. "As long as you don't kill me and my guys, we're fine with that."

We set a day and time to make the purchase and, ultimately, bring her down. I would bring Det. Iggy Vasquez with me to make the purchase. Iggy was bench pressing about 450 and was roughly the size of a refrigerator. If there was to be any bullshit with the bikers, he was a good guy to have in the room with me. We planned to position a couple of officers near the door, and when I gave the cue—*"all good things must come to an end"*— they'd bust through the door and take down Janet and whoever else she had with her. I figured the four of us would be able to get control of any situation inside. I was wired so the outside team could monitor the deal and hear my cue to make entry, and we headed to Motorcycle Mama's apartment.

We entered the unit and found Janet alone, seated at the kitchen table. She didn't waste time.

"Gimme the money."

We handed it over and asked for the case, which I figured wasn't in the apartment since I didn't smell any nitro from the shitty load. She couldn't have stored it there—it would've made her sick.

"Where's the case?" I asked.

Janet gave us directions to a trailer park where she said she'd stored it. She already accepted our money for the stolen dynamite, so I figured we had enough to take her down. We stepped toward the door, and I waved goodbye.

"Well, Janet, all good things must come to an end." I awaited detectives Danny and his brother Joe Benitez to make entry as planned.

But they didn't.

Janet sat there nodding, waiting for us to leave. Maybe I was too quiet or there was radio interference in the transmission to the cops outside.

"Like I said…all good things must come to a fucking end already."

Nada.

Janet furrowed her brow—something was up.

I looked to Iggy and shrugged.

"Fuck it," I said, then turned to Mama. "Janet, you're under arrest."

It took her a second to realize we were serious. Then, I watched in awe as she rose, a guttural bellow roaring forth from deep in her mountainous body. I'd been to both the circus and the zoo and never heard a sound like that. She began to draw a revolver she'd concealed under a significant roll of belly fat.

"Gun!" Iggy shouted as he dove on her. They went down and I threw myself on top of them and grabbed for the weapon as Iggy bounced around on her like a kid in an inflatable house at a birthday party. She rolled us both back toward the front door where the Benitez brothers must've been enjoying a Cuban coffee or something.

The fracas in the apartment must've tipped them off that something was wrong, and they finally busted down the door right on top of us.

The free-for-all finally ended, we cuffed Janet Barnes, and I looked around for the *Candid Camera* crew. I didn't find them, but I did find a dislodged microphone wire in my pocket. The cord ran from my lower back around to right under my nipple and I'd accidentally pulled it out of the transmitter sometime before entering the apartment. The Benitezes hadn't gone for coffee after all.

I called Tom Brodie and told him the location of the trailer park where Janet told us the load was. As a couple of our guys worked on a search warrant, Brodie and his bomb squad headed out there to secure it as Iggy, the Benitezes, Janet, and I waited inside the apartment. I told Brodie to call me at that number when they found the dynamite; we didn't want to bring Janet out in handcuffs before that, lest anyone watching her apartment tip off the people guarding the load in the trailer. Brodie called me fifteen minutes later, laughing, so I knew he'd just seen some dangerous shit.

"You're not going to believe this," he began, then told me the person guarding the hot, sweaty, ten-case load had actually placed it all under his trailer. "This guy was sleeping on a time bomb." Though he was arrested, he should've thanked us for saving him from a far worse fate.

When Janet appeared in court and was found guilty, the judge heard our recordings, including her nonchalance regarding my plan for the explosives. That didn't go well for her and she was sentenced to fifteen years.

—

One of the days I was in court, a deputy came into to the courtroom and told me I had a call from someone asking for a Sgt. Diaz. I grabbed the call but was quick to correct the caller about something.

"It's *Detective* Diaz."

"No," the caller said. "You're a sergeant now."

I asked who was calling and he said it was E. Wilson Purdy, my director. At that point I knew my brethren at the department were messing with me. I replied in kind.

"Fuck you." I hung up. I was needed back in court and had no time for pranks. A short while later, I was sitting in the courtroom and was called out to the corridor, where I was told there was a phone call waiting for me. It was Maj. Steve Bertucelli.

"Diaz," he began, "the next voice you're going to hear is that of our director, E. Wilson Purdy. He wants to congratulate you on your promotion to sergeant."

My *what*?

Shit. After how I spoke to him back at the office, he was now probably calling with a very different message. Bertucelli patched the director through, and I apologized before he could even speak.

"It's alright," he said. "It's not the first time someone told me to go fuck myself."

It hadn't been a prank call after all, though it didn't mean people above me weren't laughing. My promotion came with a transfer to the Southwest District, under a captain with a terrible reputation—Robert C. "Flat Top" Windsor. I'd always heard about him but never experienced his reported absence of charm until I was interviewed by him for the sergeant job. I'd rushed out to get a haircut before going to his office in the Southwest District, as Windsor earned his nickname by never changing his hairstyle since leaving the Marines decades ago. I walked into the room for my interview and before even greeting me he said, "I hope you plan on getting a haircut."

I *had*. And made sure it was short and tight!

I told Windsor I would, though the barber would draw blood if he went any shorter.

I glanced up at the large fish mounted on his wall. He saw me looking.

"Looking at my catch?" he asked.

"Yeah," I said. "It's a beautiful blue marlin."

He slapped the desk, shocked.

"You're the only son of a bitch to come in here and recognize that as a blue marlin. At least you know your fish."

That ice breaker disarmed the grouchy guy and our meeting started without any tension. He was at ease, but it could have easily gone another way.

Moments before, when I was outside waiting to be called into his office, some of the detectives out in the hall told me about his fish.

"He loves when people talk about it," they said. "He's really impressed when someone compliments him on catching a sailfish that big."

Initially I thought that was very helpful of them. They could've easily been standoffish with the new guy being hired to be their boss. Instead, they tipped me off about the sailfish, which, as you now know, was actually a marlin. The pricks were sending me in to make me look like an idiot. Fortunately, I'd done my share of fishing and knew a blue marlin when I saw one.

Though our meeting started well, Windsor didn't pull any punches.

"You're starting this job already behind," he said. "You don't have a very good reputation, coming from OCB and all."

I knew that would be the case. OCB got dirty looks from every other bureau in the police department because we were considered untouchable. OCB had the authority to investigate anyone else in the department, including Internal Affairs, the supposed cops of the cops. We were seen as too powerful, too privileged, and basically hated by every other unit.

I had a friendly face there—Corrine, Windsor's secretary. Previously, she'd worked for my first captain when I was in Central District. She knew I was a hardworking officer and liked me very much. So, she was the first person I went to after starting in Southwest. She must've seen I was stressed.

"Raul," she said, "you'll do a good job up here."

"I appreciate that. But I'm gonna need some help."

She smiled. "I'll take care of you."

I'd just been assigned to supervise the worst squad in the district, so I took her up on that instantly; I asked her to round up all the personnel files for everyone who'd be working under me. The first thing I looked at was where the officers in my new squad had worked prior to being transferred to Southwest. I was pleasantly surprised to find that six of the seven guys under me had come from my old Central District, which I'd mentioned was the worst in terms of crimes committed. Two of them I'd known as brothers of men I had been with in the academy before working with them in Central. If you survived Central, you were the best of the best.

One of the first things I did in Southwest was remove this acting sergeant in favor of Bill Bruckner, one of the officers from Central who I knew to be a great cop.

"I'm sorry," I told the outgoing acting sergeant, "but I'm running this as if it were *Central* District." Anyone in the department knew what that meant—we were about to hit the pavement with a fire that few officers in districts other than Central had ever seen. Those guys around me would respond to my running the operation like we were hitting the chaotic streets of the city's most violent district. I'd been assigned to Southwest in February of 1977, and within months we were the top squad in calls answered, tickets, and felony arrests. We were running at top speed, every day and night. This is when I got lost in my own city and had to employ Dr. Rodriguez's breathing technique.

Truthfully, once the guys knew I'd come from their old district, that did half the work for me. They knew what I was made of, having worked in hell, and they assumed I'd be a good boss. They raised their game for me, especially after they saw I made a proper and fair appointment below me. It also didn't hurt that some stories about my unorthodox tactics in Central had preceded me to Southwest and might've painted me as a little crazy.

On paper, my new assignment looked great. Southwest was more affluent than much of the city and didn't come with the stress of Central District. It wasn't the streets that were the issue in Southwest—it was the personnel. And I had no doubt that one man in particular thought I'd be swallowed alive trying to manage those Southwest officers under Windsor the Terrible.

The hiring of a sergeant cannot be controlled by superiors most of the time, except in the rare case of specialized units. Most often, when one passes the sergeant's test they are ranked and promoted in that order. However, *where* that new sergeant is assigned is very much the recommendation of those above them. I was certain my placement in the troubled Southwest district was due to Lt. Tommy Lyons's dislike of me.

—

The year before Lyons sent me to work for Windsor in Southwest, our unit in OCB had started an investigation regarding a bomber named Antonio de la Cova. Two informants came forward, but they told Lyons they didn't want to work with me. They claimed I was too close to the Cuban exile community and the activists working in it, and then they mentioned my father-in-law Musculito's involvement in Watergate as the icing on the cake. I wasn't surprised by these two—I'd suspected them to be agents of Cuba and I never trusted them or their intel prior to that anyway.

It didn't take much convincing of Lyons—I knew he thought I was just another Cuban who couldn't divorce himself from the legacy of the Cuban people, right or wrong. He was all too happy to keep me from pertinent details of the investigation.

Then on May 6, 1976, Lt. Lyons had me accompany him to Washington to speak to a US Senate subcommittee led by Senator James O. Eastland on terrorism in Miami. When Lyons was called upon by chief counsel Richard Schultz to open the proceedings, he read from a long prepared statement. He never told me I should prepare something along the lines of a statement or statistics or anything like he presented. He made it sound like it would be just a basic Q&A and as a result, I was tap dancing my ass off to try and provide the committee anything of value. I don't know if I looked as unprepared as I felt, but that was not how I operated. I knew right there that this prick was still out for me.

The one good thing that came out of that trip was my meeting a man who eventually became a mentor. Al Tarabochia, an Italian immigrant, had been a Dade County Sheriff Deputy and was now the lead investigator for Eastland's Subcommittee. We hit it off from the beginning and we had lunch together. It was during lunch that Al asked me "Raul, why did you become an American citizen?"

I was surprised by his question but replied that I did it to show my gratitude to this country for granting us asylum and a new home.

Al shook his head. "Not me. I became an American Citizen because I'm convinced, after everything this country has overcome, that God is American. I want to get to the Pearly Gates and be able to say 'Hello, God. I am Alfonso Tarabochia, born in Italy, but I am an American citizen too.'"

I never forgot that.

One afternoon, Lyons called me into his office after rolling the Musculito reference by De la Cova's informants around his mouth for a while.

"I want you to document your father-in-law as a confidential informant," he said. This might seem an innocuous request, but at that time, I was looking for the devil in the details. In almost every police department, confidential informants, or CIs, are documented to maintain a record of their reliability or lack thereof. This practice is very useful, as long as the informants' identities don't fall into the hands of corrupt officers. And the unfortunate reality is that many an informant's life has been compromised by crooked cops.

"No problem, sir," I replied. "Just as soon as you document your wife." He stopped in his tracks.

The department once had an investigation into Eastern Airlines flight attendants running a prostitution ring. The case began with information a CI had given us. Lyons's wife was a flight attendant herself, though not part of the ring. But she sure sounded like an informant to me. I took a gamble, and Lyons dropped the matter on the spot. Though from that day on, he detested me.

It all pissed me off because back in '75, I made that asshole look like a star when I recovered that massive theft of liquor while Bobby Gonzalez slept.

—

In September of 1977, I was yet again pulled from my uniform assignment to head something else. This time, Capt. Windsor asked me to organize a VIN unit for his district. VINs— short for vice, intelligence, and narcotics—were specialized units with initiatives that focused on those issues. Larger investigations, complicated ones with multiple agencies that could go on for months or years, fell under OCB. The VINs were all about quick arrests and seizures that could be touted around as impressive statistics.

Windsor hated VINs, and I understood why. Too often they were cobbled together with random officers who other guys in the unit knew or liked for whatever reason. This guy was from General Investigations, that guy was from Motor Patrol, and now suddenly they're a detective in a VIN. No training, no preparation, no doing anything differently than they were doing yesterday. They were just wearing different clothing.

I went to Windsor and told him I would take the assignment under two conditions.

"First, I want to be able to select my own people. And second, I want three months to train those coming to work in my VIN. We can be operational come January 1978."

He agreed, grateful that I'd put that much forethought into the position. My early focus on working with as many outside agencies as possible was coming back to serve me again. I sent my VIN recruits all over the place to learn all the disciplines they'd need to really be effective investigators. They'd do two weeks with DEA, then two weeks with Customs, and another two weeks at the ATF. Then they were off to FDLE, the state investigative agency, for even more training. I phoned in favors with all the investigators I'd worked with in those agencies. When my VIN went operational in the new year, we'd hit the ground running—fast.

Undercover work was one of the things I had my guys focus on. I knew we'd be doing a lot of it, and my unit needed to be well versed in how to do it right. They needed to know the lingo, which varied depending on which segment of the population they were dealing with. Working with Cubans was different than working with Blacks and that was different from how the whites did business. My guys needed to know the roles, how they each operated, and even much simpler things, like how to dress for each of those groups.

I stressed the importance of including other agencies in all our operations.

"Whatever you hear, it doesn't matter how small you think it might be, pass it on. If you hear about guns, you pass it on to ATF. If you hear about the numbers rackets, you pass it on to OCB. If you hear about narcotics, you pass it on to DEA." It was imperative they learn how they all work together, and I was also very aware I was doing a big favor for those agencies in keeping the stream of information flowing.

Undercover investigations can put a cop in the most dangerous predicaments in our vocation. I always told my guys not to fall into the trap of trying anything the dealers were offering. I said not to do that shit you see on TV where a cop wets his finger, dabs it in a little powder, then rubs it on their gums to identify cocaine or heroin. There was a ton of PCP being cut into shit out there and I didn't need some officer in my unit freaking out and telling me there were spiders all over his goddamn face as we walked into the station.

Though one night in particular, I became a very poor student to my own lessons. We did our first buy of a kilo of coke over in Kendall, right off US-1. We went in as planned and showed our money, but the girl hosting us wasn't in a rush. She started pouring drinks and it seemed we were in for a social affair, made all the more enticing by the skimpy blouse advertising her ample assets.

"Ever had a torpedo?" she asked me. We hadn't seen any cocaine yet; we were sitting around waiting to close the deal. So, I played along.

"No, never did."

She stepped out of the room for a second and returned with a request and her hands behind her.

"Lay your head back."

I did. Maybe foolishly, but hey, we needed to kill time. Plus, I could overpower her pretty easily if I had to. She was no Janet Barnes. Most *men* weren't.

What I didn't plan to overpower was the blast of coke that she blew up my nose through a straw. Holy Moses; that stuff shot right up to my brain and my hair stood on end. I was wired the whole night, which made all the shit I got from my unit more unbearable.

"Hey sergeant, so much for not touching any drugs on the job."

Once we were operational, I got my obligatory phone call from Sleepy Gonzalez, I mean *Bobby*. He was unhappy back in the airport and seaport assignment. He was being pressured to produce numbers, and Bobby didn't ever maintain an informant network like I did, nor did he have me there to cover for his ass when his laziness went into full operational mode. I listened to him whine for a while and told him I'd make a call. I asked Windsor if he could bring Bobby down to Southwest with me, and he approved it. My shadow was behind me again.

My unit was crushing it. Within one year, we received the Departmental Unit Award for having seized more narcotics and more money than the other six VINs combined. Impressive.

Kind of. There's something you should know about crime statistics—they're bullshit. I don't know if there have been significant changes in their reporting, but when I was working, they were unreliable. Here's a perfect illustration of how departments would mess this up. Let's take a real bust—Rudy "Redbeard" Rodriguez. Rudy was a big player, and we raided his Banyan Dr. home and seized fifty-four kilos of cocaine and $913,000 in cash. This was a Miami PD case, though we were assisting because they didn't have jurisdiction. Of course, each department must document the haul, and for that we would prepare and file an AOA report, for "assisting other agency." Each department files their statistics with the FBI and when the Bureau compiles all the annual data, they get those same stats from *both* Miami Dade and Miami PD for the one seizure.

Final tally for the bust, added to the tons of other inaccurate data from around the country—108 kilos and $1.8 million in cash, twice the actual seizure. When you consider our funding and accolades were based on those statistics, it's easy to understand why no one really complained.

—

Someone who was complaining more and more was Thania. She was a forgiving soul whose needs were unmet by my profession taking the best of me. She was very family-oriented, as were all the women in her family. She would see her mother and sister every Saturday with all the children and do lunch, take them all to the movies, and spend the whole day together. She'd never know where I'd was or when I'd get home, much less count on me for a movie date with the kids. Thania needed stability.

When she was just eighteen, she got a job with the Southern Bell Telephone Company, where she remained for forty years, rising to a marketing executive position. She was loyal that way, and hated change. Three times in my career, I had the opportunity to leave Miami Dade police, and, at her urging, I declined all the offers. One was from FDLE Commissioner Bob Dempsey, who told me I'd be able to stay down at their Miami office. But Thania was smart.

"Once you rise in the ranks they're going to throw you up in the state capital office in Tallahassee," she'd said. "And I'm *not* moving up there."

Another offer was from US Customs, which would have eventually required we move someplace else, including to other countries. So that was out.

Then there was the CIA offer. She went ballistic. Remember who her stepfather was; I couldn't blame her for feeling that way, based on what Musculito put the family through. So, I stayed put, despite my urges to go elsewhere.

Those selfish urges also permeated the sanctity of our marriage, and unfortunately, I didn't resist as easily as I had while turning down FDLE and the CIA. I was drinking more, staying out more, and spending time with other women occasionally. I was submerged in the chaos of my job and the bottle wasn't helping, though I had no inkling of that at the time. I just kept pushing, hungry for advancement and the thrill of everything the job could provide.

Thania was happy back when we first married and moved far from Ronnie's Lounge, the old cop spot I frequented on Miami Beach. Then, wouldn't you know it, Ronnie moved to a location near me in Miami, about a dozen blocks from my house. After that, I was there almost every night. Me and the guys would leave work and go there like it was an extension of our shift. I don't blame Ronnie's move; I would've found somewhere else to fuel up after emptying my adrenaline all day long even if he hadn't followed me.

Our two daughters were born fourteen months apart: Thania, or Tani, in 1978 and Thalia, or Tati, in 1979. This added some stress, but truthfully, my job kept me so consumed that my home life was becoming somewhat foreign to me anyway. My career wasn't a nine-to-five thing, and whatever hours in the day the investigations weren't swallowing, I was swallowing at the bar. I wasn't running from home; when you're pumped full of adrenaline from chasing the demons of society all day, you need a come-down. The camaraderie and liquid relaxation had a way of placing the bothersome things we saw into a drawer. Going straight home would have brought them into the house. That's how I looked at it.

—

THANIA: I think his downfall was that he wanted to please everybody, except he could not. It was sad because he really did not understand the thing about families is that there are some things that your kids have to be first rather than anything else. For an example, Raul was a night person and I'm a day person. So on the kids' first Christmas, I was so excited. I said, "The kids are gonna wake up early and see all the Christmas gifts, I can't wait." And Raul said, "What do you mean?" I said, "They're gonna get up and they're gonna see the gifts, and they're gonna open them." He says,

"Oh no, just tell 'em to wait until I get up at one o'clock." That's not gonna cut it. The kids come first; there has to be a connection with the kids. He worships the girls now, but my daughters did not have that [with him].

TANI: My dad wasn't always there. He was there when we needed him, of course, and he was always there for fun. But he was also there if I needed to talk to someone. My dad is a really good listener. I know me and my mom clashed big time and whenever I had a problem, I could call my dad, and I could sit with him for hours and talk to him and he would just listen.

TATI: Whenever I go get him like a birthday card or a Father's Day card, it's really hard to find one for him because a lot of them are like, "My dad's always been there" or "He's the helper." He's not a handyman. He'll call somebody to fix something.

My mom worked, you know? My sister and I were the first ones at school and the last ones to get picked up. He never once ever took us or picked us up from school.

I played soccer and I ran track in high school and out of the four years, I think he went to like one Saturday practice that I had for soccer, and one track meet.

THANIA: Oh, I'll take them to ballet, I'll take them someplace, you know, whatever. That was not his thing.

TATI: My mom is a godsend. I think my sister and I are here in this world because my mom wanted us. She lives and breathes me and my sister. Everything that she has done in this world has been, and still is, for my sister and me.

Whenever I need anything, I call my mom. I was once in a car accident on the avenue that my dad lives on. I was less than a block away from his house, and I called my mom.

THANIA: He was not my idea of a husband. I was not the kind of person that would tell him, "Hey, you have to do this." I just expected him to go ahead and do it. But if you knew the Cuban men at that time, their mothers used to do everything for them, and so the wives were supposed to do everything for the men, regardless.

So, I worked six weeks after I gave birth; my daughters were fourteen months apart. I had to work, take care of the kids, do the lawn, you know, everything. So, it was sort of like we started drifting apart.

—

Despite my marriage becoming a failure, I considered my tenure with the Southwest District to be a success. Then in July 1979, a woman would walk into my life and change the face of crime in the city with a singular event.

CHAPTER EIGHT

GRISELDA BLANCO

You always remember the first time you hear the name of a woman who ends up having a significant effect on your life. For me, one such occasion was on a July afternoon in 1979.

I stood in the rear parking lot of Dadeland Mall sweating my ass off with about twenty other cops from Homicide and the Southwest District. It was quiet now; the momentary chaos that had begun at 2:20 p.m. was over, leaving only the detritus of another crime scene. Though this one seemed to be different—I was looking at an absolute cop-killing machine parked in the lot.

Two young Latino men lay dead inside Crown Liquors in the strip mall, both riddled with automatic gunfire. A couple of workers were injured in the assault, which appeared to be another drug hit. The two assailants had also sprayed the parking lot with gunfire before fleeing, putting the public at unnecessary risk. Considering the hundreds of casings we found, it was a miracle more pedestrians hadn't been indiscriminately hit. This was cowboy crap, walking into a business and lighting up the whole place just to get one or two targets, not to mention the bullshit in the parking lot after their mission was accomplished. That was just maniacal.

But that's not what gave me pause. Rather, it was the vehicle that officers had found in the back of the mall while waiting for the Crime Lab to arrive. The white box van seemed to be a commercial vehicle, with the name "Happy Time Complete Party Supply" and accompanying phone number stenciled on the sides. It had been left there with the doors open after two men were spotted running from it. Bystanders had called it in.

Inside lay a cache of weapons, but more alarming were the modifications that had been made to the interior of the rear storage section. Portholes had been drilled into the back door, which had bulletproof kevlar vests screwed to the inside. It took me two seconds to realize these shooters made an armored war wagon which they'd abandoned in their haste to flee the scene.

The muzzle of a machine gun could easily fit through each of the ports, allowing them to fire out the back at anyone pursuing them, which—you got it—would've been us. There were also a couple of small sliding windows on each side of the van, near the top, allowing the shooters to spray targets on both sides of the truck. They had a goddamn tank, and I wondered how many more of these were out there waiting for us.

We towed the truck to the Southwest station and *Miami Herald* crime reporter Edna Buchanan was already on the case. I brought her inside the garage to see the war wagon.

"Oh my god," she said as she climbed inside and saw the reinforced walls.

"This is a serious signal of what's to come," I told her. I wish I'd been wrong. Dadeland and the associated war wagon are often considered a turning point in the Miami drug wars. They signaled cavalier and uncivilized violence was being imported from South America to replace the clandestine, and dare I suggest, more professional practices of the Cuban cocaine kingpins.

The day after the Dadeland scene, me and my team in VIN sat around the station discussing the events of the previous day. We kept going back to the savagery of the scene—the spraying of an entire liquor store with the intention of blowing away not just the two targets who'd been followed in their Mercedes and into the store, but anyone else unfortunate enough to be present. Agent Charlie Cecil of the DEA had been working closely with us and he was listening to us recount the scene. He'd sat quietly, until the conversation paused.

"Griselda," he said.

I looked around at the other blank faces. Who the hell was Charlie talking about? I thought maybe he was late for a date.

"Huh?"

"This is her," Cecil continued. "Whatever happened at your Dadeland scene, Griselda Blanco was behind it, or part of it."

Charlie Cecil was familiar with the cocaine cartels in Medellin from his work with DEA in Chile and Colombia. For some reason, Charlie had adopted our VIN unit and spent a great deal of time at our office. He was the most helpful friend we had in the US government. He took one look, or one listen, at our descriptions of Dadeland and didn't hesitate in matching the MO to the woman who would soon grab our city by the balls.

Within a couple of days, Metro Police Chief Charles Black called for more stringent immigration laws as he announced the Dadeland target had been identified as German Jimenez Paneso, a top-level Colombian drug operative. As more pieces of the puzzle began to connect, I couldn't shake Agent Cecil's certainty in identifying the increasing violence as a fingerprint of the Colombian gangs. Soon the Miami newspapers were all over the story of a potential drug war from Colombia having found its way to US soil.

Paneso had been a top guy in one of a handful of Colombian drug gangs identified by our criminal analyst June Hawkins. A few weeks prior to Dadeland, Paneso's maid, Esther Ramirez Rios, had been found strangled to death in a field. Consistent with what we began learning about the Colombians, the lives of innocents were proving to be of no consideration. Ms. Ramirez's murder was perfectly worthwhile to them as it served as a message to Paneso from a rival gang. It was business.

Paneso got that message loud and clear. Six days after his maid was found, an incident occurred that I'd earmarked as the real tipping point for the forthcoming storm that would paralyze South Florida like nothing before. Dadeland was bad, but I felt something brewing even beforehand.

At around noon on April 23, 1979, homicide detective Mike McDonald was driving on the Florida Turnpike when a black Audi 5000 flew past him, speeding in the shoulder of the highway. McDonald likely wouldn't have pursued if there hadn't been a man leaning out the passenger window firing a .45 caliber submachine gun at a Pontiac Grand Prix flying beside it in excess of 100 miles per hour. The detective called it in and gave chase.

That chase went on for ten miles on US-1 with gunfire alternating between the two suspect cars firing at each other and also shooting at the pursuing Metro police cruisers. It all ended at US-1 and Caribbean Blvd. when the two cars stopped and the men got out and began shooting at each other in the intersection, then some fled on foot when the police cars pulled onto the scene. The men were soon apprehended, but the scene got more interesting when officers opened the trunk of the Audi for a routine search of the vehicle and found a hogtied corpse. The body was that of Jaime Suescun, a key player in the rival gang that had murdered Paneso's maid just days before.

Reckless shootouts in broad daylight with dead bodies in trunks were a new level of ruthlessness. But the thing most prominent in my mind was how they'd so cavalierly turned their guns on police. Schools in the area were contacted and told not to dismiss children until police were confident they'd apprehended everyone responsible, lest the open-air gunfight resume. This entire scene was third-world nation shit.

Incidentally, the Audi carrying Suescun's dead body was registered to German Jimenez Paneso. His murder at Dadeland would just be the next move in a bloody game of tit-for-tat. I knew Miami was headed for more trouble and would not be the same for a long time.

—

Griselda Blanco Restrepo was born to a sex worker on February 15, 1943 in Colombia, and grew up in Medellin amid the widespread poverty common to the area. By all accounts, her childhood was horrific, as she'd participated in a kidnapping at age eleven and shot the young victim to death herself when the family failed to produce the ransom. She was sexually abused by her mother's "Johns", a victim of a horribly abusive upbringing.

She became a pickpocket on the streets of Medellin and purportedly began turning tricks herself at age fourteen. She married a smalltime criminal while still a teen and had three children before divorcing the man, who was killed a short time later. Her second husband, Alberto Bravo, was her conduit into the narcotics trade. They moved to New York City in the 70s and began importing marijuana and cocaine. In 1975, she returned to Colombia to evade federal DEA charges when she and thirty associates were indicted in Operation Banshee. She then got into a dispute with her business-partner husband and shot him to death. She was on her third lucky husband by the time I'd heard of her.

Griselda really spread her wings once coming to Miami in the latter part of the 70s. She was entirely unfazed by murder, and it became her primary tool for doing business as she used it to thin out competition, settle old scores, and erase debts. And anyone who was perceived to have slighted her in any way was clipped handily.

Blanco had a team of hitmen at her disposal and is even credited with having invented the practice of putting assassins on motorcycles. It allowed them to be nimbler on the streets, maneuvering and shooting better than in a car, and escaping much more quickly than on foot.

Once establishing herself in Miami, Blanco's operation was reportedly trafficking over 3,000 pounds of coke a month at its height. It turned out the two rival gangs in the German Jimenez Paneso saga had the same boss—Griselda Blanco. They belonged to separate factions within the same organization, proving Agent Charlie Cecil right about his Dadeland theory, times two.

Before I knew it, I was ensconced in the world of the Colombian drug trade. Up until then, my VIN had been focused on various kinds of organized crime, not only narcotics but vice as well. We were busting massage parlors and bingo halls, but I stopped all that small shit when I saw what was happening with the Colombians coming into the area. The level to which they were taking the violence associated with their growing control of the cocaine business was too much of a priority—I decided to fully focus my guys on narcotics.

We needed to grab these guys on the street and start pushing them around. We started shaking the tree and looking closely at what fell out. If we ran into a guy that looked Colombian carrying two beepers, we'd stop him, identify him, and pass that information on to the DEA or the OCB. We helped those agencies, but also helped ourselves by keeping the info on these individuals for future use. Understand, we were suddenly being invaded by

Colombians in the Kendall section of the city, and many of them were involved in the coke trade.

We had to resort to drastic measures if we intended to make a dent. We were behind the eight ball because we had no Colombian informants to help us with our investigations—we didn't have time to develop any. We were in the dark as to how their operation worked, so we began finding these guys on the streets and following them, looking for their *caletas*, or stash houses. Eventually, by continuing the practice, we got some insight into how they operated.

A cartel member would buy a house and put a couple with a child or two in there and just tell them to stay out of the garage. That's where they'd keep the loads and do the transfers, as we'd see cars and trucks coming and going, pulling in and out. In time, we started popping them and bringing in some good-sized narcotics seizures. More importantly, we finally began to develop informants.

Here's how to flip a Colombian in 1980. If you considered how callous and ruthless these guys were, you might've thought coming down twice as hard on them might crack them. Maybe beating them up a little or threatening them with violence would soften them. But I didn't do that; didn't need to. The ruthlessness of their own people was the weapon I employed.

We'd bust them, take the coke, and let them go.

Sound crazy? The only thing that was crazy about it was how quickly some guy from the brutal streets of Medellin with probably ten murders under his belt would start shitting his pants. He'd now have to go explain to his bosses where fifty kilos of their coke went. You think a cocaine kingpin would entertain one of his runners saying a million bucks' worth of product had been confiscated without an arrest as proof? Only a moron would think they weren't ripped off by that guy, and most of the people near the top of these cartels were not morons. Actually, I didn't know Griselda Blanco's

IQ, but the more I learned about her organization the more brilliant I thought she was. Heartless, but genius.

When we busted these guys and I told them to leave, they would beg me to put cuffs on them.

"I'm not leaving!"

"Well, I'm not arresting you," I'd mutter, ready to head off and go about my business. They'd start softening as I walked to my car.

"No, no, no, no…please!"

"See you later."

"Then give me a receipt!"

"I'm not giving you a receipt."

That was usually all it took. I figured given the choice, they'd fear staring down the barrel of their boss's gun more than mine.

One afternoon I had a Colombian informant call me with a tip that there were twenty kilos in a drawer in a room at the Ramada Inn on 77th Ave. in Kendall, waiting for their buyer. The room was unoccupied when I got there, and it looked like the last guests had bolted in a hurry. For them to leave twenty kilos behind there must've been a serious threat they'd gotten wind of, most likely a police raid, if this scene was legit.

The crime lab returned a report citing very low purity on that load, which told me that my CI had likely cut it, left with ten kilos of the original load, and pumped up the other ten I found with laxative, the most common cutting agent, and left it to be found. He was ripping off his boss, and he thought I would be an unwitting accomplice; he'd tell the cartel that the room was busted, and the cops took the coke. Meanwhile, he had stolen half the load valued at $500,000.

The next day, this guy was ringing my phone.

"Diaz, why isn't this in the papers?"

"Just another drug bust. They're getting too common."

"Hey, you gotta make a press release, man!"

I told him I'd see what I could do, and instead of doing anything, I waited a day. He called back, crying.

"Raul, please! They're going to kill my wife and kids! I need proof that their load was seized!"

I should've told him to take back the ten kilos he ripped off if he was really concerned. But instead, I did him a solid and called Edna Buchanan, and within a day there was a small story in *The Miami Herald* about the twenty kilos we'd seized from the hotel. I needed as many informants alive as possible.

—

I began reading everything I could get my hands on about the Medellin cartel. I knew Griselda couldn't be the only one doing business here. She was always touted as the most violent part of our new problem in Miami, but she was not the only problem. My always working well with other agencies and having connections in them assisted greatly. I read reports on Griselda, Pablo Escobar, the Ochoa brothers, Jose Rodriguez Gacha, and Carlos Lehder—the major movers out of Colombia at the time.

Traditional portrayals of organized crime tended to show separate cartels or groups operating autonomously, so insular that they battle with each other for control. In this case, the Colombian drug lords were smart enough to realize that, while they were ruthless with competitors who did them wrong, they needed each other to penetrate the US. They were all intertwined in each other's operations, which made it even harder to trace the path a product had taken.

Take, for example, Carlos Lehder. He was a big-time cocaine trafficker in his own right, but more importantly, he provided a crucial service to the other Colombian operators when he bought an island in the Bahamas called Norman's Cay, which became the base of his entire operation. Loaded flights out of Colombia could now land there safely and unload their kilos into boats or smaller planes that would then head into Miami.

Loads from several different traffickers were packed together on the flights out of Colombia, each delineated by a unique marking. This efficiency eliminated the need for each individual trafficker to run their own flights, thereby cutting the risk. It saved money too, as only one pilot was needed for multiple loads in one trip. When a flight landed in Norman's Cay, Lehder would pay the pilot for the entire load, and then sort all the kilos by markings—Ochoa's bricks had an "8" stamped on them for *ocho*, for example. Lehder would receive packages for his own operation in those deliveries from Colombia as well.

The various organizations wouldn't only transport together; they also helped each other by providing services. One group might have direct access to the cocaine factories in Bolivia, where they'd buy the base and process it. Then Carlos Lehder would handle the transport to the Bahamas, and still another boss would arrange for the speedboats to pick up the loads and get it into Miami, where someone else had a crew ready for the pickup. It wasn't unlike a supply chain for any consumer goods—factories handle production, an international shipper flies it out to a distribution center, it's sorted and placed on smaller vehicles, where street level carriers get it in the hands of the happy customers, and everyone along the chain makes money. It was a surprisingly symbiotic relationship between merciless generals.

At Metro we had no shot of nailing these guys on the waterways; that was up to the Coast Guard or Customs with their fast boats. So, I used to wait until they were at their most vulnerable, here on land, before I made my move. I did use a valuable tool to get the job done—the extraordinary authority of US Customs.

My team and I would drive by Black Point Marina in South Dade or Matheson Hammock Marina, any marina in the county really, and look for big trailers. We'd sit on it until a boat came in, and then I'd call Customs. They would determine if the boat had returned from international waters without reporting and being cleared. If they hadn't, Customs then had authority to search and seize the boat. But why settle for the boat when I could have so much more?

I took the longer game and allowed the traffickers to hitch the boat to the trailer and get on the road. Customs would come along with me and follow the target to a house and then we'd move in. Customs didn't need warrants to search the boat, and they also had the authority to "extend the border" to encompass the residence, meaning we could search it all.

After everything was said and done, Customs would make the seizure of 300 kilos and our department would write an AOA—"assisting other agency" report—and we could then claim the 300-kilo seizure statistic as well. This was one of the reasons my unit was so successful in getting as much cocaine as we did. My district was loaded with marinas, and I tried to use every one of them to my advantage. Understand why my playing nice with outside agencies all those years wasn't crazy?

It turned out one of the most reliable pilots running loads for the cartels was my old friend Rene "Toto" Nunez from the Lords days. Rene became their go-to specialist for flying loads in foul weather, though not because he was especially skilled at it—he was just fucking crazy. He'd fly into a tornado if he was offered enough money. Rene eventually got busted and ended up in jail. It had been many years since I'd spoken with him, and I really didn't know what became of him until he called me from prison.

"Raul, do cops have dogs that can sniff through walls?" he asked me like we'd been meeting for lunch for the past decade.

"Yeah, we do."

"I need a favor." Rene was about to lose his house, a massive estate on the bay, and he wanted me to search the premises with a dog. He and his wife had hidden a few million dollars in the walls and underground in the yard, but they were high when they did it and couldn't remember where it was. Would I be so kind (and unethical) to get a dog and search the walls and the yard?

I politely told him to fuck off and that was the end of it.

An interesting side note—musicians Gloria and Emilio Estefan became the next owners of the house. I'm not sure if they found anything interesting while making holes in the walls to hang platinum records, but Gloria, if you didn't and are reading this, I'll let you know where to send the Christmas card.

Federal authorities had no choice but to admit their limitations in stemming the flow of illegal immigration from Colombia and the resultant drug violence. Raymond Morris, the district director of the US Immigration and Naturalization Service in Miami said, "We would have to stand on the seacoast hand in hand to come close to stopping them."

And just as we were trying to get control of that, another immigration situation was about to exponentially add to the havoc. And this next wave of problematic immigration was not only legal, but invited by the US government.

—

I couldn't believe what I was seeing as I stood beside my friend Willy Cueto in the park by Florida International University. Willy was working for the CIA at the time, and we were watching thousands of Cubans entering the makeshift processing center set up beside the college. Except these new immigrants were, well…different.

"No way these people are Cubans," I said to him.

He shook his head. "I've never seen Cubans like this."

But they were, and they were wild, just crazy. The new arrivals, *Marielitos*, as they'd come to be called in less than complimentary terms, were Fidel's latest gift to the Unites States. We were a compassionate nation, to be sure, but telling Fidel Castro that we'd grant asylum to anyone he sprung from Cuba, no questions asked, was insane. Naturally, Castro sent his most dangerous criminals from the jails and mental institutions to the shoreline at Mariel Harbor and on May 1, 1980 took President Jimmy Carter up on his offer to adopt them, provided they could get here.

Well, they got here—an estimated 125,000 of them between May and October 1980. Finally, the Carter administration had to cut off the agreement. Approximately 92,000 refugees in that wave landed in Dade County. As Willy and I stood there watching the processional of gaunt, tattooed, disheveled souls—some talking to imaginary people, others answering them—the weight of what was happening landed on us both. We knew this group of people would soon be making our already difficult jobs absolutely impossible.

We felt the impact from the moment they hit the streets. Miami and Miami Beach began getting hit with a surge of rapes, robberies, murders, and all sorts of violent crime. It became a decodable formula—a Colombian was usually responsible for a boat seized with a hundred kilos of coke, but when a seventy-year-old woman was raped on the side of the road, a Marielito was responsible.

If the Colombian coke wars and Mariel invasion weren't enough of a challenge for us, 1980 got even worse with the McDuffie riots. And it was only May.

Arthur McDuffie was a Black man who died from brutal injuries sustained while in police custody after a traffic stop. Five of the officers charged were acquitted at trial and in response, on May 17, a large protest erupted into violence in the Central District and Liberty City that lasted two days.

In addition to the mounting crime from the Cocaine Wars and random violence the Marielitos were causing, now we had two days of horrific statistics to add to our scorecard, kicking off with eighteen homicides in the first twenty-four hours of rioting. Those numbers were brutal for the department because any open cases affect the statistics of a homicide unit. Open cases go against the cases cleared by arrest, thereby producing a gauge on the effectiveness of a department. Needless to say, our number of open murders had given us a shit metric to work with, and the new riot killings absolutely buried us. Though I wasn't in homicide, the entire department was affected by such reporting.

But something more significant was brewing in the homicide unit. Troubling allegations were surfacing about some of the detectives, and they were serious enough to warrant federal investigations. The more the FBI probed, the more they began to find. It came to a head in spring 1980 when suspensions were doled out to six detectives pending the results of the probe into their roles in the Mario Escandar cocaine ring. Federal investigators found members of our department had run interference for Escandar and his operation and were used as muscle for him. They were also ripping off cocaine from crime scenes and turning in bags of sugar to the evidence room, figuring no one would ever need it for court. They gave the real coke right to Escandar.

In April 1980, the feds expanded their search to include more officers and a former judge-turned-Assistant-US Attorney. This investigation would infamously become known as the Cocaine Cops case and ultimately snag eight Metro-Dade homicide detectives, which resulted in horrendous press. It was headline news every day in South Florida at the worst possible time for our department.

Julio Ojeda was the detective most involved and would eventually be convicted on eleven counts, the most of anyone on trial. I had known Julio since Nautilus Junior High, but on the job I wasn't around him enough to know he was dirty.

However, one curious exchange came to mind once I learned he was arrested. One night before any of this came to light, my VIN unit and I went to a new watering hole at a hotel near the airport, and some cops from the other units were there. I happened to be standing behind Ojeda and a couple of other detectives who were bullshitting freely. Det. George Pontigo turned to Ojeda.

"We should buy this place, man," he said.

I laughed to myself. *How the hell are they going to pull that off,* I wondered, but didn't consider it anything more than a couple of cops talking shit after their shift. That is, until I found out about Ojeda. They probably could've bought the place and five others like it. Incidentally, Pontigo would be flipped by prosecutors and testify against the other Cocaine Cops.

In June, the maelstrom of trouble in the homicide unit landed firmly on my lap when I answered a call from Maj. Bob Windsor who had a small request of me. It would change my life and bring me right into the centrifuge of madness.

CHAPTER NINE

THE MAJOR LEAGUES

"Raul," the major began humbly, "I have a very serious morale problem in Homicide, and a loss of trust from federal and state agencies."

It was blowback from the Cocaine Cops case. The remaining investigators had been betrayed by their own brothers in the unit, which was embarrassing and demoralizing. Above them, administration was having issues engendering trust from cooperating agencies, and the remaining homicide detectives doing the daily grind were burning out. The wall of open murders continued to fill, and investigators were becoming more frustrated and planning their retirement, if they were nearing the requisite age, and resignation if they weren't.

"What do you need from me?" I asked Windsor.

"I need someone who can motivate our people here. I don't give a shit whether or not you know anything about homicide. But I need you here to rebuild the bureau."

Windsor had been my captain at Southwest District and had trusted me with starting their VIN. I was honored, but this was a Herculean task for sure. Things were as bad as they'd ever been and now Windsor, the coach I most trusted and considered a godfather in my professional life, was asking me to put on the jersey and quarterback this team.

If the existing investigators in the unit who would be under me didn't already have enough to bristle about, my having been promoted to acting lieutenant while still only holding the rank of sergeant might've given them such. I expected sideways glances, but I also knew it would cease once they saw what I was bringing to the table. Ironically enough, the one thing I *wasn't* bringing to the table in Homicide was homicide acumen.

Maj. Windsor knew I didn't have the experience, but that wasn't what he needed me for. He prepped me for my interview and advised that the panel would be asking questions related to homicide investigations. I soon found myself seated before Capt. Marshall Frank and three others. Sure enough, the biology test began.

"What are petechiae?" Frank asked me, seeing if I knew the term for the tiny hemorrhages in the whites of a victim's eyes indicating death by strangulation. I didn't at the time, and I respected everyone in the room enough not to bullshit them.

"I don't know that, but if you want to talk about the effects of a bombing on the body, I can tell you. I can also tell you the value of proper scene processing, because no scene work is more detailed than bombings. We needed to find the smallest piece of wire, or blasting cap fragments scattered all over the place after detonation. And I can talk about fingerprinting with you too, since I made the whole case on Rolando Otero with his print."

Capt. Frank squinted. "So why are you applying for homicide?"

Honesty always wins.

"Because your boss told me to."

The captain smirked because he'd obviously been called by Maj. Windsor and told what to do, but the others in the room just looked over at Capt. Frank, who thanked me and dismissed me.

On my way out, I saw Bobby Gonzalez seated by the door, waiting to go in.

"What the hell are you doing here?" I asked.

"Well, they have an opening, and I knew you were interviewing, so I figured I'd try too."

"But you're only a sergeant."

"So are you."

He didn't get how this stuff worked. "Bobby, I was *asked* to come. Formality, you know?"

He shrugged. "Well, I'm gonna try too." God bless him.

I got the position and was assigned to head a Homicide platoon as an acting lieutenant, and was pleasantly surprised when on day one I had two veteran detectives step into my office.

"Raul, we're glad you're here. We need your help."

The two men, Dets. Ray Nazario and John LeClaire, were trying to reach an important informant regarding an open homicide they had, but this guy was proving slippery. When they mentioned his name, it was obvious why they were standing in my office.

"We came across the name Ricardo Morales in our investigation, and we've been trying to find him for three weeks."

I picked up my phone and dialed Monkey's beeper and entered my number. He called right back.

"Where are you?" I asked.

"The Mutiny Club."

"Okay. I'm coming over with two guys from Homicide."

"I'll meet you here."

Just like that.

That's what I brought to Homicide, in addition to my working relationship with federal agencies. I might not have known what petechial hemorrhages were, but in one minute

I handed a prized informant to two detectives to close their case.

There was certainly jealousy regarding my appointment; there were sergeants who'd been there for ten and twelve years whom I'd leap frogged. I'm sure they rolled their eyes when hearing some Cuban sergeant was put in charge, but no one knew the conversation Windsor had with me nor his reasoning for the decision. I certainly wasn't going to tell them, "Your boss put me here because of all your shitty attitudes," though I didn't need to. In time, many detectives knew they had a secret weapon in me.

Only one officer ever said anything derogatory to me about my appointment, and it was the last person I ever expected to hear it from. One afternoon, my good friend and drinking buddy, Sgt. David Rivers, was in my office discussing a case he'd just caught. I told him to head to the scene and call me if he needed anything.

"Because you know so much about homicides," he mumbled on his way out. I was shocked.

I stepped out to the squad room and called him back into my office. I closed the door and spoke calmly.

"You know, since I got here, I was wondering who would be the first one to criticize me for my inexperience working homicides. And I expected it to be any of those guys out there except you."

"I'm sorry." He knew he fucked up.

"Don't let it happen again, David. Now, just go outside and do the right thing."

He stepped out of my office and turned around in full view of the others in the unit. "Lt. Diaz, sir, I apologize for my misconduct."

He was man enough to do that in front of the squad, so it was easy to forget the infraction. Incidentally, Rivers remains one of my very good friends today. I also helped transfer another old friend to my unit—who else? My shadow, Bobby Gonzalez.

Skepticism over my appointment wasn't reserved for the rank and file in my unit. One night while drinking at the Alibi Lounge in the Holiday Inn, another one of our watering holes, Chief Charlie Black slid up to me with Slick O'Keefe in tow. Slick was an ex-Marine and legit badass; he was regarded as a sort of hitman of cops—if you had to be put in check, Slick would come for you. Charlie was Chief of Detectives at the time but had taken some shrapnel from the Cocaine Cops case and had a reputation as a tough guy as it was. These two approaching me at the bar meant bad news. Black glared down at me like a shark, flashing a predatory grin. His mouth may have been curling at the edges, but his beady blue eyes weren't smiling.

"Do you have balls enough to come up to my office?" he asked me out of the blue.

"Sure," I said. "I have enough balls to go anywhere with you."

"All right. Come on." He led me out into the lobby with Slick walking right behind us.

We got in the elevator in silence and took a ride to the top floor, then headed down a long hallway to what I naturally assumed would be a hotel room. But Black opened a door and led me out onto the roof in the dead of night. It was quiet, dark, and we were very much alone.

"Come with me," Black muttered as he walked me to the very edge of the building, ten or twelve stories above Miami. He faced me and I glared right back at him, not even blinking during the impromptu stare down. I didn't know what this was all about, but Black was weird like that. I didn't think he would try and hurt me, but there was some test at hand, so I just locked eyes with him and held out. Finally, he sighed.

"Diaz, you got balls," he said finally. "Not many people would do this with me." And that was it. He just turned and left, and I had passed muster in his mind. It didn't matter whether or not I was a good investigator or a reliable brother in uniform; only that I had accepted his challenge and had a set as big as he had. From that day on, I got a warm greeting anytime he saw me.

"Hey, Raul, how are you? How's everything." He became the nicest guy in the world to me.

If I had been afraid of criticism or cared more about having friends than I did about doing the job, I never would have taken the position. I knew how screwed we were after the Cocaine Cops debacle, plus the Marielitos and Cocaine Wars. But at the time, I truly felt Homicide was the most natural place for me to be, where I could use my contacts to be really productive. After working Narcotics so effectively, the DEA treated me differently than the other officers, and I had already received my staff instructor badge from them for the Southeastern region of the US. Though I was employed by Metro, I was a part of DEA and they were a part of me. I could bring those advantages to Homicide just as I'd done in Narcotics, which was beneficial because the two were so closely intertwined due to all the drug murders.

The second reason I took the assignment was Maj. Windsor himself. He was my rabbi, my mentor, and when you find someone like that in a job and they want you on their team, you run, not walk. In turn, Bob Windsor gave me full autonomy in solving the problems in the unit.

My first job upon walking in was finding out what I had available to me in the unit. I was a lieutenant in charge of a regular platoon, which consisted of two or three squads, depending on what time of day it was. There were two or three sergeants and anywhere from fifteen to twenty investigators. That's what I had to work with, which I didn't feel was sufficient based on what was happening on the streets. I needed a position where I didn't belong to just one platoon; I wished I was in a position to be available to every detective in every squad in every platoon in Homicide. I started mulling over ways to bring something like that to fruition, though I couldn't set pen to paper on it just yet. I was just too damn busy. Between the Colombian illegals and the Marielitos, we spent as much time trying to identify the dead bodies as we did suspects. We didn't just have *who-done-its*—we had *who-is-its*.

Here's a typical murder case in 1980 in Miami. You'd find a body either in an apartment, a house, or out in the boondocks. Most of the time it was shot several times or cut to pieces. Maybe you'd find a car, maybe not. Then you'd find the deceased's ID, which was false, of course. The house address listed on it was also fake. So after hours of investigation, we had nothing more than we did when we greeted the body.

We'd send that body off to Medical Examiner Dr. Joe Davis, and maybe two or three days later, he'd get a call from an attorney. Dr. Davis would notify us and the attorney would come to our office with a passport picture of the deceased. The lawyer would say, "This is the guy that you found at Kendall and 107th Ave., and I have his family in my office. They want to come and take the body back."

Well, before they did that, we had to interview them, obviously, because we had no other leads. The family's answers would be as follows:

"I don't know."

"I don't know."

"I don't know."

And in the end, we still had jack shit after this waste of our shrinking resources. We never got any leads from those interviews. We were closing so few cases that we stopped tracking our percentages. Why demoralize ourselves any further?

The drug wave brought a new brand of crime to Miami as well—kidnappings. An American kid, probably late teens, had been fronted a kilo of coke by one of the Colombians and the kid got ripped off on his deal and had nothing to pay the fronted load with. The cartel wanted their money back, so they snatched the kid and made it known his return would only happen if they were paid.

Kidnappings fell under the Homicide Bureau's purview, and they were particularly time sensitive. We set up a command post in an empty apartment in the guy's complex right away and waited in his apartment with his wife for another call from the Colombians. I got on another phone and worked all my contacts in Narcotics. Eventually, the party responsible called on the phone and began negotiating. I knew how the drug business worked, and I was able to keep them talking to us while I stalled for time.

I'd called my contact in Southern Bell's security department and asked for a trace-and-tap, which is basically an emergency trace in lieu of a warrant. My telling them it was a life and death situation was enough to justify it, and whenever the kidnapper called we would try to get a trace. Until we did, I needed to keep the Colombians at bay, and the American alive. They called back.

"I'm trying to get the money together for you," I told them. "These are regular people—they don't know anyone with fifty thousand dollars. You have to give me three hours to call more people."

This went on and on. I worked them for about six hours when the phone company finally gave us an address. When the Colombian called back, I told him we had the money ready, and the person to whom I'd been speaking abruptly hung up. He didn't give us a meeting place or anything, so we just sat with the American guy's wife and waited while our recording equipment sat cold.

I stepped away from my team into the courtyard of the complex for a stretch and a smoke, when I saw a familiar face coming toward me.

Holy shit. It was the American kid. Did he escape? Did they cut him loose?

He was walking very slowly for someone who'd just been spared his life, and as he approached I saw the shell-shocked expression on his face. Something wasn't right.

Then I saw a head directly behind his, peeking out around him.

"Bad guy!" was all I managed to yell to my guys. There was no time to explain as the man walking behind the hostage reached around him, raising a gun. The terrified victim was now a moving shield.

I drew my weapon and identified myself as police. That was the invitation he needed to start firing on me, and he did, leaning to his right, around his shield. It was insane.

I couldn't stand there just taking fire without returning anything, so I started shooting to the clear left side of the victim. He dropped to the ground during the exchange and the Colombian turned and took off upon losing cover. I hoped the kid hadn't been hit in the crossfire, but I had to pursue the shooter while I had eyes on him. My guys could check the kid when they came out of the apartment.

I ran after the offender and, fortunately, the moron ducked for cover into the very apartment we'd set up in, and was greeted by ten of my fellow officers with guns drawn. The guy dropped his weapon and was arrested. Thank God the hostage was okay; the poor guy had fainted when the guns started going off. It probably saved his life, and I took a minute to offer a nod of gratitude in Saint Michael's direction myself, again.

—

The Pablo Melo incident was an important catalyst for expanding our investigative machine. We'd encountered Melo while initially looking for another hitman, Paco Sepulveda, Griselda Blanco's brother-in-law. She was so well insulated that if we had any chance at bringing down her organization we'd need to chip away at the people shielding her. And I can say unequivocally that would have been impossible without the incomparable criminal analyst June Hawkins.

Within two months of the July 1979 Dadeland massacre, June was brought into the overtaxed homicide department in an effort to coordinate information and sift through the complex web we began to uncover that extended back to Medellin. She was amazing at her job and worked her ass off to find new sources who could help her paint the picture, though so much of her work would lay dormant. There just weren't enough investigators to follow up on all of it, and the ones we had were busy processing new scenes all the time. Though it was understandable, once I sat and looked at what June had been compiling, I saw we had a real opportunity that was being overlooked. I did wonder how much of what the department had been ignoring was due to her being a female in a greatly male-dominated profession, especially back then. I think they were ignoring her as much as they were ignoring the memos.

June was a dedicated investigator who'd been laboring away in Internal Affairs, handling bullshit like officers who get sued because they broke a latch on someone's fence while chasing a perp. Chief Black called her up to Homicide because, other than her obvious skills, she had one asset lacking in our department—she was a female who spoke fluent Spanish. She could sit with the women we came across in our investigations and establish a rapport that a Hispanic man could not.

Such was the case with a woman named Olga who'd been friends with Griselda Blanco and, while not a part of her organization directly, had been in its periphery. She wasn't in trouble with us, but June would run a name by her and be able make some connection to the intel she was compiling. Olga couldn't provide very current information, as she hadn't been around Griselda for the past couple of years. But she helped June figure out who was who, who was related to whom, and who had a problem with whom from some grudge extending back to Medellin. When I got to Homicide, June had notebooks and three-ring binders exploding with all this information that I knew would be useful connecting the dots for many of our open cases.

One such connection involved Griselda's aforementioned hitman brother-in-law, Sepulveda. He was wanted on a warrant out of New York for several murders, and we got information he was staying at a hotel in Key Biscayne. I grabbed June and Bobby Gonzalez, and we sat surveillance on the place, waiting for a glimpse of him. After a while, a guy built very much like him left the hotel room and got on a Vespa-type motorcycle and we pulled him over. It wasn't Sepulveda, rather a Cuban Marielito, who had a gun on him, so we charged him on the spot. He flipped pretty quickly; we showed him some photos and he identified Paco Sepulveda and said he was still back at the hotel. I radioed for a dozen more detectives to get into the area right away; I wasn't taking any chances after finally locating him.

Shortly afterward, I got a call on my radio from one of the other detectives watching the hotel—Sepulveda and a couple of females were leaving in a Cadillac, heading west. Perfect—only one way out of town, so I immediately headed further west and blocked off the street.

I got out of my car and stood beside it with my gun drawn, eyeballing the car coming toward us. It kept coming, head-on, then veered off the road to my left, and slowed down as he passed me so closely I had to turn sideways and press my ass against my door. As the car crawled past, its window was rolled down and a MAC-10 machine gun was pointed at me.

I dove to the ground in what little space I had between our cars and opened fire on the Caddy. Bobby started shooting too, but I called it off when I remembered we'd been told by surveillance about two ladies in the car. They sped off.

We gave chase and I asked the dispatcher to raise the Crandon Park bridge—the only way out of Key Biscayne. This fucker was done.

He swerved left, into the Jamaica Inn parking lot when he realized there were five cars behind him and a raised bridge ahead. He hopped out of his car, and the first detective he ran into was BJ.

"Big John" Parmenter was the size of a small skyscraper, and he loved me, fortunately, so when he got a clear shot at the punk who'd just pointed a MAC-10 at his guy, he took it. BJ slugged Sepulveda in the face so hard it knocked the bridge out of his mouth, and he hit the pavement, unconscious.

Except, upon closer examination, it wasn't Sepulveda at all.

We'd just apprehended Pablo Melo, who looked so much like Paco Sepulveda that our informant on the Vespa had looked at our picture of Sepulveda and confirmed he'd just been with him back at the hotel. He really thought it was a photo of Melo.

We picked up Melo from the ground and he was arrested and brought down to the station. We searched his car and uncovered the MAC-10 that had been shoved in my face, a MAC-11, and a Smith & Wesson Model 59. We then got a search warrant for his apartment and found some cocaine, some emeralds, and a tape recorder under the bed. Turned out Pablo was fond of recording his trysts with women, and we had some fun playing it back for him at the office, loudly enough for the squad room to enjoy. Melo had initially given us a phony name, but Charlie Cecil of the DEA, who'd initially given us Griselda's name and was deemed an "honorary homicide detective" because of how often he was in our offices, pulled me and June aside and gave us his real identity.

Melo was surprised that we had found it and knew the lady on the cassette tape wasn't the only one screwed. He'd have no bond, and the gun charges alone from ATF would've sent him away for decades, so he agreed to flip. Now we had someone else on our team who'd worked closely with Griselda's brother-in-law.

Not fully, though. The cartel guys were scared shitless of Griselda, and Melo thought he could tread water giving us little drips and drabs of info. He said he knew Griselda, and had worked with her a little, but didn't go into anything actionable. However, he was helpful in converting more of June's raw information into working intelligence. He'd tell us some guy's nickname and identify another guy from a photo June had in her files. We continued to paint the picture with what he gave us, but we knew he wasn't giving us Griselda directly, or even Sepulveda, whose brother Dario was married to her.

Unfortunately, we didn't have much time to work with Melo because he got a lot harder to find. I was surprised to learn that he'd bonded out of jail, which required access to some serious money. I assumed it was fronted for him by one of his bosses, and when I next ran into him I asked where he got all that money.

"You guys missed the sugar," he said with a smirk, then told me about the thirty large emeralds hidden in the sugar bowl in his kitchen. Oh well.

Other than teaching us to check every cooking ingredient during a search warrant, what the Melo shootout did for us more than anything was give me a real-world example to take to the Major as evidence that we were outgunned. In that one exchange alone, Melo had sixty rounds each on the two machine guns and twenty-eight rounds in the pistol. So here we've got one guy with 148 rounds, while the other eleven of us with badges had .38 Special revolvers. The score was Melo with 148 vs. twelve detectives with a combined 72. I walked into Maj. Windsor's office armed with this lopsided data, ready to advocate for the detectives in my unit.

"I can't believe this," he said after I told him those numbers. "So, what do you want to do?"

"The least you can do is give the officers in Homicide authorization to carry semi-automatic handguns."

He thought for a moment, then brought his hand down hard, smacking the desk.

"Bullshit!" he bellowed. "I'm giving you *fully* automatic weapons."

When I was first offered the job in Homicide, I'd told Thania the best thing about the assignment would be my safety. She'd become more vocal about the shootouts in which I was involved, and I had been able to sell this new position by telling her that when I got a call from now on, the body would already be dead—I wouldn't be pulling my gun anymore. She wasn't wrong to be concerned. I had two beautiful children at home who deserved to see their father every day. I didn't have a very good explanation for why my safety seemed to be on the table again, and she didn't much want to hear it anyway.

—

I sat at Versailles Restaurant awaiting Ray Havens. Previously, Ray had been a sergeant in the airport and seaport security project and later a lieutenant, but he moved on to become the lead investigator in Janet Reno's State Attorney's office. He kept in contact after that, but he'd never asked me to meet him for lunch. I figured this get-together would feature something of significance to discuss.

We met up and exchanged the usual pleasantries. Then after we confirmed the wives and kids were alright, he asked me a weird question.

"Do you know who the biggest bookie in your area is?"

I didn't. But I made an educated guess. "The Valenti brothers?"

"Nope." He shot each of my guesses down and finally said, "It's Mikey."

"Never heard of him."

"Sure you have."

I thought. "No, I really haven't."

"You actually know him very well."

The only Mikey I knew well was my brother. But it couldn't be him.

It was.

I knew my brother gambled but I had no idea he was taking action as well. He was a good handicapper; it got to the point where some bookies in town wouldn't let him bet with them and he had to place bets through friends. But this was a surprise to me. Ray had come to me as a courtesy because of our history, but his office was ready to put the screws to Miguel.

"Raul, I need to either talk with him or arrest him."

I said I'd arrange a meeting between them and called Miguel as soon as I left the restaurant. It was true; he started taking bets and he'd had a few bad weeks after his layoff guy took off. When bookies saw too much money being laid on one side of a game, they'd go to another bookie to try and lay off some of those lopsided wagers. If not, they could get killed if the team getting the heavy action won. Well, that's what happened and people were looking for my brother for winning payouts he couldn't make.

It had gotten bad. He told me people were calling my parents' house and he feared for their safety. Miguel had only one way out.

"You have to call Ray," I told him. He did, and after providing them with some information for their ongoing investigations, Ray told him to get out of town. He owed a fortune in payouts and had just given up everyone Havens asked about, so he headed west to California where my aunt and uncle who originally took us in had moved. He stayed with them until he got on his feet, which was pretty quickly.

He found a job selling used cars at a Chevrolet dealership after answering an ad in the newspaper. In six months he was an assistant manager, and in a year he was general manager of the dealership. The guy had never sold a car in his life prior to that.

He became so successful selling low margin at high volume in low-income areas that he began buying radio time. His commercials were about five seconds long. "Do you want to buy a car, but have bad credit? Call Miguel." He gave the phone number and that was it. He was able to run that thing twenty times in a day for what it would've cost for a long-ass pitch.

—

Jaime Guillot Lara was a leading smuggler of all things contraband. He'd been doing it his entire life—he started by smuggling TVs and refrigerators into Colombia for sale on the black market and eventually moved on to pot, pills, and coke. He found Cuba to be the ideal hub for his cargo, a place where he could safely land and disseminate loads onto fast boats and other planes destined for the US.

Raul Castro, Fidel's brother and the number two in command, and Adm. Aldo Santamaria, commander of the Cuban Navy, were all the reason Cuba was a safe haven for Lara's distribution network. The communist regime in Cuba was supporting the guerrillas in Colombia, like the M-19 rebel group. Lara was permitted by Adm. Santamaria by order of the Castros to land his ships in the country in exchange for his shuttling weaponry back to Colombia and arming the rebel forces.

In 1979 I got a call from one of my sources who had a friend named Carmen who wanted to talk to me. She'd reached out on behalf of her boyfriend who had a problem with international implications. Her man, Jaime Guillot

Lara, needed to make a permanent safe landing in the US. His arrangement with the Cubans had been sniffed out by the Colombian government and he was now a wanted man. He thought I'd be someone he could bargain with, so one afternoon in my office, Carmen dialed the phone and handed it to me.

"Jaime wants to talk with you."

I took the receiver and chatted with this complete stranger about family and the Old Country. Then we finally got to his smuggling operation. He told me how well connected he was with the Cuban government and could basically hand us the top echelon for their complicity in this scheme. It was first-hand information and could result in indictments against one of the US's most targeted enemies for international crimes against our nation. In exchange for his information and testimony he asked for US residency and immunity for the crimes to which he'd be confessing.

This was a great deal. Yes, we'd be giving asylum to a confessed drug smuggler, but the reward outweighed the risk. I met with Bill Fernandez of the DEA and "BW" of the CIA and gave them the whole setup. They put the wheels in motion, but it was shot down at the top—President Jimmy Carter did not want to cut a deal with a drug smuggler. Lara couldn't stay in Colombia, as he'd be arrested the minute they found him, and he wasn't welcome here. So, he landed in Cuba.

Though we couldn't make the deal happen and get an indictment against Raul Castro and Adm. Santamaria, the information we'd gotten still had value. BW at the CIA called me with a strategy; they wanted me to leak the information we had to the press and begin a smear campaign to lay the groundwork against the targets for future use. I called Edna Buchanan at the *Herald* and fed her the story, which ran on the front page the following day under the headline "Miami Drug Smuggler Ran Guns for Castro to Guerrillas, Agents Say." Then, the head of the DEA, Peter Bensinger, publicly refuted the story. Our nation's chief drug enforcement agent said they knew nothing about the operation of one of the biggest international drug smugglers in the world.

This sucked, big time. Not only did we look incompetent on the law enforcement side, it put Edna in a shitty situation. She'd taken my word and ran a story without one additional source to substantiate what I was telling her. We had a great relationship, and I know she didn't think I was full of it, but maybe my source was. She had taken a leap of faith for me, and now the DEA lied and made her look unreliable. I went back for Fernandez.

"Listen," I said, "Edna was very cooperative in doing that for me. We need to get her straightened out." The right phone calls must've been made when I hung up with Fernandez because the following day Secretary of State Alexander Haig publicly confirmed the information in the article as accurate, stating Cuba was involved in "epidemic drug smuggling." That got Edna cleared.

I'd already gotten my promotion to Homicide and moved on from Narcotics when the case finally bore fruit. Lara was arrested in Mexico, and in 1982 charges were brought against Adm. Santamaria and others for smuggling drugs into the US.

—

One afternoon I got beeped to call the office and I was told Miguel Reyes was waiting to speak with me about something very serious. Reyes was a prominent member of the Cuban community who I'd developed a personal connection with. He was president of the Artemisa Association, which represented people from the town of Artemisa in Cuba living here in the US. He was also a close friend of my father-in-law, who was also from the region.

I met up with Reyes, who was in a horrific situation. He'd gotten a frantic call from his daughter that she and other members of the family were being held hostage by a pair of Marielitos. They'd beaten and raped the two women in the house and were holding them, an elderly grandfather, and a baby in the home. They were asking for an astronomical amount of money in exchange for their release.

"Be honest with me," I said to Reyes, "are you involved in anything you shouldn't be?"

"No!" he protested.

"Narcotics?"

"No, no, I swear to God."

I wasn't being insensitive. If he wanted to see his family alive, it was imperative I knew all the details to determine how to handle the situation. But I believed him. I'd known him a long time and there was nothing in his life to indicate a red flag, from the car he drove, to the clothes he wore. Additionally, it didn't seem to be in his character, but I had to ask. Money makes people do weird shit.

The kidnappers told Miguel that everyone in the house would be killed if he spoke to the police, so he asked me not to go over there. I couldn't jeopardize the family inside, so I had to approach this differently.

The first thing I did was order the house surrounded; I didn't want these guys to get away, so I had my homicide investigators and police officers from that district discreetly placed all around the block. Then I got on the phone and dialed the Marielitos, posing as Miguel for a call that lasted hours. The scene in the home was awful. The men had been drinking rum and doing cocaine all day long and I could hear them screaming at the women who were crying in the background. The kidnappers were becoming more erratic, and I had to get the hostages out of there.

I ordered the Special Response Team (SRT) to set up a sniper across the street and put marksmen along the side of the house, on the other side of the neighbor's fence. I kept the kidnappers busy talking while we got set up, and eventually we had a female officer from SRT speak to them in Spanish, telling them she was the female hostages' sister and pleading for their release. No luck.

I got back on the phone and convinced them that I—Miguel—didn't have the money they were asking for. Eventually the kidnappers told me they'd messed up and chosen the wrong house and just wanted a clean escape. They asked for a car to be left in front of the house, running, with doors open and keys in the ignition. I told the caller I needed some time to make that arrangement and hung up and had a car delivered and left at the curb. I called them back and told them it was ready, though neglected to mention the two punctured tires they couldn't see from the house.

"Okay," one of the offenders said. "We see it. We're coming out with the old man and if we see anybody out there, we're gonna fucking kill him right there." They hung up and the front door opened.

I radioed the SRT team. "They're coming out. The moment I tell you, you take them out. No questions."

The first kidnapper came out with the old man beside him as promised, a gun at his ribs.

An SRT sniper radioed. "Lieutenant, I can take him down."

"Where's the other guy?" I replied.

"I don't know."

The kidnapper and the grandfather were inching their way down toward the street, the gunman's head on a swivel checking out the area.

"Give him a minute," I told my sniper. The other coked up kidnapper was still inside with the rest of the family. If we hit the guy outside, the one inside might start shooting up the hostages.

Before the first kidnapper and old man reached the car, the next guy came out holding the baby on his chest like a shield, a gun in his other hand.

I radioed the sniper. "You still have the first guy?"

"Yes."

"Okay, take him out and everyone on the perimeter swarm the guy with the baby."

The first guy reached the car and stepped from the old man to grab the door.

POP. He went down.

The second kidnapper heard the shot, then turned and ran for the house, dropping his gun in the process but still holding the baby.

An SRT officer leaned over the fence beside the house and put two rounds in the guy's head. My team was upon him before the baby could hit the ground. In a matter of seconds it was over.

We still had to clear the house. It was reported that there were two offenders, but maybe that was inaccurate. SRT advanced on the front door, and I followed. The first officer made entry and began yelling.

"Freeze! Hit the ground!"

Oh shit. There were more inside with the women.

We all piled inside, and I realized everyone was safe, as the life-size statue of St. Lazarus likely posed no threat to us. It was standing right on the other side of the door and scared the shit out of the SRT officer.

"Whatever you do," I told him, "Do not shoot him. I don't need the bad luck."

And I didn't. Without my realizing it, the guys in Homicide were all walking a little taller lately, holding their heads a little higher. The Pablo Melo shootout, the rescue of the American kid who was kidnapped, and this scene at Miguel Reyes's house sent word out to the street that we were not to be fucked with. You could sense a change in the attitude of our bureau, like "God damn, we're *back*." We began getting requests for transfers into our bureau for the first time in a while. A year before, that had been unthinkable.

—

On May 1, 1981, the body of a man was found chopped up and packed in a cardboard box on the side of the road at SW 152nd St. and 130th Ave., near the gate to the Metrozoo. Homicide responded to the scene and found the man had been shot to death recently, likely within a day.

Six days after the body in the box, we were called to a murder in the parking lot outside the crowded Midway Mall during a Mother's Day sale. A car with four men had rolled up beside a fifty-something Latin man and shot him to death at 8:45 p.m. I rolled onto the scene a little later and as I talked with Det. Ray Nazario about the murder, his eyes kept bouncing over to the backseat of my car. Ray was clearly distracted by the pile of all the clothing I owned stacked to the roof in my backseat.

"Having problems?" he asked.

"Yeah."

When I was done examining the problem laying in a pool of blood on the ground, I drove *my* problems to my parents' house. Before responding to the murder of who we'd later identify as Octavio Mejia, I'd packed my stuff and moved out of Thania's and my home for good. It had all become too much for her—the drinking, the shootings, and the endless work hours. Who could blame her? We had two little children at home who deserved stability; the stability I was definitely not providing. I could have done better by them. I *should* have done better. But I was so deeply fixated on my career, maybe even obsessed, if I'm being truthful. No human being in the world would have been able to handle me in those years.

Earlier that morning, after Thania had dressed for work, she'd sat down on the edge of the bed beside me.

"I want out," she'd said. "It's not working."

It wasn't. There was no argument to be made. Even if I'd wanted to pull myself away from work, I wouldn't have been able to with the frequency at which the drug murders were happening. That was made abundantly clear when I couldn't even get thrown out of the house by my wife properly without being dragged to a damn murder at Midway Mall.

—

THANIA: Most of the Cuban men were the same—they did not see the women as an equal. A lot of my friends got divorced. Only a few stayed. Because the woman had a lot of responsibility as far as making sure that the man [felt that] he did everything correct, plus taking care of the kids, and taking care of the house. But the men, not so much. They were womanizers. They used to have two and three families in Cuba. Where they found the time was beyond me, but that was another thing. My dad had two families. Where did he have the time? I have no idea.

They always thought that they were better than the women. But I was madly in love with Raul. He was my whole world. If I said, "Oh, look at the sky, how beautiful and blue it is." And he would say, "No, it's dark. What are you talking about? It's black." I would say, "Oh, you know, you're right. It's really black." Because I would see everything through him. But when I started to grow up, then things changed. I don't think he could handle me changing. I think that that's when we really started to have all the problems.

I was working for the telephone company, and I got promoted. We were having like a company party or something and Raul was talking to my boss, the one that promoted me. Raul said, "I don't understand why you promoted Thania. She's not qualified." And I just froze. Raul didn't realize I heard it. I said to myself, something is not right here. Everybody in the company appreciated what I did and how I handle my job. And I was doing everything in my house too—I worked, took care of the kids and what have you. I didn't get a "you're doing a good job." But I wanted validation.

—

I had to compartmentalize my mind and focus on the chaos in the streets. The inhumanity of the murders in Miami was only escalating that year. Oscar Piedrahita, whose young son had just drowned a few days prior, was shot to death in his driveway while hosting a repast for mourners. Piedrahita, who'd been handling Griselda's exports out of Colombia, had been foolish enough to kidnap her teenage son Osvaldo in exchange for a million-dollar ransom. She paid it, he was returned, but the issue was far from over in her mind. No matter what industry we're talking about, you don't mess with someone's kid.

Nestor Garcia was a dealer who'd stolen five kilos of cocaine from Osvaldo, ostensibly unaware who his mother was, which was the signature on his death warrant. He was shot to death entering his vehicle in a shopping center on Kendall Dr. After that, June and I responded to the murder of Garcia's partner, Miguel Perez, who was machine-gunned in his car at the intersection of US-1 and Lejeune Rd.

Then Alfonso Arrubla, who was suspected of ordering the murder of one of Griselda's friends, was murdered on November 28. On November 30, a young woman was found shot to death on the side of the road. Her name was Lilian Trejos, and she made the mistake of threatening to provide information about Griselda's organization, in which her jailed husband Diego was working.

In a roadside hit gone wrong, the intended target Jesus "Chucho" Castro's life was spared, but that wasn't the case for his young son riding in the back of the car that was shot up. The little boy was hit multiple times and died. In a troubling and heartbreaking post-script, Castro drove his son's lifeless body home after the massacre and bathed him, dressed him in a little tuxedo, and laid him down with a flower in his hand in front of the Yahweh Temple. He made an anonymous call to the police to report the location. Castro had run afoul of, you guessed it, Griselda Blanco, and she told her main hitman to shoot him upon seeing him. He did.

That hitman was named Jorge "Rivi" Ayala, and before his capture he'd carried out twenty-nine plus murders for hire, nearly all believed to be for Griselda. She was so well insulated that in all my investigations that year, Rivi never showed up on my radar. He was captured after I was gone and he finally came clean, helping to close all those open drug murders. Remember, when many of those bodies were fresh, we could barely identify them unless one of our CI's knew the face, and that's where their intel ended. None of them would dare mention Rivi, or worse, his bosslady.

It was around this time that I became aware of Rafael Leon Rodriguez, or "Amilcar", whom you met in the introduction when he began shooting through his windshield at us. The Venezuelan hitman and drug smuggler was being sought for murders all over the globe, and was under investigation for as many as twenty in New York and Dade County alone. News reports called him a "one-man terror squad," and I began to collect as much info on him as I could.

The problem was that the chain of events causing a single murder could be spread all over the world. A homicide in Colombia would trigger a homicide in Queens, NY, which would trigger a homicide in Dade County, which would trigger a homicide in Los Angeles. There might've been so much linked to our one case in Miami from elsewhere from before we caught the body. Then aftershocks of the first killing would happen in locations outside Miami, leaving those investigators in other locations clueless. They likely wouldn't contact federal agencies in what was probably considered just a local murder. Additionally, those departments certainly wouldn't have contact with each other regarding these cases unless they'd uncovered a specific link, and most times the nature of so many of our *who-is-its* prevented that.

If anyone was going to nail the likes of Griselda Blanco, they'd need to be as organized as the Medellin cartel itself. That's exactly what I prepared to do as I walked into DEA administrator Peter Bensinger's office and put crosshairs on all of them with something called CENTAC-26.

CHAPTER TEN

CENTAC-26

The DEA had been assembling CENTACs for several years. A CENTAC, abbreviated from Central Tactical Program, was just that—a centralized unit that culled information from various agencies and put it at the fingertips of any investigator anywhere in the world. Remember, this was a time before electronic databases of any kind. If one agency didn't specifically communicate with another, neither would know what information the other one had on any given target. But as participating agencies would agree to join a CENTAC, they'd all be sharing the same brain, in essence. Investigators in New York could know what investigators in Miami or Colombia knew, and could identify items of evidentiary value for a specific investigation.

This was exactly what we would need to hit these cartels where it hurt. These traffickers and assassins were coming from all over the place, and they were likely committing crimes there too. Agencies elsewhere no doubt had information that would aid us, intel that we might not have even known we needed. I'd amassed connections in other agencies from my years of cooperating with them, but if I was to make this a reality, we'd need a godfather for the project. We needed agency muscle and, most importantly, we needed funding. I already knew I had to look beyond local law enforcement.

I sat down and wrote a proposal that explained the problem, its genesis, the geographical data, and what resources were needed to stop the ongoing violence, particularly in Dade County. I needed to include guidelines for choosing the person to lead this specialized unit. I wrote that they couldn't be below the grade of lieutenant, should be Hispanic, and experienced in narcotics, counterterrorism, and homicide. I all but included my height, weight, and eye color as prerequisites.

Peter Bensinger was the DEA administrator who'd served both Presidents Ford and Carter's administrations and was kept in that spot under President Reagan. Right after the inauguration in 1981, I went to Washington armed with my proposal. I'd first presented it to Bill Coonce, a supervisor at the Miami regional office of the DEA, and it made its way up the ladder to Bensinger himself.

"Okay," he said. "Go ahead." After a ten-minute meeting, CENTAC-26 was a reality.

We now had the DEA as our sponsor. They labeled it an official CENTAC and slapped the next numerical tag on it—26. We now had the might and support of that agency, and they were on board 100%, complete with a "zero budget" designation which meant money for anything I deemed necessary, from cars, to radios, to overtime. Recall that I hadn't been able to get Lyons to put an officer on Emilio Milian when he basically saw a guy put a bomb under his car, which then blew his legs off, so having support like this was a godsend.

Bensinger assigned Dick Jarrett as our liaison to the DEA, and we were off and running. Jarrett already had ten or fifteen CENTACs running under him, so he was experienced. He was there to handle the administrative side while I ran the operational.

I immediately sought to strategically attach departments and agencies to our CENTAC who were relevant to the cartel investigations we had in Miami. By the time I'd assembled my roster, I also had people from FDLE, and the PDs of both the City of Miami and Hialeah. DEA brought in the LAPD and New York State Police. I had direct access to ATF agents as well as DEA agents stationed in field offices in New York, Miami, and Colombia.

We began compiling data from our open cases, everything from the MOs at crime scenes to nicknames and phone numbers collected from suspects' and informants' address books. Once we funneled those through the CENTAC-26 partnership agencies' computers, a picture began to emerge that we were dealing with a single group. This was not the Cubans we'd been dealing with since the 70s. One group was causing all this shit in the city and making it the least happy place on earth.

For example, we would find an address book with a bunch of phone numbers that belonged to a victim or suspect. I would pass that on to our criminal analyst June Hawkins who would, in turn, make copies and send that to Lois Goodall, the analyst at the DEA. She would compare the phone numbers to what they had in their database and return reports to June notating who was calling whom. It truly made our investigative world smaller.

If anyone were to put up resistance to my proposal and need convincing, *Time* magazine had just pleaded my case better than I ever could have done. Their November 1981 cover story "Trouble in Paradise" had announced to the world that Miami was the last place law-abiding citizens who valued their well-being should visit on their next vacation. Crime in this city was exceeding the typical big city risk that anyone took visiting a metropolis.

By the end of the year, gun sales in the city had risen 46%, with a record 66,198 weapons having been purchased. Tourism was the city's leading revenue driver, a nine-billion-dollar-a-year industry, and now hotel occupancy rates had slumped like the dead bodies on our streets, dropping 25% in a single year. Miami's fall from greatness was becoming epidemic and now the global media was covering it.

—

My staffing moves went well for the most part. One hiccup came when Maj. Jack Rafferty handed me a couple of men I hadn't handpicked—Timmy Davis and Sgt. Nelson Perry. Timmy I didn't mind, though I knew he wasn't the brightest star in the sky from my days working with him in South District. Sgt. Perry was another matter. He'd previously been on a governor's task force on organized crime and wound up investigating a friend of mine from the Lords. He was wary of me, and we just didn't get along after that, but he was put in my unit by the major. I had no choice but to work with him.

One day after roll call, a couple of my officers approached me with a problem.

"It's Timmy Davis," they said. "He told us he found an unattended briefcase at the airport while picking up his sister."

No big deal there, but they continued. Timmy had seen the man put down the briefcase, go through his wallet, get his luggage, and then walk off. He watched him leave, then went and grabbed the briefcase.

"What did he do with it?" I asked them.

Timmy told them he took it. "I thought my ship had come in!" Timmy had said. He'd rifled through it and when he realized it yielded no fortune, he'd given it to the airport's lost and found desk.

There was a real ethical dilemma here. We'd just gotten over the Cocaine Cops case and I didn't need any guys with questionable morals working for me. But maybe the story got bungled. I went to Sgt. Perry, the other recent addition to CENTAC and no fan of mine, and told him to look into the matter and get back to me. I approached him a few days later.

"What's going on with the Timmy Davis thing?" I asked.

He asked to talk with me in private. I told him to meet me in my office in ten minutes and we could be alone. He came in and started spewing the strangest shit I'd heard to date in any department in which I'd worked.

"You know, we have all these Cubans in the squad, and we have you, a Cuban lieutenant, and you guys are talking Spanish."

I was confused. "Yeah. And?"

"Well, sometimes I don't know what the hell you're talking about."

"So?"

"Well, you could be stealing millions and I wouldn't know anything about it."

I realized I was dealing with the investigator of the century, thinking our singular deceptive effort after pilfering millions would be to talk about it openly, but in Spanish. We were on a road that I wanted an exit from. I'd always suspected my ethnicity had something to do with his dislike of me, especially after finding out his target of the Cuban organized crime investigation had been a friend of mine a long time ago when we were teens. But I kept it professional in the moment.

"Okay, sergeant," I said. "We'll get to that in a second, if you want. But what did you do about the Timmy Davis issue?"

He shrugged. "Nothing."

"Why not?"

"Because of what I just said."

"Because I speak Spanish?"

He was adamant. "Yeah. Why should I look into the Timmy Davis thing when a lot of shit could be going on with you Cubans."

"Well, I asked you to handle the Davis thing." He wore a mask of stone-faced arrogance as he leaned back in his chair. I was beginning to simmer, but I asked again, calmly. "Are you going to do it?"

"I ain't doing a fucking thing about Timmy Davis."

I stood and ended the meeting. "You should find another place to work because you're getting the fuck out of here."

He smirked. "The major put me here. He will never transfer me."

I left the room before I exploded. I knew Maj. Rafferty didn't give a shit about CENTAC-26 because we had started under Bob Windsor, and he might try to defend Sgt. Perry. I went to see him anyway. I recounted the story and told him I wouldn't stand for the kind of attitude Perry was giving me.

"Major, he refuses to follow my direct orders, and I'm going to charge him with insubordination and have him demoted or fired, unless you transfer him."

"Lieutenant, I'm the one who put him there."

"That's why I'm asking you to remove him."

He hemmed and hawed. "Sgt. Perry already told me about this and it's really a he-said-you-said kind of thing."

I slid out my small tape recorder. Good thing I used the ten minutes in my office before the meeting wisely. I pressed play and sat back as the major listened to my entire conversation with Perry. I stopped the tape when it was done.

"Okay," Rafferty said. "He's gone."

And he was. I replaced him with Sgt. Al Singleton, which was the best move I ever made. Blade, as he was known for his tall, slender frame resembling a single strand of grass, came from Homicide and brought an old-school expertise to our unit. He was a master of door knocking and interviewing, as well as the crucial crime scene work when the body was still fresh. I knew this guy would be fastidious and ensure our dotted i's and crossed t's would result in convictions and closures.

Though Blade's interview skills were top shelf, not all my guys were blessed with that instinct. We arrested one of Griselda's hitmen named Miguelito Perez after a brazen hit at Miami Airport. Papo Mejia was one of Griselda's former enforcers who'd ripped her off and declared war on her, therefore landing on her shortlist of targets. She was offering top dollar for him and anyone in his crew, and Rivi Ayala oversaw the elimination of eleven of Mejia's soldiers. But the prized pig, Mejia himself, had thus far escaped her clutches, despite Rivi blowing up Mejia's house with a bunch of dynamite on Killian Parkway. The house happened to be empty that night.

Then they got word that Mejia had boarded a flight to Miami alone. Griselda ordered Rivi to stab him with a bayonet so he could bleed to death "like the pig that he is." The one wrinkle was that she wanted it done *inside* the airport. Rivi later said he considered that a suicide mission and passed it on to the one guy he knew would do it—a Marielito named Miguel "Miguelito" Perez. Remember, many of these exiles were the lowest of the low in Havana and would eat their young for the right price. Miguelito's price was $250,000 and he headed to Miami Airport with a concealed sixteen-inch bayonet.

There are cops all over that airport, on every floor, in every area. It's unimaginable to me that Miguelito thought he could stab someone to death in the main concourse of a busy airport and get away. Well, he tried. Mejia came off the plane, walked down the concourse, and was grabbed in a chokehold by Miguelito from behind, and stabbed six or seven times with the weapon. As onlookers screamed in horror, Miguelito dropped the body and the bayonet and ran. He was tackled by pursuing police and was in custody in an instant.

He was brought into one of our interview rooms in handcuffs where he sat in a chair reverse style, with the backrest against his chest. During the tense interview, one of my guys in the room reached across to slap Miguelito who leaned back too far and fell off the chair. Unfortunately, an electrical outlet had a loose plate and in an unlikely act of misfortune, Miguelito's handcuff hooked the loose plate and slid inside. Holy shit—he began thrashing about like a frantic chicken as a few hundred volts shot through his body. One of my guys got up and kicked Miguelito's hand free from the socket.

On another occasion, Joe Diaz and Bobby Fiallo, two of my guys, were interviewing a suspect who'd insulted my investigator's mother. The two cops charged at him, each from opposite sides of the perpetrator's chair, the suspect leaned back, and one investigator ended up clocking the other in the eye. Fiallo came out holding his face and passed me.

"Lieutenant, this is no fucking way to work," he said. I couldn't argue with him.

I realized I had to work on interview tactics with my unit, as well as the power of persuasion over the fist. I always did my homework on a suspect before going into the room. I looked at our records and saw if they had a family, someone who might be able to trigger some concern, perhaps fear, and make them cooperate. If I could drop family members' names and addresses when I told the suspect or witness I was ready to have their mother, wife, and sister deported back to Colombia, it tended to be more credible. They usually talked.

We were pulling out any tactics we could think of to get to Griselda. She kept herself so hidden that we had to widen the circle around her more. That's when we realized her niece was having a fifteen-year birthday party, a *quinceañera*, at her parents' house. If Griselda was going to be there, we couldn't take any chances. We loaded up and stormed the place. We pulled everyone out and lined the backyard lawn with face-down Colombians as far as the eye could see. This poor girl who'd done nothing wrong just had a police raid added to her special day. She'd never understand how important it was that we arrest her aunt before any more innocent people were killed.

Then the sprinklers came on.

It was shit timing, but the automatic system activated and watered the lawn and an entire family. The birthday girl was bawling as her beautiful pink dress was saturated in the mud and worse still, Tía Griselda hadn't even attended her quinceañera.

—

I was holding a briefing with my unit in a classroom in the station before going out to serve a search warrant. The warrant was for firearms used in the commission of a murder, so I was taking time to review the plan with them, taking all the precautions I could to ensure all the officers' safety. We were all business when the back door opened and a guy walked in with a TV cameraman in tow.

"Whoa, whoa," I said. "Who are you?"

"I'm Geraldo Rivera."

I had no idea who he was before hearing his name, and even less so after.

"Oh, okay. I still don't know who the hell you are."

"I'm a reporter for ABC," he clarified.

"Well, you or *anyone* from ABC can't come in here and interrupt my briefing."

This guy wasn't leaving. "You don't understand...I'm Geraldo Rivera. I've covered three wars."

"Wonderful. But we're busy fighting the Cocaine Wars in here, so you need to go back out that door and return to whoever told you that you were allowed in here."

He did and returned with Commander Pete Cuccaro, who pulled me to the side.

"This guy applied for a ride-along with you for a news story they're doing," Cuccaro said.

"Yeah, but tonight we're doing a search warrant on a gun trafficker's house. It's too dangerous."

Then Cuccaro used his most deadly phrase.

"Please just do me this favor."

Pete and I had been academy mates, so I caved. I told him to have this Geraldo guy sit down in the back of the room and wait until I was done with the team. Then I'd talk with him. I did a quick interview for him and put Sgt. Rene Bello and Ralph Granda, two of my best guys, with him for the operation. We all headed out to the cars when I noticed a stretch limo in our lot. The back window was down and I could see a lot of scurrying when all the officers passed the car, like they were stuffing something into the seats. I took a second glance and recognized the two ladies in the back— they were prostitutes who'd hung out at the Mutiny Club with the other dopers and smugglers.

"What the fuck are they doing here?" I said out loud to anyone near me.

"They're with me," Geraldo said, getting in the limo.

"Hang on," I said. "You can't bring hookers on a police operation."

"They're not hookers," he said with a straight face. "They work with us down here."

Imagine how this shit would look—my new, high profile CENTAC unit arrives to a bust with a couple of hookers who then get shot by a trafficker. Geraldo kept them away from the target house, we made our bust and recovered some guns, then he left with his footage and hookers. Everyone scored that night.

Seizures like that were good for numbers, but nailing Griselda was still like catching the big fish as far as our open cases were concerned. She was proving to be an elusive swimmer. We were patient; there were a host of other dangerous players operating right under our noses that I felt we could pick up rather quickly given our new coordinated effort. We decided to make a list, kind of our own "Most Wanted", and start with those names.

And the first name on that list was Rafael Leon Rodriguez, or "Amilcar".

—

Amilcar, nicknamed so after the Carthaginian general Hamilcar Barca in the Punic Wars, was a dangerous man. He'd been wanted for a double homicide out in Miami's horse country, but also had charges pending in New York, Bolivia, and Colombia for murder and narcotics. He was a major drug dealer as well as a hitman, and therefore a fine candidate for the number one spot on the auspicious CENTAC-26 most wanted list.

When we first started tracking Amilcar, I went to Monkey Morales for some intel on him when I learned they'd both worked for the Venezuelan intelligence agency, DISIP. Morales said Amilcar was an expert marksman, having been trained from boyhood by his father, an armorer in the Venezuelan army. Morales said he could light a match tip by firing a .45 at it from thirty feet away. We weren't taking him lightly and had been looking for him for a while.

One of the informants that June Hawkins and I had developed was married to the daughter of Burton Goldberg, owner of the Mutiny Club. Prior to marrying her, this informant had been married to a beautiful Colombian model who Amilcar had stolen away. He knew better than to exact revenge against Amilcar on his own—Amilcar would've wasted him in a heartbeat. But maybe he could accomplish it with a little assistance.

He and Amilcar had reconnected in Miami and were now friendly to one another, though the jilted husband hadn't forgotten the bounty to be paid. One afternoon, Amilcar called him to hang out at the Mutiny, and the ex-husband accepted. Then he called us.

"I hear you're looking for Amilcar," he said. "I can get him for you. I'm meeting him at the Mutiny today."

I took him up on that and decided this advanced notice of his whereabouts was the advantage we needed to grab our Number One. I wasn't taking any chances. That meant all hands on deck—ten cars in total—and let's throw a plane in there too for air surveillance. He'd eluded us so far, but we were about to build a fence around him, and this is where you and I began the story.

I put one guy inside the Mutiny itself to keep an eye on the target and position my remaining cars along Bayshore Dr. in both directions, so we'd be on him the moment he left. Plus, we had that plane.

My guy in the hotel saw a Latin male who fit Amilcar's description inside the lobby, however, we were working off only the single photograph of him that we had. We spotted him leaving the club and followed his car along US-1 and eventually to Miracle Mile in Coral Gables, right before Lejeune Rd. Then, we lost him. All of us—ten cars and a plane, which was called away due to its proximity to landing patterns at Miami Airport. I expended every curse word I had, in two languages. I told everyone to fan out and keep circulating—someone was bound to come across the car.

Better than that, I saw him walking across Miracle Mile, back to his car. I radioed my location to the team, and we got back on him. We followed until his driver stopped the car curiously in the middle of the road, in front of the Burger King filled with students from Coral Gables High School. As I mentioned earlier, I made the call to take him down right there, and that's when they started firing at my guys, right through their own front windshield. Officers dove out of the way as they were pelted with shattered glass, and Amilcar and his driver leapt from the car and bolted on foot.

Amilcar got fifty feet from the scene before pulling open the driver's door of a car waiting at a red light. He shoved the driver aside and sped off in the car, while his accomplice continued on foot, gun still in hand across the busy intersection. One of my guys, Gary Yallelus, pursued him in his unmarked car when the driver stopped running, turned to the car, and raised his gun. Gary didn't even try to hit the brakes—that fucker got plowed over before he had a chance to fire a bullet at my investigator. That's how CENTAC-26 rolled.

Meanwhile, Amilcar sped down to Biscayne Blvd. before cutting across some side streets, eventually losing us again. He pulled over and got out of the carjacked vehicle, but not before turning to the terrified driver.

"Here," he told the man as he slid a Rolex off his wrist and handed it to the citizen. "I'm sorry I made you go through this, but here's your payment." Amilcar took off on foot and the victim found a pay phone and called us right away. We responded to the location and took the man's information, as well as his fare for the ride. He was pissed, but the Rolex was evidence.

"I never should have called you guys," he said.

"You just never should have told us about the watch," I offered in return.

Amilcar had gotten away. He made calls to our informant over the next couple of days and we finally got a trap-and-trace on the guy's phone so we could get the location of all the incoming calls. Amilcar was smart. He was making all the calls from public phones and would only talk for two or three minutes before hanging up, driving to a new location, and calling back to continue the conversation. I started looking for a pattern, tracking the locations to see which direction he was traveling.

Two calls, second one west of the first. I sent my guys west, ahead of the last location.

Next call, south of that. I sent them south.

Dets. Joe Diaz and Bobby Fiallo spotted him pulling into a parking lot of an apartment complex at NW 45th Ave. and 10th St. Amilcar and his companion, Luis Garcia, a Marielito wanted for the murder of a woman in Hialeah, got out of their car. The moment Diaz and Fiallo pulled their car into the lot, they jumped out and started firing on these guys. No "Stop! Police!" bullshit. These two lowlifes would've started blasting right there in the lot, and if anyone was going to get the first shot it was my guys.

The two bad guys bolted up to the second floor of the complex and Garcia was caught right away. Amilcar kept going as Joe Diaz and backup officers pursued while Fiallo cuffed Garcia. They searched open doors for Amilcar, and eventually found him in a laundry room, crouched behind the washing machines.

Joe radioed that they'd cornered him.

"Shoot right through the fucking machines," I replied. That was all Amilcar needed to hear.

"Me rindo! No disparen!" he shouted from behind the machines, surrendering and begging us not to shoot. He slid his .45 pistol across the floor to Joe Diaz.

We interviewed Amilcar back at my office where he spoke openly about his criminal history. We knew he killed a guy in Lima, Peru so we chatted about that first. Then we got a call from Roy Black, the powerful, high-priced attorney to the superstars of the underworld.

"Stop talking to my client," he said. I took that as an opportunity to have some fun.

"Come on, Roy. He's telling us about the guy he killed in Peru—we have no jurisdiction there."

"I don't want you saying another word to him."

"You're spoiling everything for me, Roy. He's already offered me fifteen million to let him go."

"No more talking!" Black yelled into the phone.

"At least let me get him up to twenty."

Black was shitting his pants. He thought his fee was heading into my pocket.

That was it for the hitman; he was convicted and sentenced to life. Comically enough, Amilcar went on to file a complaint against me alleging I tried to extort fifty million dollars from him that day. We'd recorded the interview so it never went anywhere, and Roy Black got his fat payment, I'm sure.

Getting Amilcar off the streets was great for society as a whole, but having the head of our list's number one hanging on the wall was a victory for CENTAC-26. It was a harrowing ordeal, the entire shootout and chase, but our take-no-prisoners approach had announced us to the city.

—

One of the first effects of CENTAC-26 going operational was a reduction in homicides. It was a natural byproduct of how we were working, and not so much from targeting individual suspects in open murder cases. Actually, it came as a result of our targeting homes.

Solving murders may close cases, but the homicide is still on the books as having happened. Being proactive and locking up killers *before* a body hits the ground keeps the homicide off the board and someone lives to wake up the next day. But short of having a crystal ball, how would you know who was going to kill someone? Well, you wouldn't. But I think we were able to do exactly that in a very roundabout way—by hitting stash houses.

It was a gradual build. When we hit people on our list, we made note of addresses in their little phone books and started going by the locations. We were looking for any indicators of drug activity, but we didn't always see something that overtly signaled that. Many times, we saw regular families, with kids and a Chevy in the driveway—Americana. Except none of them seemed American; they all seemed like they arrived yesterday.

As I'd mentioned earlier, the cartels would put families in these houses as a front, then once the sun went down, the cars and trucks would come and go all night. We learned that by talking to neighbors. We also learned that these families were there all day long; none of them worked and the kids weren't in school. We ran the license plates of the cars in the driveways and they all came back to bullshit addresses. The false registrations gave us probable cause to raid the houses. That was the mother lode.

We, along with DEA and the VINs assisting us, were hauling drugs and money out of those stash houses, and more importantly, we locked up the guards. When the trigger men for the cartels weren't out clipping people, they were guarding these places. We rounded up as many as we could, and we didn't stop there. We locked up the couples that were installed in the houses and had social services come and get the kids. Immigration would come in and if the charges weren't sufficient enough for us to try them here, they were immediately deported.

By 1982, we'd cut the number of homicides significantly. Then, late at night on December 20, I laid in bed watching a movie when I got a phone call reporting a homicide that we couldn't prevent. This one hit a little closer to me than most of the others I'd investigated.

CHAPTER ELEVEN

LAST CALL FOR MONKEY

I'd been seeing less and less of Ricardo Morales over the past couple of years. When he returned from Venezuela in 1977, he fell in with a group of Cuban cocaine dealers that had been on our radar. Morales was brought into an organization operated by Carlos "Carlin" Quesada—one of the earliest and fastest growing Cuban importers and distributors in Miami, after Carlin splintered from his former partner, Rudy "Redbeard" Rodriguez. It was a coup for Quesada to land the legendary Monkey Morales, the man with connections to all US federal law enforcement agencies and an expert in counterintelligence. But it was decidedly a step down for Morales.

The sad reality was that too many of the CIA trained mercenaries who served Brigade 2506 and the Bay of Pigs landed in the newest entrepreneurial industry in Miami. The US government had discarded them, turned them loose in South Florida to fend for themselves, and many found employment the easiest way they could. Their benefactors in Washington D.C. had instilled skills that would be valuable in the smuggling trade, and the exiles already had a built-in network from their past work. They all knew each other, frequented the same spots, like the Mutiny Club, and helped each other out with employment.

Morales had been very helpful to me on many investigations before he went into a life of excess and started running with the dopers from the Mutiny Club. He was no longer helpful to me once he went that way. Additionally, the personal side of my collaboration with Morales was deteriorating. We'd become very close, very quickly, but now he was becoming just too damn much. He was always a handful, a certified purveyor of chaos for all agencies for whom he assisted. I could usually deal with all that. Lately, though, Morales was using cocaine, guzzling Johnny Black, and popping more Quaaludes as nightmares from his service for the CIA in the war-torn Belgian Congo began to haunt him. He was paranoid, skittish, and just not the brilliant, personable guy he once was.

Morales was arrested while escorting a load of marijuana and began providing information to the State for their case against Quesada and thirty defendants in what became known as the "Tick-Talks" trial after City of Miami Police put a bug in the wall clock in Quesada's living room. Morales requested placement in the US Marshalls witness protection program, which was granted. He gave Janet Reno's State Attorney's office all the info they needed, and Morales was sent to live as Guillermo Anibal Martinez, first in Houston, then 216th St. in Bayside, Queens, NY. The world-famous operative tried it for a few months and soon after applying for a job at a gas station, called his FBI handler George Davis.

"Fuck this. I'm leaving."

Living quietly incognito was too much for the adrenaline-addicted mercenary to handle. Risking his life as the Monkey was worth more than hiding as Guillermo and pumping gas. He called me and said he was heading back to Miami, and George Davis paid his fare. I'm sure the US Marshalls loved that.

Never one to shrink from the spotlight, despite having left the protection of the WITSEC program, Morales became more boisterous and brazen than ever. His story had been covered by two national publications that year, *Newsday Magazine* and *Harper's*, and he went on Francisco Chao's TV show *En Un Hora* and openly laid blame for the Cubana Airlines bombing at the feet of the Venezuelan government, including its president Carlos Andres Perez and the DISIP intelligence agency. He criticized the CIA for its role in the international chaos in which he'd been embroiled. He was spiraling and in a very public way, the exact opposite of how the expert operative would have handled business a decade before.

Worse still, he began circulating the fact that he was working on a book that he promised would name names. Everyone I knew who'd admired Morales or showed him loyalty was now bailing. He was a massive liability.

The late-night phone call that took me from my viewing *On Golden Pond* was from reporter Jim McGee of *The Miami Herald*. He told me Morales had been shot in the back of the head at Cherries Bar inside Roger's on the Green restaurant. I can't say I was shocked by this, though I was disheartened. Morales was brilliant. But he'd wavered so far off track that he alienated everyone and expended every available avenue for survival. He was one of those rare individuals, so perfectly fitted with God-given gifts for his chosen profession, or, more accurately, the profession that chose him.

—

The initial story we got was that Morales was involved in an altercation with someone at the club—possibly the owner Rogelio Novo, possibly a bouncer. None of the twenty-or-so witnesses interviewed said they'd seen anyone actually pull a trigger. Some said they saw an altercation, some said they saw nothing. Only one person claimed to have seen the shooter. Initially, anyway.

Nancy Lamazares spent the evening hanging out with Morales—yes, the same Nancy from earlier whose husband German was found shot by Eladio Ruiz and, yes, the one with whom I'd had a fling. Nancy's most recent ex-husband, the former medical student Juan Cid, was a silent partner in the club and she'd been barred from the premises. It was curious to me why she showed up there and paraded Morales around. There were a thousand clubs in Miami she could've taken him to.

At first, Nancy said she'd seen Rogelio shoot Morales. Afterwards, she came back and said she didn't see the shooting. One thing that no one was conflicted about was that Nancy had taken a drink outside without paying and started a commotion in the parking lot that the bartender and others went out to settle. Might she have created a diversion to take everyone's eyes off Morales and whoever was in the bar?

The case was being handled by an excellent homicide investigator name Steve Roadruck, so I felt it was all in good hands. Eventually, the bouncer, Orlando Torres, a former Cuban police officer, confessed to shooting Morales in the back of the head to protect owner Rogelio Novo when Morales shoved him. The police department eventually requested the DA formally drop the charges against Torres as they felt it was a justifiable homicide.

No one was happy with the bar fight explanation. I personally think Nancy set Morales up. For whom, I couldn't say; I wasn't investigating this. It just all looked too professional, and Morales should have known better than to leave himself exposed like that. The guy was an international agent who'd survived a car bomb that detonated with him inside. He was shot in the head and in the back on two different occasions. He was arrested for crimes but never tried due to his affiliations with US agencies. If I were to testify to anyone having nine lives, it would have been Ricardo Morales.

Moreover, he was experienced enough to look for big trouble. Maybe the kind coordinated by a familiar local girl wouldn't have landed so overtly on his radar. No one knows, and a lifetime of investigation would've been needed to uncover who was really behind this fake bar fight. That local girl and her shenanigans came with a lot of baggage and usually ended up getting someone in trouble.

Everyone was cleared in the Morales shooting and moved on with their lives. My phone rang one night not long after it all settled down, and I realized Nancy hadn't moved on from *me* just yet.

Shortly before the Morales murder, Nancy had come to me with some information about her marijuana smuggler ex-husband Juan Cid. She had an axe to grind with him, and wanted me to investigate him for some financial improprieties. I told her I didn't handle that, and I put her in touch with Raul DeArmas at the IRS.

Sometime after that, she reached out for some advice.

"I got subpoenaed for a grand jury," she said.

"Okay. What's the problem?"

"I don't know what to say."

"About what?" I asked.

"About you."

"What about me?"

She wanted to know if she should tell the truth about our having dated and slept together. I didn't think it was anyone's business, professionally speaking. Nancy was never a suspect for anything I was investigating, nor was she a convicted felon that I would have been cavorting with. As far as cases I'd actually investigated, she was only a witness in the Morales's murder and her ex-husband German's years before that.

"So just lie," I said, carelessly. The question of Nancy and I had no legal conflicts, and as such, it was no one's business.

But I thought about it after hanging up. It pissed me off to think this kind of thing would even come up, so I thought of the perfect way to make it unpalatable for the courts. I called her back.

"Fuck this," I said when she answered. "If hearing about us in bed is really important to them, tell them everything, right down to the size of my dick."

"Huh?"

"Yeah, go all the way. Tell them how damn good I am."

I'm usually pretty good at sensing what's coming down the road and should have heard bells going off, but at that time I was too distracted dodging body blows from others.

CHAPTER TWELVE

TAKING FIRE

I was invincible.

That state of grace was beyond the confidence that my guardian angel instilled by helping me out of dangerous situations. My career path to that point had yielded accolades, professional praise, and concrete results, and it all lifted me. I'd always walked with a conviction and self-reliance, never one to second guess myself. Being put on plane and sent to a strange land without your parents as a kid will do that.

With CENTAC-26 now an undeniable success, it was further confirmation that I'd taken the right path in my ten years on the job. I advanced quickly and rose to meet each challenge, which just reinforced that bravado. I didn't wait for answers or permission. I acted on instinct, which most often proved correct whether or not I was doing things the "right way." I wouldn't be stopped.

Unfortunately, my marriage to Thania was a casualty of that. Work was demanding, but I think she would have dealt with that, as difficult as it was. It was more the bluster and machismo that killed us, and it was both of those things that instilled the confidence to be successful in my career. There was no way to achieve what I'd wanted to in law enforcement while still being available for my family. It's like a deal with the devil, and I had no idea I'd signed one.

I didn't hate my lifestyle. Maybe it's crass to admit it, but I have to be honest. I went to the Mutiny Club among the most successful cocaine kingpins and celebrities who spent lavishly, carefree. It didn't cost me a dime. I was Lt. Raul Diaz, and everything in Miami was on the house. Even my membership to the exclusive club was gratis. My power didn't come from the money those other guys at the Mutiny had; it came from that four-inch piece of shiny tin I could flash and open doors to the world.

Speaking of those guys, we may have been on opposite ends of the playing field, but I always had their respect. I got along with them outside of our respective careers, notorious guys like Quesada, Rudy Redbeard, and *los muchachos*, Sal Magluta and Willy Falcon, because I didn't treat them disrespectfully. There were a lot of cops that got off by hitting the blue lights behind them whenever they'd see one of their extravagant cars on the road. They'd pull them out, make them spread their legs, and frisk them in front of the beautiful girl in the passenger seat. They got off on embarrassing the kingpins. I never did that. It was classless and cheap. I didn't need to hit them below the belt; I played by the rules of "man-code." I knew I was better at the game than those dealers, and I'd win in time.

My name was in newspapers and on TV newscasts as a leader in my field, seen as brave and rebellious in a profession that usually honored tired conformity. I didn't score touchdowns or sing hit songs, but in Miami I was becoming a superstar.

Shortly after my divorce, I met a young lady who worked at the State Attorney's office. She was stunning from a distance and more so as I approached. I introduced myself and we started going out for a while. At one point we were talking about our mutual attraction.

"You know the one thing I first loved about you?" she asked.

I assumed it was my winning smile or well-coiffed black hair.

"Your arrogance," she said.

There's a lesson for all you single guys out there.

Everything was working for me—I had it all. And the moment you feel that way, you can no longer see the forces aligning to deliver equilibrium to your universe. Those destructive elements always enter through a door you leave open yourself, distracted by your all-consuming self-involvement.

—

Anyone in a high-profile position of any kind is subject to some harassment. The bigger you get, the more parasites can feed off you, and this was the turn my career began taking after I got a lot of attention for spearheading CENTAC-26.

Every accusation against a law enforcement officer must be investigated. That can really tie up the accused, whether or not they did anything wrong. Those on the periphery of law enforcement, like attorneys and reporters, as well as cops themselves, know that and can abuse it if so inclined.

I was no stranger to internal investigations. It's a reality of the business if you head up the ladder. If you climb quickly, as I had, they come faster and more furiously.

I became aware of a departmental investigation into me regarding an informant of mine and supply of Russian-made grenades that he allegedly showed me. My failure to report it or do anything about it would've made me culpable, but he'd alleged it happened while he was signed out of jail by my unit. I'd gotten word that both me and Bill Fernandez of the DEA were under investigation for supposedly having seen this illegal weaponry and doing nothing about it.

It all started with Larry Visuña, an informant of mine whose information had brought us down an investigative path that ultimately led to Amilcar being charged with the double murder. Visuña was doing time for trafficking a load of marijuana in Tampa and he called me for a lifeline. The guy had an FBI rap sheet that was just slightly fewer pages than the New Testament. I told him to be patient and see what his lawyers could do. He was in too deep for me to help.

One afternoon shortly after this call, he was taken from the jail for an "on-location." On certain occasions, prisoners needed to be taken to meetings with the State Attorney or US Attorney and we'd sign them out under our name and transport them back and forth.

Visuña told defense attorney Doug Williams—friend to all with pending drug cases and archenemy to whomever arrested them—that a pair of CENTAC-26 investigators had taken him home to have lunch with his family while signed out for an on-location. It was there he said he'd shown the grenades to the investigators. This information got to Juan Perez of the DEA, whom I'd known from his days back in my department though I never socialized with him. Perez started to look into this accusation and arranged an interview with Visuña, who was hesitant to name the detectives. Perez pushed and got a little clever.

"Then just tell me this," he began, "do their last names start with D and F?"

Visuña nodded.

It was no secret to Perez that Bill Fernandez and I were teamed up at the time, since CENTAC-26 was being run out of the DEA in Miami where Perez was employed. Perez and Williams used their "D and F" intel to force an investigation into me and Fernandez.

Reporter Jim McGee of the *Miami Herald* got his grubby little hands on this info, no doubt leaked to him by Williams. The defense attorney was likely attempting to engineer a PR offensive against me and Bill to soften up the department for an acquittal of his client or outright dismissal.

When I found out that Bill and I were being investigated, I checked into this and saw that Visuña had, in fact, been signed out for a trip to Asst US Attorney Jerry Sanford's office by Joe Diaz and Bobby Fiallo.

D and F.

I called them into my office and asked if they knew anything about this. "You need to come clean with me," I said. "I'm being investigated for this bullshit."

They glanced at each other, then to me. "Lieutenant, can we go for a beer after work?"

Shit. This wasn't going to be good.

We went to Ronnie's and they confessed. They'd taken Visuña to have lunch with his family and while there, he told the detectives he wanted to show them something.

"Wait here," he said as he went into the bedroom and came out with the grenades.

"Put that shit away!" D and F barked. "And don't even mention that you have them."

I dropped my head into my hands at the bar when they recounted this. This was trouble, and I was pissed. "Why the hell didn't you tell me about this when it happened?"

Visuña was a witness for us in the Amilcar case, so Diaz and Fiallo feared jeopardizing the case by having that impropriety on record. I got it, but now it was all fucked times ten.

"Okay," I said once gaining my composure. "Honest mistake. But listen…we never had this conversation—not *then*, when it happened, and not *now*."

I told them they were likely going to be called into Internal Affairs anyway. They clammed up and no one was able to prove I had anything to do with that grenade incident and it was all dropped. Head DEA administrator Francis Mullen looked into the matter and publicly cleared me and Bill in the matter.

But Doug Williams didn't stop there. This guy had a hard-on for me, and his puppet Jim McGee was happy to splash anything Williams fed him into the newspaper. I worked with a lot of defense attorneys who were former prosecutors like Williams and I always had respect for them. He was the exception. He was brilliant, but he used that mind vengefully. Witnesses were paid by Williams's clients to do whatever was required for a charge. In one instance, one of his clients bought a Corvette for Larry Visuña's wife in exchange for Larry providing false allegations about me. This vendetta against me stemmed from when Williams was a prosecutor and lost that case against Monkey Morales when I revealed the sole witness in the shower wouldn't have been able to see Williams standing in the courtroom even if he were taller than Napoleon.

Williams's next magic trick reached back those very eight years; he pulled a bullshit accusation out of his hat that alleged I had been present with Monkey Morales when he shot Eladio Ruiz to death on his doorstep. Williams was currently defending Juan Cid, Nancy Lamazares's ex-husband and silent partner in Roger's on the Green where Morales was killed. Cid was going down for an IRS case spearheaded by Raul DeArmas of the IRS's Criminal Investigation Division. Cid held it against me personally because I had put Nancy with Raul when she called me out of the blue. I had so many damn namesakes in law enforcement those days it was hard for anyone named Raul to score any narcotics in Miami. DeArmas had a strong case against Cid, and Williams would've certainly needed some magic to get his client off. The sleight of hand they planned had involved Nancy.

I got a call from a good friend who I won't name in FDLE, Florida's state investigative agency. We chatted a bit and then he took a serious tone.

"Raul," he said, "I have faith in you, so there's something I gotta tell you off the record."

He told me I was being investigated by Agents Danny Benitez and Sergio Piñon at FDLE. I knew Benitez had it in for me back when I tried to bring Bobby Gonzalez to OCB and Maj. Bertucelli had mixed up the two last names and brought Benitez instead. Danny's ass was hurt when I told him that I had no intention to work with him, and I'd requested Gonzalez. It wasn't my fault white majors couldn't correctly decipher Latino names.

Well, now Benitez was out of our department, working for Florida's State agency, and had his chance to play tough guy. He could look into Lt. Diaz, the CENTAC-26 big shot, using Nancy's cassette tape as his weapon of choice. That random call she'd made to me about her being subpoenaed by a grand jury was recorded by her at her ex-husband Juan Cid's behest.

A couple of things about Cid: he's extremely smart. I mentioned he had been to medical school before running with the wrong crowd and getting into smuggling. He was a good kid when I knew him years before this, but nothing corrupts like that Miami money. He figured if he could get me and Nancy on tape confirming that we'd had a relationship, it would invalidate any cases she and law enforcement were in bed over. No pun intended.

When Cid was indicted in the IRS case his ex-wife had precipitated by coming to me, he confronted Nancy and gave her the opportunity to make it right. She'd gotten the ball rolling, so he told her she'd be able to stop it on its way downhill by recording me admitting to improprieties. In exchange, he promised her the $60,000 she needed to get all her jewelry out of hock. Cid told Benitez and Piñon the plan, and they hooked her up with the recording equipment.

Well, she had more than just my admitting we'd slept together on tape—she had me telling her to lie to the grand jury about it. They obviously hadn't recorded the second call when I told her to tell the truth and mention my prowess between the sheets, or they just discarded it altogether.

I didn't know those details when my friend at FDLE had called with the tip, but I had lots of questions. I called Rolando Bolaños, the head of FDLE and another good friend, figuring he might be able to shed some light.

"I understand you're investigating me," I said.

"Raul, even if we were, I couldn't confirm that. I'd give you a 'no comment.' But honestly, we're not investigating you."

I said, "Well, Danny Benitez and Sergio Piñon are."

"Nah." He refuted that out of hand and reminded me that any investigation conducted by a state investigative agency into anyone in law enforcement had to be approved by the governor himself. Bolaños would certainly have to approve it at the regional level before it went to Tallahassee.

I was insistent and told him I trusted my source. So, he hung up with me and went into Benitez's desk, and there it was—an entire unauthorized file on me. It was non-government sanctioned and, therefore, illegal, though not prosecutable.

The thing gnawing at me the most was a very bothersome feeling that this was all done from the inside. All of these agencies conducting the investigations—DEA, Internal Affairs, FBI, FDLE—didn't talk to one another. Without organized coordination, each could launch their own investigation of me for the same allegation and jam me up for years, making me repetitively refute the same charges. Only someone on the inside could've known that kind of disorganization could be weaponized against a cop. And only someone close to me, another cop, would have enough details about my life and career to drop the right names to make these things seem believable.

—

Bobby Gonzalez and I were invited to lunch by the deputy chief.

"I spoke with the director," he began, "and he wants two Latin police commanders. I want it to be you two."

I think he expected me to jump at the chance. I knew better how the bureaucracy really worked. "I really appreciate it," I said, "but what is a police commander going to do?"

"Well, the police commanders will work under a major or a chief, learn about supervision."

"What kind of staff am I going to have?"

He shook his head. "You'll have no staff."

"So how am I going to learn about supervision if I have nobody to supervise?"

He didn't have an answer for me, so I summed up the whole offer for him.

"I really appreciate your considering me, but, in so many words, I'm going to be somebody's secretary. No thanks."

Bobby emphatically agreed with me, steadfast comrade that he was. We left that meeting with our dignity, bolstered by our commitment to the challenge of the job, and not taking some bullshit position that would keep us sitting on our asses all day long. Some guys would like a cushy job like that, getting paid for nothing. But not Raul Diaz and Bobby Gonzalez.

Two days later the department orders came out and I checked the list.

Promoted to police commanders: Jesus Bencomo and Bobby Gonzalez.

I called Bobby immediately and chewed him a new asshole.

"Damn, Bobby, we both turned down the offer together. What the hell?"

He babbled about the deputy chief going to his house that night after he left us and explaining things more clearly to him. Well, that was it, as far as I was concerned. Bobby was one of "the boys" now.

I shouldn't have been totally shocked. I'd begun having a recurring thought that I couldn't shake, like a bad dream that would creep up on me. I began to believe Bobby Gonzalez was behind the investigations I was under. No one ever mentioned his name, but I was seeing this sneaky, greedy side of him, and as I rose in the ranks he always needed my help more and more. That can be demoralizing, and I think it chipped away at his self-worth. I was a symbol of everything he wasn't. Taking me down would have elevated him, in some twisted way. Bobby was my friend for a long time, a fellow Lord, but I sensed his ethics were eroding.

One afternoon, Bobby called me randomly and invited me to meet him at his brother's house. I walked in and followed him to the dining room, where there sat a bottle of Johnny Walker Black on one side, a bottle of Pinch Scotch on the other, and a bucket of ice in the middle.

"Bobby," I said, "if this is a duel, you're going to lose."

We drank and talked, both of us frustrated with our respective positions in our careers. Me, because of the investigations, and him for some reason that wasn't making sense. I asked him what the problem was.

"Raul, I'm pissed off because I want to retire as a millionaire." It was very left field.

"The only way you can leave this job a millionaire is if you do things that you're not supposed to do."

He laughed and raised his glass. I returned the gesture. *"Salud."*

In actuality, Bobby and his wife were sort of living like millionaires already. She'd bought a storefront and began selling designer clothing and expensive purses. That couldn't have been a cheap startup, and the girl personally began spending money like crazy. I didn't know her to have a job prior to that, so Bobby must've been getting shitload of overtime or something.

My former academy mate, Pete "Do Me a Favor" Cuccaro of the Public Information Office, who'd saddled me with Geraldo Rivera all night, called me one day during the thick of the investigations into me.

"Raul, will you do me a favor? This McGee guy from the *Miami Herald* is a real pain. He's calling all the time, asking questions about you. Will you get him off my ass and just sit down and talk with him, once and for all?"

I made a big mistake and helped Pete out.

—

I invited Jim McGee to my office on January 14, 1982 to answer any questions he had and, hopefully, end this campaign against me. It was obvious he thought I was crooked and every time he printed my name it further reinforced that for readers. Pete thought if McGee sat with me for twenty minutes he could fire every question and allegation at me, at which time I would give him a dose of truth and set him straight once and for all.

"Let's start with Nancy," he said. I knew right there that this whole meeting was another attempt to glean something for defense attorney Doug Williams to use at Juan Cid's trial. Their ploy to use Benitez and Piñon at FDLE for this purpose had failed when they didn't get clearance to investigate me, so now Williams would use his puppet at *The Miami Herald*. He wasn't fact-finding; he was fishing. This was bullshit.

I got angry and set him straight about Nancy never having been a CI of mine, and all the other crap he brought up that Williams fed him. Williams went as far as accusing me of having been present when Monkey Morales shot Eladio Ruiz on the doorstep. I knew that was rooted in his embarrassment from Morales's trial when his key witness was asked to take off his glasses and admit he couldn't see the nose on his face without them.

McGee sat in my office and parroted every desperate charge Williams could cook up and throw at me, without ever mentioning his source. He didn't have to; it was patently obvious. When McGee started reaching back to the 1973 murder of Nancy's first ex-husband German Lamazares I knew exactly where he was going, and I knew it was designed by the defense attorney. By getting me to admit to sleeping with Nancy back when Lamazares was killed by Eladio Ruiz, they could hint at my role in Ruiz's murder by Morales since we were close at the time. Makes for some good noir fiction and compelling courtroom drama—a girl's husband is shot by a business partner, she starts screwing the investigating detective and gets him to kill her husband's killer. Ridiculous. I was pissed off and done with McGee, so I wrapped up the interview. When he left I had to restrain myself from finding Pete "Do Me a Favor" Cuccaro and kicking his door down. Hard to believe that today he remains a great friend, but I'm having second thoughts right now.

I was not found to have ever violated any laws or my oath as a whole, but the process of defending myself was harrowing and I was drinking more than ever. CENTAC-26 was everything I knew it would be, but most of my time in the past year had been dedicated to these bullshit charges. I was angry at the pettiness of so many in my own profession.

Edna Buchanan, the venerable Miami crime writer at the *Herald* went to bat for me with her colleague.

"You're wrong about this guy," she told McGee as his typewriter became increasingly familiar with my name. "I've known him since he was a kid in Miami Beach PD." It didn't matter. McGee kept on.

Listen, I wasn't without flaws. I've already admitted to an abundance of arrogance and self-absorption, but I never went out of my way to professionally screw someone over. There have been officers who worked for me that needed disciplinary action, and I've certainly been turned off by the behavior of some investigators around me. But I never went behind anyone's back and did them dirty to a superior. I handled any issues with peers to their faces. How foolish of me to expect that professional respect to be reciprocated.

I'd shown Bolaños at FDLE that their investigation into me and Nancy was unlawful, and to that point I'd batted away every allegation ever brought against me. But it had eaten up so much time and energy, and turned me very dark. Now it was over, every allegation answered, and every investigation settled.

Then, in late 1982, after all the other investigations were concluded, I was notified by Internal Review that those Nancy allegations had now generated an FBI investigation. This was puzzling because anything of value Nancy had told investigators had come up more than a year ago in the FDLE investigation. That meant the Bureau had sat on that information for almost eighteen months before doing anything about it. It was almost like they stood on the sidelines watching every bullshit investigation try and wear down my defenses before charging onto the field themselves.

Distracted by the sandstorm of controversy I'd found myself in, I'd forgotten about Lt. Tommy Lyons, my archnemesis who I'd never forgiven for denying Emilio Milian police protection, and every other shitty thing he did. While I'd certainly never forgotten him, I overlooked the significance of him leaving the department and being hired by the Federal Bureau of Investigation.

CHAPTER THIRTEEN

END OF SHIFT

"Lt. Diaz is reportedly the subject of accusations he once urged a witness to give evasive testimony, according to a motion filed Tuesday in a Dade County court.

Defense attorney Douglas Williams asserts that an officer, later identified as Diaz, allegedly 'counseled…witnesses to be evasive and dishonest' when giving testimony."

Jim McGee's December 15, 1982 article "FBI Probes Homicide Supervisor" in *The Miami Herald* introduced the Nancy tapes to the public and I was soon contacted by Maj. Windsor.

"You have to get out of Homicide," he said. "That will be the action taken by the department for your talking with the press about an ongoing investigation, even if it's about you. You violated that particular policy."

I couldn't fault him. He knew my value and didn't want to lose me entirely, but they had to do something after that was written in the paper. That was the way they planned to handle it—if anyone asked what disciplinary action had been taken, they could say I was transferred pending the results of all the other investigations.

I was called into Chief Willie Morrison's office in preparation for the transfer. He had been my sergeant back when I'd gotten a complaint from Ms. Georgia Jones-Ayers—the Black activist who'd mistakenly thought I was harassing that pimp. Morrison had looked out for me then, calling that complaint an "honest mistake" and brokering the meeting with Ms. Jones-Ayers. He'd moved up and was now a division chief in charge of all specialized units, like Criminal Investigations and the airport district; I hoped he would be as fair this time as he had been years prior.

"I understand you're to be transferred," he began. "Before we do that, I want you to know you can probably save yourself from that."

He had my attention.

"How?"

"I know that you know who saw those Russian hand grenades."

The D and F incident. Morrison went on, right where I thought he'd go.

"And if you give me those names, I'll be able to say that you helped us out on that investigation."

Morrison knew my character and had to figure that this was a long shot. He waited, then I spoke.

"Years ago, when I was a rookie patrolman, I had a sergeant who, when I had made an 'honest mistake,' let me finish my new departmental probation." I looked at him and let it sink in. "Do you remember that, Willie?"

"I do remember that."

"Well, I want to thank you for that. But as far as I'm concerned, the Russian hand grenade was another 'honest mistake' made by two professionals who were more concerned about the outcome of our homicide case than they were about some Russian hand grenades."

He nodded slowly, a glint of understanding in his eye. "Where do you want to go?" he asked.

"I don't care."

"I have an opening for a lieutenant at the airport. You'd be working for me."

That was all I needed to hear. I had a place to go where someone wanted me.

—

I never worked a single day for the police department. If that old adage about never working a day in your life if you love what you do is true, then my statement stands. Now, I was separated from my baby, CENTAC-26, and not long after going to the airport detail I started to fall apart physically.

I wasn't doing myself any favors. I was drinking every night, more so than I ever had before, which was a lot. The stress of my divorce from Thania coincided with all these investigations and I didn't even have a damn car. I'd been driving the county police vehicle for so long I didn't realize that when I turned it in, I would have no means of transportation. Thank God my daughter's godfather, Dr. Jacinto Baralt, who was also my physician, built an apartment onto his house for me.

—

THANIA: He never drank at work. It was always afterwards, but no matter how much he drank, it never went against his being a hundred percent okay. It was like drinking water. It was like he was immune to alcohol. It was unbelievable because no matter what he did he always had a drink in his hand, and you would think after a while he would be tipsy, but that was never the case.

TATI: Whenever we got into the car, whenever he had to drive anywhere, he always made a drink to-go. Always. When we were going to eat or to a friend's house, he would take a drink with him in the car. And I know in his office he had a bar there. But I can never say that I saw my dad drunk. That was something; he held his alcohol very well.

—

I was in physical pain and my body was breaking down. I developed sores in my mouth and all down through my colon. I landed in the hospital for six days and after testing me for everything under the sun including this scary new thing called AIDS, nothing turned up in the results. But there was no doubt I had some autoimmune disorder, and it was becoming dangerous. Dr. Baralt sent me to another doctor he'd gone to medical school with that he called "The Professor." He was known as the best in the field, and after more negative tests, even he waved the white flag.

"You're out of my hands now," he said. But he told me I had to see one more doctor—my old psychiatrist, Dr. Rodriguez, who'd treated me for stress and given me the breathing exercises I'd used when I got lost in my own city.

Before I was discharged, Walt Murphree, one of the Internal Affairs investigators in charge of my case came to visit me in the hospital with another detective friend of mine.

"We need to talk," he said, "but not here."

He helped me into a wheelchair and pushed me out to the street.

"Raul, I don't understand your case," he confessed. "There seem to be so many people pulling the strings on this."

"Who?" I asked.

"That's the thing—I don't know! There are all these invisible entities, and I can't even see the strings."

Then I went somewhere that must've floored him. I told him who else might've been orchestrating much of it. "The Cuban government."

"How's that?"

I had a few reasons for this belief that might've felt outlandish to him at first glance.

I explained that I might've just been some local police lieutenant, but there were a lot of important people that were getting very nervous, and I was the cause of a lot of it. First, there was the case I'd started against Adm. Santamaria of the Cuban Navy, a man very important to the Castro regime, who was eventually indicted for importing narcotics into the US. Prior to that, I prompted Edna Buchanan to start the character assassination campaign against the Admiral and the Castro brothers. My name was all over that one.

Then, of course, there was Juan Cid who was facing the IRS case with DeArmas. Cid was very close to the controversial Rev. Manuel Espinosa who first used his pulpit to call for the easing of sanctions against Cuba before local vitriol and violence by the anti-Castro groups in Miami forced him to change his tune. Cid and Espinosa had traveled openly back to Cuba multiple times. Who knew what support they were seeking to use against me when it seemed the Nancy bullshit would die on the vine?

Another one of Doug Williams's clients also had strong connections to Cuba. Aguedo Borrego had been smuggling marijuana through Cuba into the US and could have also easily been a bagman and messenger from the powers that be in Cuba to Douglas Williams. It was certainly in the Castros' interest to get rid of me, and they certainly had the means to do it using the people around me.

My doctors finally got to the bottom of my health scare. After years of my working at an unreasonable and abnormal stress level, my new position at the airport reduced that to nearly zero. One might think that was a good thing for my health, but crazily enough it had the opposite effect. My stress levels on the streets of Miami conditioned a constant adrenaline supply to flood me daily. Then, in one moment, it was all gone, and my immune system had become dependent on that blast of adrenaline. Without it, I was left unprotected and vulnerable to anything my body encountered. It sounds nuts, but when the constant threat to my life was removed, my goddamned body stepped in and decided to try and whack me instead. How fucked up is that?

Finally, the Nancy investigations that came as a result of the phone call set-up were squashed, including the late FBI one. Then, unbelievably, I got word from Internal Affairs that the FBI was now investigating something else. They were looking into an allegation from Nancy that a decade ago I'd smoked pot with her and Eladio Ruiz. Despite this new allegation appearing ridiculous and desperate to anyone with common sense, any complaint must be pursued to a conclusion. I guess this was supposed to have happened at some point before Ruiz killed her ex-husband German, and obviously before Monkey had dropped him on the doorstep.

You'd think a wayward detail like that with no substantiation could be ignored. It was tied to someone who'd generated previous investigations with her ex-husband Juan Cid's defense attorney that were found to be without merit. Yet, this bizarre little tidbit from a decade ago was worthy enough to merit the FBI further tying me up after learning all the other charges were put to pasture.

I got in touch with a friend in Internal Affairs. I didn't intend to interfere in their investigation of me and I didn't ask for any favors, except one small one. I wanted the names of the FBI agents who brought the investigations after sitting on information for a year and a half. I just wanted confirmation of one thing, and I got it when my friend gave me the names—Special Agents Jack Hexter and, yes, Tommy Lyons. The lengths some will go to act on a petty grudge is astounding.

That's when I knew it would never end. Regardless of what happened with that pot smoking allegation, the next obstruction of my advancement would be right around the corner. The worst part of it all was the helplessness. I'd always fought for myself, defended myself in the face of any adversity. With pending investigations, all one can do is wait while those who've aligned against you fill the investigators' notebooks with bullshit. You couldn't speak up and say what you really wanted to. It was frustrating.

I was already dejected from having to accept the airport detail and unjustly leave CENTAC-26. Throw in the hospital stay, my divorce, and the fact that I didn't even have a damn car, and I'd reached my end. I put in my resignation for later that year; I wanted to leave a good few months to be exonerated in the investigations and not look like I was running from them.

I wouldn't be able to evade the efforts of my enemies in US law enforcement or the Cubans forever. Imagine being betrayed by government agencies of both the US and Cuba. At last, there was finally one thing they both agreed on— they wanted me gone. I'd just do them the favor in lieu of a career of sidetracks and distraction. I choked down my pride, and in May 1983 I put in papers to retire in September, at the ripe old age of thirty-three.

Slowly, my body began to recover and become more acclimated to the patterns of a normal person. Shortly after putting in for my resignation, I was directed to The Top of the Airport, a restaurant befitting its name, by Dade County Manager Sergio Pereira and Hialeah Mayor Raul Martinez, who was like a brother to me from our college days. Pereira told me he planned on having me promoted to major in six months if I'd reconsider my resignation. He thought that was suitable enough time for all investigations to wrap up. At worst, I could get an administrative slap on the wrist for talking to McGee about an active investigation, or for telling Nancy to lie, maybe a three-day suspension.

"Namesake," the mayor said, turning to me. "Take the deal. Sergio offered this in front of me, and if he doesn't follow through, he will have to deal with *me*."

I smiled, genuinely touched by their gesture. I let it sit for a moment, earnestly evaluating if it did anything in me, in my soul. Would it be enough? They waited in respectful silence.

"Sergio," I began, "do you remember when you and *La Rubia* were getting divorced?"

He made a face at the mere mention of "The Blonde".

"Oh, yeah," he said.

"I asked if you could try to work it out so you didn't have to leave her. Do you remember what you said to me?"

He shrugged. I reminded him.

"You said, 'I just can't live with her anymore.' Well, I just can't live with this department anymore."

He nodded, slowly. I turned to the mayor.

"I can barely put this uniform on in the morning. I used to love it. Now, I fucking *hate* this uniform."

My hosts accepted that, and Sergio raised a glass. We solemnly exchanged a toast to our final cocktail as co-workers together.

So, in September of 1983, I officially ended my career in law enforcement. I would do no more damage to those I loved, or to myself. I would try not to, in any case. I was still standing, but on wobbly legs. My marriage to Thania and my chance to be with my girls in their youngest years were down for the count, though. They were school-age at the time of my resignation, and I'd missed so much of their lives already. My name was in print forever now, and not in a fashion I'd be happy with them reading about when they got older. I'd now have time to reconnect with them, to write my own story with them at least. Jim McGee and his typewriter would do no more harm.

In a more selfish way, I mourned the loss of CENTAC-26. They still carried on without my guidance and eventually connected Rivi Ayala, the most cold-blooded hitman ever to poison Miami's streets, with a bunch of the unsolved murders we worked. Remarkably, though, that wasn't until 1985.

Long after I'd retired, I finally got my hands on the hard copy of memo between the FBI and our department's Internal Review team with Agent Tommy Lyons's name typed right on it for all the world to see. Years later, I was in touch with Tommy Lyons who was adamant that he had nothing to do with that final investigation. Fortunately, I'd kept the Internal Affairs memo with his name on it. That allowed me to send it to him and tell him what he could do with it.

Unwittingly, I'd dropped bodies in my wake too; how different was I from Rivi Ayala? The main difference was *his* victims were strangers and mine were the people I'd loved the most. And the most significant casualty was me.

CHAPTER FOURTEEN

AFTERMATH

I'd reached out to a pair of retired narcotics detectives from OCB a few months before the shit storm hit full force and I realized I'd been marked for a professional death. Truth didn't seem to matter—those responsible had already benefitted from my production in arrests and seizures.

Juan Cayado and Tommy Dazevedo had left the force and founded the Intercontinental Detective Agency, or ICDA. They mostly handled cases for criminal attorneys, which was an ironic twist. They were always good guys to me and when I approached them about my situation, they were kind enough to let me buy into their venture. We became equal partners, and I kicked off the next phase of my life.

As a private investigator, I was doing the exact same thing I was doing as an investigator for the police department, but without the benefit of the badge and a whole department to support me. That's what the entire job entailed—reviewing the evidence of a crime allegedly committed by our client or redoing a crime scene investigation that the police had already done. We went out to the scenes. We interviewed witnesses. We talked with the local, state, and federal investigators. We examined all the evidence. We got access to almost anything we needed through the discovery process or through a court order.

The next step was to look at both investigations—the police's and ours. If there were discrepancies, we reported them to our client. We didn't take sides. Either the facts matched and fell within the law, or they didn't, and we reported them regardless. I realized very early on that Tommy and Juan were the best investigators I'd known. Their interviewing techniques were incredible and I learned a lot from them.

Here's an example of an early case. I was contacted by very good defense attorney named Robert Hertzberg, another former prosecutor, regarding a homicide in Liberty City. His client had been charged with the murder, though he was insisting he'd returned fire only after the deceased had fired his .45 first. The problem was the detectives recovered no casings or projectiles from the victim's gun, and therefore could find no corroboration of that story. Had the victim fired, the casing would have been ejected somewhere and the projectile would've hit something—a wall, window, or the defendant himself. But the police found no evidence that the deceased had fired a gun.

I visited the scene with a great homicide investigator I knew from the force named John LeClaire. We arrived and I started looking around the house.

"Boss," he said, "whatever you do, please don't make me look bad."

"I'm not here to make anyone look bad, John. Let's just go look around."

He unlocked the door and we stepped into the house. I knew from the reports where my client said he was standing in relation to the victim. I walked to where the deceased would have been, looked around, and saw I was standing beside a cabinet, slightly taller than me.

"Grab me a chair," I said to John. He did, and I stood on it to check the top of the furniture piece. There it was—a .45

casing. When a casing ejects at that velocity, it can bounce around for a bit. I handed it to John.

"Fuck!" he shouted.

"I'm just glad you're here to witness it, John."

He was becoming more anxious. I replayed the proposed scene in my head a few times while I looked around the apartment. In particular, I was most interested in the victim's point of view, since his location in the altercation had now been confirmed by the shell.

"How'd you guys get into the house?" I asked.

"The door was open when we got here. Uniformed officers were the first ones here and made entry."

"Did you guys secure the location when you left?"

"Of course. We pulled the door closed and locked it with the key."

That, of course, meant the door was left open the entire time the crime scene techs processed the scene; the very door my client said he was standing near when he was shot at.

"John, close the door for me."

He did.

A .45 slug sat burrowed in the door.

John dropped his head, shaking it slowly. "I knew you were going to fuck me up."

"I hate to say it, John, but your lab guys fucked up."

And that's the essence of what we did at ICDA—re-investigate investigations. Only now, I was doing it for the defense instead of the prosecution.

I would've been foolish to think I'd truly escaped my role in law enforcement. One day, a good friend of mine who'd worked for the CIA's infiltration team with my father-in-law called me. His son had gotten in a bit of trouble with a group of Colombians when he ripped them off for a kilo of coke. The going price on that was sixty thousand dollars back then, so his father knew they were staring down the barrel of a loaded gun. The drug dealers came to his father's business looking for the money, which he didn't have. So, he called me.

I didn't know who these guys were, there were new names and on the streets every day, but chances were they knew me, or had at least heard of me. Only a couple of years prior I had declared war on their entire industry and sought to lop off their heads. You tend to remember someone like that.

The father gave me the Colombians' phone number and I called and invited them to the ICDA offices. Two guys came in, both of them real cowboys from the hills of Colombia, complete with cowboy hats and boots. One of them was wearing a satchel over his arm that was too big for a handgun, and likely housed an Uzi or MAC-10. I invited them into the conference room and we sat.

"My friend cannot pay sixty thousand," I told them. "I know what the real value of a kilo is and he may be able to pay that." I also knew that on top of the amount their boss had told them to collect, they had added a few bucks for themselves.

"We're going to tell this to our boss," the spokesman for the group said. "That's not going to be good news."

I slid my business card across the table to them. "That's fine," I said. "But please tell your boss that you are negotiating with me. My name is right there on the card. Make sure you read it to him."

They left and returned a few days later. We sat in the conference room again.

"Our boss knows who you are," they said. "We have been given his permission to negotiate that price with you."

After a little discussion we got it down to fifteen thousand. I never asked who their boss was and they never offered it. But my time on the job certainly contributed to getting my friend and his son off the hook. I firmly believe they didn't give me the benefit of the doubt solely because I had been a cop. Rather, they knew I was a fair cop, one that didn't embarrass these guys when I had to deal with them, nor was I dirty. I did a job, and, yeah, I did it well. They were doing theirs, and obviously they were good at it too, given they were still freely walking the planet.

That didn't mean I wasn't a target for others. Remember Julio Ojeda, the Cocaine Cop that had remarked he wanted to buy the club we were standing in back in 1980? He'd been brought down and locked up, so I was pretty shocked when I was in my ICDA office, and my secretary said he was in the waiting room. My wheels got turning pretty quickly and I asked my partners Juan and Tommy to go into Tommy's office and open their intercom line, and I did the same at my desk. They hit the record button on a cassette deck, and I led my former co-worker into my office. He was overly friendly and even gave me a hug after having served his time for embarrassing the entire department and making our lives a living hell as we tried to do our jobs. Then he got down to business.

"Hey, Raul, you still have contacts in the FBI?" He obviously didn't know how fond I was of that organization, given all I'd been through, but I played along. I could see the whole thing laid out before me. It was like playing chess with a kindergartner.

"Yeah, Julio, of course."

He leaned in. "Listen, I can get us money for information about a witness."

"Eh, not interested." I played hard to get.

"What about for twenty grand?"

I paused, thought. "Hey, if I can help you out, I'll be more than happy to." I told him to let me work my people and call me in a couple of days. I wanted to have a little fun at the FBI's expense, truth be told. I'd gotten word from a source that Ojeda was working as an informant for a federal prosecutor named Pat Sullivan.

Ojeda called back as planned.

"Julio, my FBI friend is in some training class and I can't reach him. Give me a few more days."

He did, and was then dissuaded to hear my fictitious friend in the FBI had left school and gone right on vacation. I said he was unreachable for at least another few days, but I'd be sure to connect with him when he was back. After giving him the runaround some more, I told Ojeda to come to my office again because I needed to talk with him in person.

I told him we couldn't proceed. "That name you gave me to check out was flagged."

"Flagged?"

"Yeah, my guy in the FBI said they've flagged him at the request of the US Attorney's Office in Miami, and anyone making an inquiry about it would need to be investigated."

I never saw him again. Though I did see Pat Sullivan, who was more than happy to let me know how I'd messed him up. Apparently, the government wanted to know if any active agents in the FBI were still helping me after I left the job. You see, I knew enough about the Bureau to figure out what was going to happen. The moment I told Ojeda that my contact was attending classes, the Bureau would start checking how many of their agents were attending courses for the Bureau. When I told Ojeda that my contact had left for vacation right after school, the Bureau would start looking at those agents whom they had identified as going to school and match them against those on vacation. There's no doubt in my mind that some agents fell under suspicion.

The US Attorney's Office and the FBI should have known that Julio Ojeda would never have come into my office of his own volition. He and I knew each other first from middle school and then on the job, but we were never friends. I had helped him with some cases, but we never socialized. In all those years, I had certainly never hugged him.

As tempted as I was to say hello to Agent Tommy Lyons while my partners were recording the conversation in the other office, I didn't. There was no doubt in my mind this was an effort by him to hang something on me after everyone else had come up short. The fact that there was nothing to hang seemed to be of no consequence. There is professional jealousy and skullduggery in all careers, and if the fact that police would do it to each other scares you, it should. The time and effort wasted trying set up a clean cop could have been used investigating someone who legitimately needed to be off the streets.

It may seem that Lyons had struck out yet again in his most recent time at bat, but he actually hit his grand slam. His efforts had forced me into retirement from a successful career. What we'd done with CENTAC-26 had only scratched the surface of what I wanted to do. Fortunately, investigators like Al "Blade" Singleton, June Hawkins (who he'd later marry), Rene Bello, Ralph Granda, Joe Diaz, Bobby Fiallo, Jorge Plasencia, Tommy Reilly, Doug Stephens, Vic Anchipolovski, Michael Diaz, Gary Jackson, Gary Yallelus, Carlos de los Santos, and Jim Chambliss and their concerted efforts would continue to pay dividends.

Griselda Blanco was a tough nut to crack. It wasn't until three years after my launching CENTAC-26 that Rivi Ayala's name began coming up as the hitman in so many of the unsolved Cocaine Wars. He was revealed when Blade and his guys headed out to Los Angeles with the DEA to debrief Max Mermelstein, a white guy who was very high up in the Colombian cartel. Nailing Rivi and getting him to talk was the conduit to getting Griselda, which eventually happened in 1985—another tree which bore fruit well after I'd planted it and had to abandon the farm. It was a long winding road to slaying these monsters, but it wouldn't have been possible if not for the coordinated efforts that CENTAC-26 had given birth to.

Stepping into the ICDA offices also introduced me to yet another new phase of my life when Elly, the stunning company secretary, greeted me at the front desk.

ELLY: When I met him, I was working for Juan and Tom, and Raul was about to retire from Metro. He came to work with us and they assigned me to him. He was very nice. At that time, I didn't have anybody serious, I just dated a lot. So finally, one day he asked me out. He was a very kind man. He was very generous and very attentive.

—

In late 1983 I got involved with a CIA investigation into Nicaragua's involvement in narcotics trafficking. Ramon Milian Rodriguez, a client of ICDA, approached Tommy and Juan and told them that he had been contacted by Tomas Borges, a minister in the Sandinista government. Borges asked Ramon if he was interested in helping Nicaragua set up a process to launder their money. Ramon already had pending charges in South Florida US Court for money laundering, and was willing to become a confidential informant to help his case.

He recorded his conversation with Borges, and I was approached by my partners and asked if I thought the CIA would be interested. I contacted a friend with whom I had worked the Adm. Santamaria case and asked him. He said the CIA was definitely interested, and sent another agent to pick up the cassette. Sometime later, I was told the CIA had put everything on hold because the DEA had an ongoing investigation into the Sandinista government working with Colombian cocaine magnate Pablo Escobar and someone with whom I'd soon become acquainted, though posthumously, named Barry Seal.

After working at ICDA for five years, I bought out Juan and Tommy and took over the company. I soon landed a high-profile case with the Barry Seal investigation. Seal was a commercial pilot for TWA that had landed a far more lucrative gig when he began flying loads of drugs into North America for Pablo Escobar's Medellin drug cartel. After getting arrested by the DEA, he cooperated with them and kept flying in loads that the government monitored via surveillance equipment installed in the aircraft. They recorded some real powerful people loading bundles onto Barry's plane—high-ranking Nicaraguan soldiers and Sandinista government officers.

Seal got a vastly reduced sentence in exchange for his cooperation: five years' probation on a charge of conspiracy to distribute 462 pounds of cocaine—otherwise a life sentence. Then, some asshole local judge in Louisiana gave him a death sentence.

In addition to the probation, Barry Seal was sentenced to a six-month house arrest. While that still may seem inconsequential given the crimes he'd committed, it announced to the world exactly where the witness that turned on the most violent cartel in the world was living. On February 19, 1986, Seal was machine gunned to death on the street in Baton Rouge, LA.

ICDA was contacted by the criminal defense attorneys for one of the men arrested for the murder, Luis Carlos Quintero. He was the alleged shooter, and the defense wanted us to look at all the State's findings in the case against him and co-defendants Miguel Velez and Bernardo Antonio Vasquez. I headed to Baton Rouge to meet up with the defense team and Henry Bonecase, an investigator for the public defender's office there, and started investigating. Henry was a good guy, but this stuff, Colombian cartels and open-air machine gun assassinations, was outside his purview.

One afternoon, I was at the courthouse looking for some documents relevant to the case when I noticed a blonde making eyes at me. Actually, it was a little more blatant than that; she was smiling and openly giggling at me while I did absolutely nothing funny. I found what I needed and headed outside.

"How you doing?" It was the blonde. She'd followed me.

I told her I was fine, and she asked if I was a private investigator. I told her I was.

"I'm actually looking to become a private investigator myself," she said. We exchanged names and she asked if we could talk again about the process of becoming licensed. I agreed, and later that night when I got back to my room at the Holiday Inn, I was met by a bouquet of flowers on the dresser. It wasn't a mistake—they were addressed to me. I opened the card.

Enjoyed talking with you today. I'd love to meet up after court sometime.

My exchange with the aspiring PI that afternoon was odd, to say the least, but this was over the top. I sensed what the Russians called a "honey trap," so I ran my fingers down the stems of the arrangement until I hit something foreign— an antenna connected to a small transmitter. Those Cajuns from the Calcasieu Parish Sheriff's office didn't seem that bright, so it might've been them. The feds would've handled this much better.

Actually, maybe not. In the course of my investigation, I learned that the FBI had been assisting in the Barry Seal murder investigation. I learned that two of the hitters in the crew sent from Colombia to handle Seal were parked across the street when the hit was going down and had photographed the entire thing before leaving for a stash house. The bosses in Medellin wanted pictures of the hit. The State Attorney's investigators and the FBI later raided that stash house with a search warrant and came across the camera.

One of the State Attorney's investigators told me that during the search, an FBI agent looking for a laugh had opened the back of the seemingly insignificant camera and pulled the film out.

"I wonder whose party I just erased?"

Colombians loved to take pictures at their massive family gatherings—it was a well-known stereotype. Well, I don't know if that agent cracked anyone up with his joke, but he definitely exposed any film that might've been of evidentiary value by doing that. Imagine…photos of the actual murder!

Whether it was locals or feds bugging my room, one thing was for certain—someone important knew I was in town. I left the flowers in the room and went to the lobby and called the defense attorney's office. I had their secretary book another room under her name and give the desk clerk their boss's credit card, whom I'd reimburse later. I stayed in the new room but would return to the bugged room and make fake phone calls. I had fun concocting alarming things to say about their evidence. Whoever was on the other end of that transmitter probably thought I was Sherlock Holmes, given all the new evidence I was "finding" that would disqualify theirs.

According to the police reports, a woman had identified my client in a police lineup at the Baton Rouge police station. She claimed to have seen the shooting from across the street, which I thought was impossible after having visited it myself, given the angle and the obstruction of passing traffic. I headed to the woman's house with investigator Bonecase in tow.

"She won't talk to me," he said. He'd tried before and she turned him away.

"Well, maybe she'll like me better," I said. We got to the house and saw her car was missing from the driveway. We sat on the steps and waited a while until she eventually pulled up and got out of the car carrying a baby. She recognized Bonecase as she got closer to us.

"I already told you I'm not talking to you," she said.

"Well," I said, "you didn't tell *me* that." I smiled at her, but she walked past us, fumbling for her keys while holding the baby.

"Let me help you," I said as I took her child, cradling it securely on my chest. I tickled its cheek as its big eyes found mine.

The mom turned to me, her door now opened.

"What do you want?" she asked.

"Miss, all I want is ten minutes of your time to go over your statement about the police lineup."

She invited us inside and brought me and Bonecase lemonades. We made small talk about the baby, then I mentioned the lineup. I told her I had a bad feeling about it and I didn't want any improprieties that I might find to come back and further inconvenience her.

"No," she blurted and stood. "I don't want to talk anymore."

"That's fine, I can come back with a subpoena. But then you'll have to come down to the attorney's office and get a babysitter and all that. I don't want to do that to you."

She sat.

"I came here as a courtesy," I said. "We can just talk right here and be done with it before our lemonades are even finished."

She asked what specifically I wanted to know, and I asked about her identification of Quintero in the lineup.

"Was he your first and only choice?"

"No."

"Who was?"

She shrugged. "Some other guy."

She'd originally written down the number of another man in the lineup, but the police officer outside the room took the paper, crumbled it, and tossed it in the garbage.

"What did he say when he did that?" I asked.

"He told me to concentrate better and look again."

"What did you do?"

"I went back in the room and wrote down another number."

It wasn't Quintero's either. The officer took that paper and threw it away too. Eventually she got to Quintero. Would've happened if they put a hundred guys in the lineup.

I wrote up the findings for my client's attorney and turned it in when I got back to Miami. As a result of my investigation, the woman's identification of Quintero as the shooter was thrown out. I've been asked if I felt bad about the only identification of Quintero as the shooter being thrown out. I didn't and I don't. I'd always played by the rules.

It turned out there were a few teams working to hit Seal. I think it was a group effort by the major kingpins, like Pablo Escobar, the Ochoas, Griselda Blanco, and Jose Gonzalo Rodriguez Gacha. They each had guys here looking to get rid of Seal, which wasn't hard after the judge left him exposed.

I felt bad for Barry. He was just a good ol' boy, a former Green Beret, a pilot who was led astray but started cooperating with our government, which ultimately fed him to his Colombian employers to be devoured.

—

My business hit another turning point with the Tanner case. Bill Tanner was a popular deejay on Power-96 radio in Miami and his arrest along with on-air talent Michael McKay sent shockwaves through South Florida. Tanner was charged with drug possession and McKay with molesting a teenage boy who said Tanner was present at McKay's house while he was there.

I was hired by Bobby Hertzberg, Tanner's attorney, to investigate the police findings and I did so until I couldn't anymore. When I started interviewing other kids who were reported to have hung around the adult men, I realized these guys were sick bastards. Attorney-client privilege precludes me from going into details, but I'd learned enough to make me sick to my stomach.

However, what troubled me most during my investigation was the parents of the boys hanging around Tanner and McKay. They were allowing the boys to stay with these grown men, in some cases dropping them off on a Friday and picking them up on Sunday. Some of these boys were preteens, and I wondered how the parents could be this clueless. The worst part was that I suspected some weren't. They were starstruck, as evidenced by one mom whose license plate read TANNER. She was a big fan of his and I concluded that some of these parents were turning a blind eye.

I went back to Hertzberg, my client's attorney.

"Bobby, I can't work this case anymore," I said.

"What happened?"

"These guys are sick motherfuckers."

If I'd kept their working case and anything I'd contributed got them exonerated I wouldn't be able to live with myself. I gave up the case and decided on the spot I was done with criminal defense cases. ICDA would focus solely on insurance cases from that point forward, and we did for three decades. Incidentally, Tanner's charges were tossed by the judge and McKay pled to a lesser charge and accepted counseling. Who knows what else those two have done in the years since then? I'm just glad I had no hand in freeing them.

—

Elly and I continued to date and were married in 1987. I made it clear that I didn't want children. It was important to establish that early on, so it didn't make waves later. She was great with Tani and Tati, and the girls had taken so well to her that I think everyone was comfortable with that decision. The detective agency was keeping me quite busy anyway, and more children would have capsized the boat.

—

ELLY: Well, I'll tell you, he loves his daughters, but he is not someone that should have had kids because he's the child.

He loves them, but he needs someone else to take care of them. It's like, "Yeah, yeah, yeah, I'm the father, but you go ahead." That was my role. I mean, totally.

So, I had to take them out and do things with them. I wasn't going to have them stay home like that, you know. So, I was more hands-on when the kids were at home with us. And it was a good relationship. They didn't notice because I was always doing things with them. But, he's not the fatherly type.

And with me, the kids never wanted me to have any kids. And I thought, "You know, that's okay." Because he's already got two and if this is what I see, why am I gonna get into something like that. It's not happening.

—

ICDA was growing, so I brought in Joe Diaz of "D and F" fame as my partner in 1989. We worked so well together in CENTAC-26 and we had a great personal relationship even after I left the department. He was as good an investigator as Tommy and Juan, and better than me. Joe would run the insurance investigations, and I would concentrate on client relations.

Comparing the rush of working criminal cases to working insurance cases is like comparing bungee jumping to pottery. I had to find other pursuits to occupy myself with while still running ICDA with Joe. I'd always been actively interested in politics but never had any interest in running for anything. Then in 1993, a guy I helped become a county commissioner appointed me to the most important board in Miami Dade county—the Community Relations Board. It was our task to develop and maintain good relations across all communities in the very diverse county.

I also began working with Bob Beamon, a 1968 long jump gold medalist, who was running a youth organization called the Miami Inner City Games. It was an offshoot of the L.A. Inner City Games and Arnold Schwarzenegger was the chair of the national organization. I was already chairman of the Community Relations Board, and I thought this was also a good fit, so I told Bob I'd come aboard. In my first year I raised $40,000, lifting our total budget to $80,000 for programs and services for the city's at-risk kids. But I knew we could do a lot better.

In 1996, Beamon was tapped by the Olympic Committee to serve as a spokesperson and had to leave our organization. While working with him, I'd met with Bonnie Reese, the executive director for the National Inner-City Games, our parent company, and Arnold himself. He offered me the regional chairmanship and I grabbed it.

At the time, we were offering our services as a three-week summer program. I hated that we gave the kids a great use of their free time, fed them, and then after a few weeks they went back to a shithole. For many kids, that snack we gave them was the only thing they'd eat for the next twenty-four hours. Arnold thought we needed a lot more time than just three weeks to influence a child at risk, and I concurred. My years working the streets showed me that firsthand. The Miami Charter became the first in the organization to add an instructional camp to the sports camp where kids could now get help with their schoolwork. We also went operational year-round, and we raised enough funds to grow our budget to $7 million and service 3,200 kids at our height. We worked with the school district to offer tutoring by teachers right in the schools.

I was blessed with teachers and administrators like Estrella Diaz, our foundation's Godmother, Alex Bromier, Linda Brown, Nelson Perez, Executive Director Jody Knofsky, and others who made my job easy. Miami-Dade County Parks and Recreation, our other partner, deserves mention, and its administrators and staff, like Willy Cutie, Vivian Donnell Rodriguez, and Bill Irvine. That's a lot of names of people you don't know and likely never will, but this is all largely thankless work, and they deserve to be recognized.

I moved on in 2012, but Arnold is still there helping run the foundation now called the After-School All Stars. Of all the things I did over the years, nothing brought me more satisfaction than seeing the effect we had on the children who needed us most.

—

My brother called me in March 2011 and asked if I'd drive up to visit him in Lake Wales, about three hours from me in Miami. He'd moved back from L.A. years ago and started a successful manufacturing business in Central Florida after buying a liquid compound that you inject into your car's tires to make it puncture proof. It's sold in the major stores, so you may have used it.

Miguel's visit was not the kind anyone wants. He told me he'd just been diagnosed with cancer, and worse still, he was on the clock. They'd caught it too late, and when they opened him up, they saw it had spread everywhere. I was stunned.

He got the best treatment available at Tampa's Moffitt Cancer Treatment and Research Center, but it was so far along. He'd been diagnosed in March, and he left us in June.

It all happened so quickly I barely had time to process it. In a flash, my best friend was gone.

I never met anyone like Miguel, and I never will even if I live 200 years. He was well spoken and wrote beautifully. When he walked into a function of any size, he owned the room in just minutes. Miguel was the guy everyone wanted to talk to, whether they knew him or not. He made friends very quickly and trusted people implicitly, much more so than I. But I blame my career for that.

When he first got back to Florida from California, I hired him at ICDA. I introduced him to my clients, and he started working his own leads. My business was up 50% in no time and I think he enjoyed it, but he wanted something of his own. That's when we started American Sealant International (ASI) and did very well.

As well as I thought I knew my brother, I got to really know how remarkable he was after he died, and I learned the actual scope of his generosity. I met a young couple and their little daughter at his funeral who sought me out when they heard I was Miguel's brother. The man pointed to their little girl.

"If it wasn't for your brother, we wouldn't have her," he said. Apparently, he and his wife were sitting at the bar in Manny's, a local restaurant, having an intense conversation about their finances. They were jotting numbers down on napkins as they tried to determine if they could scrape up enough money to adopt a child. Miguel was in the place by chance and was talking to Manny, the owner, nearby. The couple decided at the table that the $10,000 they needed was impossible, and they shuffled out after finishing their drinks, wearing the stark reality of their situation on their faces.

Manny called them a week later and asked them to come by and pick something up. When they got there, Manny handed them a cashier's check for $10,000.

"I can't tell you where this is from," he said. "It's an anonymous donation." They erupted in celebration, probably doubting the reliability of the transaction at first, though not for long. They were able to give a new life to that young lady standing beside them at the funeral. Eventually, on the girl's first birthday, they asked Manny to spill the beans on the benefactor. He introduced them to Miguel who confessed he overheard the entire discussion when he sat in the restaurant talking with Manny that night.

A little while after his death I was standing in Junior's Seafood in Lake Wales waiting for my order when the guy behind the counter pointed to my ASI t-shirt.

"Are you Miguel's brother?" he asked. I said I was, and he came around the counter and embraced me, his eyes beginning to water up. There I was, standing in a seafood joint with a man I didn't know hugging me and crying. It wasn't on my list of errands that day.

The man told me that his restaurant was in danger of going under twice in his life, and both times Miguel lent him to money to get it going again.

Then I met a man who worked for my brother at ASI who told me when he was having his first home built, Miguel paid for all the lumber for the construction. It was one story after another about how Miguel made people's lives better for no reason other than he was a gift to the world. I already knew I'd never meet anyone else like him, but what I learned after his passing was how many other people felt the exact same way about him, unbeknownst to me.

I think about him every day, just like they probably do, as well as countless others I've probably never met.

CHAPTER FIFTEEN

CASE CLOSED

I'd been retired for several years when Windsor called me. He was in a bind and wanted my help locating a former confidential informant of mine named Eddie for an Internal Affairs investigation. The CI had worked with me when Bobby Gonzalez and I were on the seaport detail, but I hadn't seen him in years. I told Windsor I'd try and find Eddie and get back to him. I drove to his house and left a message with his mom. He called me back and we met at the Orange Bowl's empty parking lot.

"Eddie, I don't know what IAD wants with you, but I'm warning you to tell the truth or those guys are going to make problems for you. Worse than that, I will personally beat the shit out of you for fucking with an investigation."

He agreed, so I set up the meeting with two of Windsor's investigators—Del "Woody" Woodburn and Mike Tabernero, both of whom I knew and trusted implicitly. They told me the reason they needed Eddie, and I was shocked.

I hadn't spoken to Bobby Gonzalez in a while. In that time, he'd become a Division Chief in Metro Dade and began aggressively pursuing his aforementioned goal of leaving the job a millionaire. Unwittingly, I'd given Bobby a valuable tool for his pursuit of the riches he realized wouldn't come from a public servant's salary alone.

Back when we were working the seaport detail, I introduced him to my CI, Eddie, who would deliver information to us. Years later, after I'd retired and Bobby was a chief, he used my CI's ID number in drawing up affidavits for fake search warrants he and his group of thieves with badges would use. The affidavits were based on alleged intel from this confidential informant; in securing a warrant, you may be asked to list cases wherein that informant had been used successfully, thus validating them as a truthful and reliable source. Well, all of that had come from our time working together.

Bobby and his brother Jose, a detective working in OCB, and others had begun cashing in on the Miami drug trade. They didn't work with drug dealers like the Cocaine Cops a decade before, but rather ripped them off. They staged fake raids with bogus warrants and carried out illegal arrests to pocket the bales of drugs and cash and turn in just a fraction of it as evidence.

The arrest of Bobby, Jose, and a handful of others happened in January 1990, and in May 1991, the Gonzalez brothers were sentenced to twenty years from a disgusted US District Court Judge Edward Davis. It was the stiffest penalty he could hand down, and he was more than justified in doing so. Their eventual arrest and indictment listed their total score as over a million dollars.

One of the things that most enraged me back when I had to defend the allegations against me was the suggestion of a betrayal of public trust. I was not a perfect cop—no one is a perfect anything. But whatever I might've done that bent the rules was in the spirit of doing my job and bringing a criminal to justice. Aggressive ambition can get the best of us sometimes, but the overarching driver is snagging that crook before they hurt someone else, or bringing down that crime syndicate before society continued to pay the price. I took the protection of the good citizens in the community as stringently to heart as anyone could. I abhorred people who cashed a city paycheck, took tax money from the community, and then turned their back on them.

Julio Ojeda and the Cocaine Cops back in 1980 and Bobby Gonzalez and his band of thieves with badges were the epitome of this crop. These guys broke the law for no reason than their own greed. To me, they were no different than a Griselda Blanco or Santo Trafficante, gangsters looking to stuff their pockets at your expense.

That's another thing that irks me—the glorification of the gangster in pop culture. I suppose people are attracted to the danger and opulence of their lifestyle, but real people lay dead in the gutters because of them. I physically picked them up as thick, viscous blood seeped out their bullet holes onto my hands. I notified heartbroken parents when we found their kid overdosed on something one of these thugs smuggled into the country. I fought to reject the image of my own kids creeping into my head at those scenes, and I nullified the burn of those events by poisoning my body with alcohol. The person watching Netflix on the couch and rooting for the "bad guy" doesn't have these scars.

I never took a dime of money that didn't belong to me. Truthfully, it had less to do with my oath to office than in my personal moral fiber. I fled a communist dictator who was doing exactly that to my family and their friends in Cuba; it is beyond me how any Cuban who watched Fidel swallow up all the land and personal assets from good, hardworking people could steal from people here. We were given asylum here, and in return we rip off the people who saved our lives? I never got it.

My old friend Bobby was not the kid I knew in the Lords. Yeah, he was always a step behind on the job and who knows how far he would've gotten on his own if I hadn't dragged him along with me on all those assignments, but I didn't peg him as a thief. When he and the other guys in his division were brought down, it drove home how wrong he was for this job. Maybe his going to sleep in the backseat of the car while we looked for the stolen load of liquor should've been an indication. But it didn't signal a criminal to me. Just, well, Bobby. And I can't forgive him. His betrayal of the job and the spirit of the Cuban refugee was more indictable to me than even the greed of a gangster.

—

Not too long ago I got a very unexpected direct message. Juan Cid reached out and asked to speak with me, "father to father."

I was really surprised. It had been decades since I'd seen him, and he really put me through the ringer with his asshole attorney Doug Williams. I didn't unload everything that came to my mind at that moment into Facebook Messenger; I don't know where I would've even started. This guy's campaign against me was a big part of my professional undoing, with his phone call set-up with Nancy. He and Williams were relentless. But something was different about this interaction—I could sense something honest, maybe even conciliatory.

I know you and I have had some problems in the past, he wrote.

No shit.

But I need your help. I'd like to hire you.

I told him I'd meet him as Raul Diaz, the father. We agreed to meet in my office and in a couple of days we were sitting across from each other. In minutes, I realized I was sitting across from a grieving parent.

His son Johnny was found dead, overdosed in a room at the Estancia Hotel, which was one of those places where pimps would rent rooms by the hour. Juan had been through a long road with his only boy's addiction over the years, but he felt there was more to this. Johnny had fallen in love with a prostitute who confided to Juan that the kid had fallen out with her pimp, who then had one of the girls give Johnny a hot dose one night when they were partying.

"I want you to find that guy," Juan told me.

It would've been relatively simple, given all my connections. I let that topic sit for a minute and instead connected with him about life and family. Finally, we got to Nancy and Doug Williams. Juan copped to engineering it all— not the Cuban government, not Williams's client Aguedo Borrego. Juan set up the whole thing with Nancy and fed all the other bullshit to Williams, who in turn gave it all to McGee for print.

Oddly, through my anger, I was lucid enough not to be mad at Juan. He was a delinquent, a criminal bent on stopping me from rolling over him. I can forgive him because he was not part of my world. He was on the other side of that line. By default, the universe had positioned us both across from each other on the chess board. What should I have expected?

Williams, however, should've known better. Defending these guys was one thing, but his using his client's fabricated traps to professionally smear me was quite another.

In the matter of Juan's son, I didn't know what to do. My handing this case over to law enforcement wouldn't have yielded anything. Any tidbits of value they would've gotten was entirely circumstantial, and any first-hand testimony would've come from unreliable sources, to say the least, given the circles Johnny was running in. I'm also sure they would've run the kid in the system, seen who his father was, and deemed this as payback for Juan's misdeeds. How hard would they have worked it?

I also didn't want to give the information I would've uncovered to him directly. He was so distraught I'm certain he would've gone to the streets and had this handled himself. That would have made his awful situation even worse. I gave Juan some bits of info, but nothing that would've pointed him directly to the pimp. In the end, I think I saved someone who'd done me great harm from doing any to himself.

—

When my brother Miguel passed, I was left with quite a mess to sort out. He was gone so quickly after being diagnosed that he couldn't wrap up his affairs as he likely would have if he was given more time. I had to deal with the trust for my nephew, his inheritance, the estate, and my brother's manufacturing business. It was all in disarray and I was the trustee appointed by the state, so I was everything.

Sorting through his affairs was more complicated because his business, ASI, was left in the hands of his ex-wife. After I deemed the financial management of the business was being handled less than responsibly, to be polite, I stepped in and took that over as well. That was located in Lake Wales, which was not a short drive from Miami. I was spending two weeks there, then returning to Miami to run ICDA and the youth organization, then going back to Lake Wales. I couldn't manage all the moving parts in my life, which is what finally forced me to leave the All-Stars foundation.

My alcoholism still wasn't on my radar. While on the job, I was too distracted dodging bullets and hunting the madmen of Miami. For the next two decades, I was building ICDA and the youth foundation, going full force and staying very busy. I was a very functional alcoholic, but when I look back now it's pretty embarrassing that I wasn't more aware of how much damage I was doing. And as is always the case with that vice, my productivity eventually began to wane dramatically, and everything in my life began to slide with it.

ICDA had a very big insurance client for whom we did a lot of worker's comp investigations. We were missing deadlines and the cases were accumulating, so finally my client called and asked to talk with me. I drove to Lakeland and promised I'd be able to turn things around if they gave me another chance. I explained how I'd become inundated since my brother's passing and my taking over his company. I explained that I had the All Stars too, and I uttered something I hadn't ever said before.

"Also, my drinking has become a serious problem."

—

TANI: The drinking when my uncle passed away hit rock bottom. That was really bad. He always had a drink in his hand, but never was he ever belligerent, acting out, all loud or crazy. I grew up in Miami. We see a lot of drunk people, you know? And he never acted that way. He was never embarrassing.

ELLY: He was such a functional person when I married him. Maybe I was in denial, but I couldn't see that he was an alcoholic. I didn't see that. He was fun. Yeah, he drank, but I didn't look at him as an alcoholic at first.

The company went down because he wasn't functioning anymore, because of the alcohol. He was so detached that one day I got to the bank and the IRS had taken everything, and I didn't know it. I was like, "What is going on?" And he didn't know either. So, it was like, crazy. It was bad. And in the end, we lost practically everything. The only thing we had was our home, thank God, because that's our retirement right there.

It became unbearable. I want to say it was twenty years down the line that he couldn't tolerate it as he used to. He would get home pissed off and I spent hours waiting. I'd have his dinner ready and if it was salty, he would go into a tirade at two o'clock in the morning. It was just unfair. And that's when I gave him an ultimatum. I said, "That's it. I feel like I'm enabling you, so I don't want be part of this. I love you very much, but I can't do this anymore."

I left for a work conference and told him when I got back, I was going to take all my stuff and go to my mom's house. But when I got back, everybody called me and said he stopped drinking.

He changed again. I mean, he really stopped drinking. It slowed him down, I have to say. It made him a little less fun—he was always the life of the party and then without it, I guess he didn't feel comfortable socializing and stuff. He was more introverted, but of course he'd made such a big change. It's actually like almost a miracle.

Something must have happened to him. You know, maybe not exactly when I gave him the ultimatum, but something happened to him that made him decide to do this. This is something you do for yourself. This is not something you do for anybody. I don't care if it's your wife or if it's your daughter—you have to wanna do it for *you*. Something must have happened to him, you know? That's the way I see it—this had nothing to do with me.

TANI: Elly called me and she's like, "Hey, I'm leaving your dad." I was like, well, that's gonna fucking suck. I was in Miami, so I went to go see my dad and I was like, "Hey, what's up? Elly says she's leaving you." He admitted that he did have a drinking problem and he was gonna seek help, but at first he was like, "I don't think I'm gonna do this." And I remember being very honest with my father and, it was probably not the right thing to say to an alcoholic, but I was so exhausted.

I told my dad, "Hey, you need to stop drinking. How many times have you pulled people over that were drunk? How many people have you seen being killed by someone who drank? That person did not wake up that morning and say, 'Hey, I'm gonna drink and kill someone.' That was not their plan."

And I told my dad, "I love you with all my heart, but I will not visit you in jail if you kill someone."

I remember him just looking at me. He was smoking a cigarette, and he's like, "Excuse me?"

He was really shocked that I said that.

—

I'd been focused on murderers, kidnappers, and smugglers for so many years that I'd largely ignored the villain that outlasted them all. Now that I was semi-retired, it was time to stare a lingering nemesis in the eye at the urging of my oldest daughter as well as Elly, who had said, "If you don't stop drinking, I'm leaving you."

I'd gotten up to consuming an entire bottle of Johnny Walker Black a night since my brother Miguel's passing. I knew in my heart they were right, so on August 20, 2012, after Elly left for a weekend conference, I was sitting alone in the backyard when I swallowed my last gulp of alcohol and looked up.

"God, I'm in your hands now."

I haven't had a drink since.

—

TANI: I remember calling my dad and he's like, "It's been two days that I haven't had a drink." And "It's been three days." "It's been a week." "It's been two weeks." So slowly he just stopped drinking. He did it.

He had talked to a whole bunch of people when he was thinking about going to rehab, but my dad's like, "I ain't doing any of that shit. That's crazy." But he was thinking he might need it; he was scared of the withdrawals because he was always drinking.

And I remember my mother was the only person who said, "Tani, when your father puts his mind to it, he can do anything. If your father says he's going to stop drinking, your father will stop drinking."

I didn't believe it. His own mother didn't believe it. My sister, his wife, didn't believe it. My mother was the only person who truly believed that my father, when he was determined [to do] something, was gonna follow through. And he did.

—

My insurance client was receptive to my asking for time to right the ship, thank God. We'd been working together for twenty-five years, and I have no doubt our history kept them with me. They knew how reliable I had once been, and they trusted I'd return to form.

I now know that cold turkey was a very dangerous way to kick booze, and my doctor was pissed at me when I told him I'd done it that way. I assured him I felt fine, just had a bit of a headache that first day. I didn't bother to mention to him that my guardian angel had some experience working overtime for me and had performed some miraculous feats before. Doc would've thought I was nuts. But it wasn't lost on me that my most important apprehension, locking up the perp in the bottle that would've eventually done me in, was made with that invisible partner who'd ridden beside me for my entire life.

—

TANI: He called me, I wanna say it was maybe a year or a year and a half after that. It was funny because he called me like four or five times in a row.

"Hey, Tani."

"Hey, dad."

"Hey, listen…um…" and it was just like stupid little things.

"Okay, dad, I'll talk to you later." He called me right back.

"Hey, I need to tell you—"

"Okay, dad, I'll talk to you later. Bye."

Called me right back and I was like, "For the love of God, dad, what is your freaking problem?" He's never done that, ever. He called me like four times in a row.

He's like, "I just want to thank you for sitting down with me and telling me how you felt that day you told me you wouldn't visit me in jail."

"Well, I felt that way, dad. I *hated* that I felt that way."

"I know."

And I was like, "I love you."

It's like little moments like that.

—

Most of the media outlets in which I've appeared have gotten things right. Sometimes they don't and that's usually the result of producers or writers not doing enough due diligence. As I've told here, there are some unflattering and incomplete telling of events in my career, and if someone relies on those alone they'll get it wrong. I've always spoken with anyone from the media regarding my time in law enforcement, and when those things come up, I'm happy to give the full story, just like I've done here.

The project I'm most asked about is the documentary *Cocaine Cowboys*. Producers Billy Corben and Alfred Spellman took the time to investigate everything in the show and put as many of the players on camera as they could. I was glad they got me to tell my part of the story myself, and I think they used me well in the film. It became very popular on the streaming channels and even had a reboot made years after release with new footage.

I was portrayed by actor Gabriel Sloyer in the Netflix series *Griselda*, which strayed from actual events a little. The actor did a fine job, but I wasn't happy with the production's portrayal of Griselda Blanco depositing a bunch of money in my bank account. That bothered me a lot because it just never happened, and while TV shows reserve the right to dramatize reality, this was a detail that was entirely fabricated. People come up to me now and say, "Hey, how much did Griselda put in there?" They're disappointed when I tell them *nada*.

Outside of their treatment of me, I found some of their creative enhancement silly. There was a scene where Griselda hosts a massive, uplifting pep rally at her house with all the Marielitos. Anyone who knew the Colombians and their relationship with the crazy Cuban criminals at that time in that business knows this is laughable.

They also placed June Hawkins's character with mine in the shootout with Amilcar, which also wasn't the case. She was likely in one of the cars that day, but she was our criminal analyst. We wouldn't have thrown her in the line of fire, but the producers obviously felt it necessary for their storyline. June and her husband Al "Blade" Singleton both consulted on the project, but in the end, Hollywood is the storyteller. "Based on a true story" definitely means *based* on a true story.

There have been a few books whose authors took the requisite time to talk with me and get their stuff straight. *The Cocaine Wars* (W. W. Norton & Company, 1988) had fair coverage of my role in Miami courtesy of author Paul Eddy who interviewed me for it. Roben Farzad's *Hotel Scarface* (Berkley, 2018), which profiled the growth of the Miami coke business through the lens of Coconut Grove's swanky Mutiny Club, also spent a lot of time talking with me about the information he was uncovering. More recently,

Monkey Morales (Post Hill Press, 2025), the biography of my informant and consistent source of migraines, stayed accurate due to my co-author Sean and Morales's son Rick Jr. doing diligent research and consulting me often. Those are the portrayals of me that stayed most true.

—

Back in 2011 and 2012 when I was driving back and forth to Lake Wales to handle business at ASI, I ended up renting a house. A retired officer named Frank Tootle who'd actually trained me in Miami Beach in 1968 and later came to work for me at ICDA had recently passed. He and his wife lived in Lake Wales and she moved when he died and kept the house vacant for a long while. She was paying HOA fees and taxes with nothing in return, so I offered to rent it from her. She charged me $800 a month, and I had a fully-furnished place to crash when I was away handling my brother's business.

It was big, right on a nice lake, and the best part was I was only ten minutes from my eldest daughter and her children. Elly would come up with me and we'd make mini getaways out of it. It was a little weird that Frank's widow left his ashes in an urn in the closet, but I made it a point to say "good morning" and "goodbye" to Frankie when I came and went.

As the years went on and the house remained unsold, it only became a matter of common sense. Frank's widow presented us an offer for a song and a dance, and we grabbed it. I'm a fisherman and would've preferred buying something closer to the ocean, like Naples or Sarasota. But being so close to the grandkids was an offer we couldn't refuse. I could deal with lake fishing as opposed to deep sea fishing in exchange for that.

A couple of years ago, we sold the Miami place and moved everything up here. It wasn't entirely like landing on another planet, it's only three hours north, but in so many ways it was like another universe. Everything I packed, personal and professional, was tied to Miami. I was cutting a fat umbilical cord, and I'm not sure I ever really believed I would.

—

TANI: I remember him telling me, "There's a book, *Cocaine Wars*, and I'm in it." I must have been in middle school, but I didn't understand [what he did]. In middle school I didn't understand it. High school, I didn't.

But then when the *Cocaine Cowboys* came out, I was like, "Oh, that's cool." And then when people started talking about it here in Polk County, someone would mention it and they'd be like, "Have you seen the documentary *Cocaine Cowboys*?" I'm like, "Oh yeah, my dad's in it—Raul Diaz." And they're like, "Oh shit!" And I'm like, "What, dude? The guy's not *that* freaking cool. He's cool, but…I don't know."

TATI: Funny story—I was in middle school, like thirteen or fourteen, and I was with my mom at my grandmother's house, for whatever reason, she was helping them with something. And my step-grandfather had the old book *The Cocaine Wars*. And I'm like, I know my dad is in that book. So I started reading just his chapters and I'm like, "Oh." So, I guess that's when I kind of found out [about his past]. I knew he owned a private investigation company, and he had all these pictures all over the wall in his office. But I never knew like the extent of what he did.

I think it's just still Dad. When people saw *Griselda*, like they reached out to me and they're like, "Oh my God, that's your dad?" And I'm like, "Yeah. All right."

But I wouldn't have ever thought my dad would leave Miami.

ELLY: We couldn't live in Miami with his retirement and my retirement. Everything in Miami is so expensive—no way. So, I said, "You know what, I'm outta here. I don't like this place anymore." It's not where I was born. I just don't like it anymore. I guess it was part of everything that happened. I mean, we almost lost it all.

I don't even want to go back there. I haven't been back since I retired. I have nothing there, even my sisters, who ask when I'm coming. I say, "No. You guys want to see me? You come up. If not, it's going to be Zoom or FaceTime. I'm not going down there." It was traumatic for me. Everything that happened at the end. I don't want anything to do with it.

—

And on that moving day, my divorce with Magic City was finalized. I drove out of Miami without a home there for the first time in over sixty-three years. God, how many ghosts were watching me leave?

Well, they can take some solace in the fact that parts of them all still live inside me—their misdeeds, their humor, their stupidity, their brilliance, their wasted potential, their danger, their excitement. The amount of drugs my eyes have seen in that city is staggering; its total value could rival a country's national budget. I swam in the hottest waters of Miami, those inhabited by terrorists and nationalists. I sifted through the detritus of their conflicted passions, strewn across the ground in burnt, exploded fragments, their violence brought about by my homeland.

Miami was also where I stared into the vacant eyes of innocents lying on the ground, killed for no other reason than who they were with or where they'd unwittingly walked. I'd taken an oath to put on a badge and protect them specifically, and on my watch the city became the most dangerous place on earth. Emilio Milian, blown to smithereens, would be the first to concur.

"This is your fault."

Maybe so, my friend. Maybe so.

Miami's newsprint had spelled words that were a great disservice to me. That part of the city had betrayed me like an unfaithful woman, but it further made me part of its fabric, intertwining me in the culture of one of the biggest cities in this country. I'm in it, it's in me.

I am also equally aware that Miami was part of my successes. My proactive team prevented crime, the amount of which we'll never know. Newspapers can't report what *didn't* happen.

Miami is also the younger officers who learned from me, who taught officers below them after I was gone. Multiply the lives they've saved, the narcotics they've seized, the cases they've closed, and there's some sort of legacy there. I humbly accept that too.

Parts of Miami may have betrayed me, but she also excited me. She was beautiful and dangerous. She made me feel a million feet tall, and also broke me down. I fought for her. I suffered for her. She showed me the best in both of us, and the absolute worst.

That was Miami. I miss her.

PHOTOS

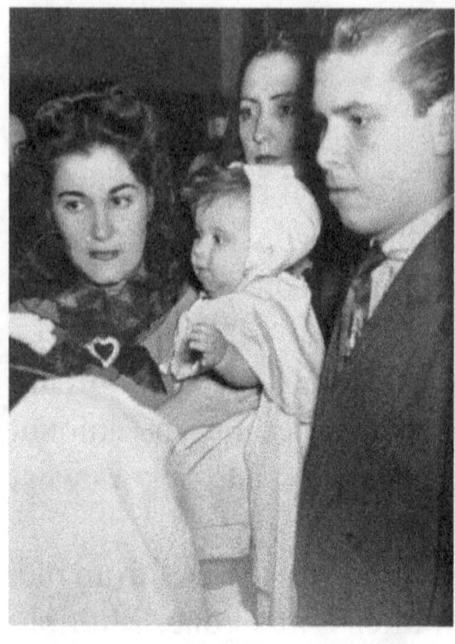

My baptism with Tia Lala and my cousin, Godfather Carlos Sanchez.

(Raul Diaz Personal Collection)

In Cuba, we got around however we could.

(Raul Diaz Personal Collection)

My parents with me and my brother Miguel.

(Raul Diaz Personal Collection)

My first collar—a barracuda, my first saltwater catch in the US.

(Raul Diaz Personal Collection)

Miguel, the star athlete.

(Raul Diaz Personal Collection)

Me and Alex "Titi" Cachaldor. The Lords was actually founded in his basement.

(Raul Diaz Personal Collection)

My father in law, Musculito, and my dad.

(Raul Diaz Personal Collection)

Mi familia.

(Raul Diaz Personal Collection)

Nothing beats the pride on my parents' faces at my graduation from the academy, 5-28-71.

(Raul Diaz Personal Collection)

The South Region VIN Unit.

(Raul Diaz Personal Collection)

Ronnie's Lounge, a home away from home for many cops, unfortunately for the wives.

(Raul Diaz Personal Collection)

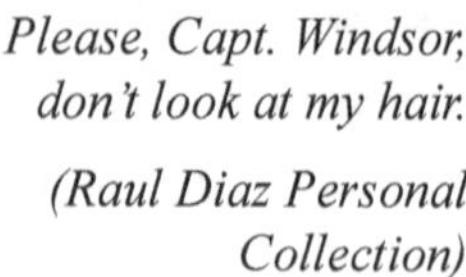

Please, Capt. Windsor, don't look at my hair.

(Raul Diaz Personal Collection)

The Rudy Rodriguez bust. Ever see $913,000 in cash?

(Raul Diaz Personal Collection)

Explaining my plan for CENTAC-26 to reporter Mark Potter.

(Miami Dade College's Wolfson Archives)

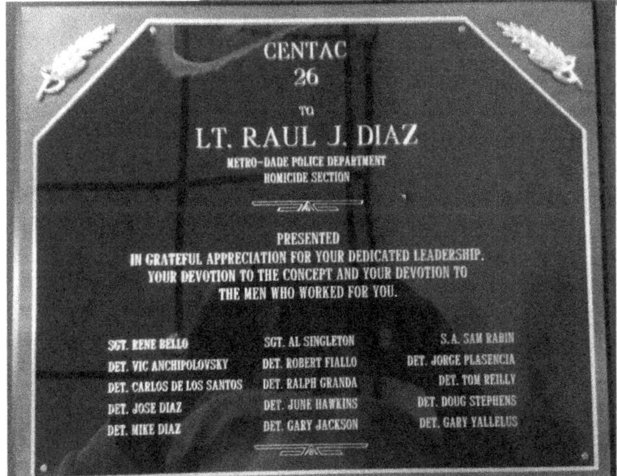

The accolades wouldn't come without a significant toll.

(Raul Diaz Personal Collection)

Planning a raid with my unit.

(Miami Dade College's Wolfson Archives)

My secret weapon, June Hawkins, and her ever-present files on every bad guy in Miami.

(Miami Dade College's Wolfson Archives)

The War Wagon that changed the face of the Cocaine Wars.

(Miami Dade College's Wolfson Archives)

Sitting on the grass and getting some sun. Six tons of grass, to be exact.

(Raul Diaz Personal Collection)

The Dadeland Massacre was a harbinger of things to come.

(Miami Dade College's Wolfson Archives)

Cozzoli's Pizza was the worst place to get a slice on 8/4/81.

(Miami Dade College's Wolfson Archives)

A young Griselda Blanco; not the last woman to turn my life upside down.

(Miami Dade College's Wolfson Archives)

It would be years before anyone learned how many people Rivi Ayala killed for Griselda.

(Raul Diaz Metro Dade files)

*Ricardo "Monkey" Morales
no doubt thinking about
creating some chaos.*
(Morales Family Collection)

*Rafael Leon Rodriguez, Amilcar,
CENTAC-26's Public Enemy #1.*
*(Miami Dade College's
Wolfson Archives)*

Paco Sepulveda, not Miss America
(Miami Dade College's Wolfson Archives)

Blade and Me, and an age old debate.
(Raul Diaz Personal Collection)

Me and Miguel, nearing sunset.
(Raul Diaz Personal Collection)

Tani and Tati—my rocks.
(Raul Diaz Personal Collection)

ACKNOWLEDGEMENTS

RAUL: Thanks to my parents for having the courage to send me and my brother to this country without any assurance that we'd meet again; my brother Miguel for being my best friend till the day he died; my Uncle Jose Miguel Couce, my aunt, Eulalia "Lala" Couce and our cousins Jose and Mayra for taking us into their home when we arrived in the US. Carlos Capote, our foster brother, for becoming our real brother.

Thanks to Coach Tarzi Kouchalakas for his counsel; all our Jewish friends in Miami Beach for offering Miguel and me their friendship, all of whom remain my friends to this date; the "Lords" for electing me to my first leadership role and remaining my brothers for life.

Thanks to Jim Kelly, Don Hasley and Freddy Wooldridge in Miami Beach PD, for the "baby steps," and to Ronnie Leonard for allowing me to make a home-away-from-home out of Ronnie's Lounge; Wayne Abernathy, Bill Powers, Julius Jackson, Tommy Dunn, and the rest of the guys in Central District for teaching me what police work was really about; Terry Polcyn, Vince Oller, Avelino Fernandez, Jack DeRemer, Bob McGavock, Jack Appleget, Dave Green, for helping me through my years in OCB; my Jewish brother, Jerry Ruddoff, and our black brother Harry Crenshaw, RIP, for their support and protection; Rene Bello, Eddie

Mederos, Iggy Vazquez and Humberto Rapado, for being great partners in OCB.

Thanks to Robert "Bob" C. Windsor for trusting me with his VIN Unit and CENTAC-26, for his support and guidance, and most of all for his friendship; all the guys in SW VIN, Timmy Redmond, Del Woodburn, Linnie Garland, Gary Yallelus, Freddy Cockreham, Marcia Reeves, and Ellen Demaso for helping us earn the Unit Commendation Award.

Thanks to Donald Matthews and Marshall Frank for their support in Homicide, along with Dave Rivers, Art Felton (RIP), Doug Buttshaw (RIP), Frank Wesoloski and all the other sergeants in Homicide.

Very special thanks to all the members of CENTAC-26: ASA Sam Rabin, ASA Michael Band, AUSA Neil Taylor, Sgt. Rene Bello, Sgt. Al Singleton, SA Jim Chambliss FDLE, Det. Gary Yallelus, Det. Vic Anchipolovsky (HPD), Det. Tim Davis, Det. Jose Diaz, Det. Mike Diaz (RIP), Det. Robert Fiallo, Det. Ralph Granda, Det. June Hawkins, Det. Gary Jackson (MPD), Det. Hector Martinez (MPD), Det. Jorge Plasencia, Det. Tom Reilly, and Det. Doug Stephens.

Thanks to Tommy Dazevedo and Juan Cayado for taking me in as a partner in ICDA Investigations and teaching me that there was a good life after the Department.

Big thanks to Joe Diaz for 20 years of partnership and friendship and huge thanks to Rebeca Ruiz for her dedication to ICDA and me; she was ICDA for many years.

Thank you to *Cocaine Cowboys* filmmakers Alfred Spellman, Billy Corben, and David Cypkin, and *Hotel Scarface* author Roben Farzad for treating me fairly in their reporting of me for their projects.

A very special thank you to my co-author, Sean Oliver, who took a chance on me with this book and without whose help and guidance I could never have been able to complete this project.

Thank you, Tani and Tati, for your unconditional love in times when I might not have been most deserving. Thania, thank you for hanging in there as long as one can reasonably expect a partner to, and for our wonderful girls. And Elly, thank you for your love, care, and patience through our many years together.

SEAN: My arrest count currently sits at zero, though I'm fortunate to have patrolled the streets of Miami for the past year by telling Lt. Diaz's story. It was a much more comfortable tour doing it from the couch.

I first reached out to Raul in 2020—six years ago as of this writing—when I needed info for the book *Monkey Morales*. He was as helpful as a cop could be working with some Gringo he didn't even know, which is to say *guarded* and *cautious*. He looked at my writing and reported an incorrect spelling of Colombia (I still blame autocorrect) and said he didn't need to read what I wrote because he lived it. And that was that.

Then something happened as we spoke more recently when I was really dug into *Monkey Morales*. Maybe he saw the level of commitment I had after six years of research, or maybe he was just satisfied I was "Cuban-broken" enough, having grown up in West New York, NJ, a former Cuban immigrant stronghold of the 70s. My love for *ropa vieja* and *papa rellena* must've convinced him. Either way, he read *Monkey Morales* and asked me to bring his story to life. I agreed immediately, though I should've made him hold out more. So, thank you, Raul. It's easy to tell stories when the subject matter is so resonant. *Abrazos*, amigo.

Thank you, Michael, Elijah, and everyone at Wild Blue Press for allowing us into your home with this story. It has been a pleasure. Thank you to editors Tanya and Audrey who already know the big secret—writers are as only good as their editors. So, if you loved this book, then you love both of those ladies as much as I do for their work.

Thank you, Thania, Tani, Tati, and Elly for allowing me into your personal lives and sharing your feelings with me. The personal side of this story, away from the bullets and blood, made it what I wanted it to be. June and "Blade" were beside Raul for an important part of his journey and their openness with me regarding that time in their careers is greatly appreciated. Mark Potter's trip down memory lane to write the foreword might've caused some PTSD, so for that I apologize and thank you greatly.

I live in a home with three other artists, and when artists love you, it makes your work and life richer. My wife Nicole has been my partner in all things creative for a quarter century and Mia and Lana have been under that learning tree for their entire lives. Screw math. This is the path. But they already know that.

For More News About Raul J. Diaz and Sean Oliver, Signup For Our Newsletter:

http://wbp.bz/newsletter

Word-of-mouth is critical to an author's long-term success. If you appreciated this book please leave a review on the Amazon sales page:

http://wbp.bz/killingthelieutenantr

ALSO PUBLISHED BY WILDBLUE PRESS

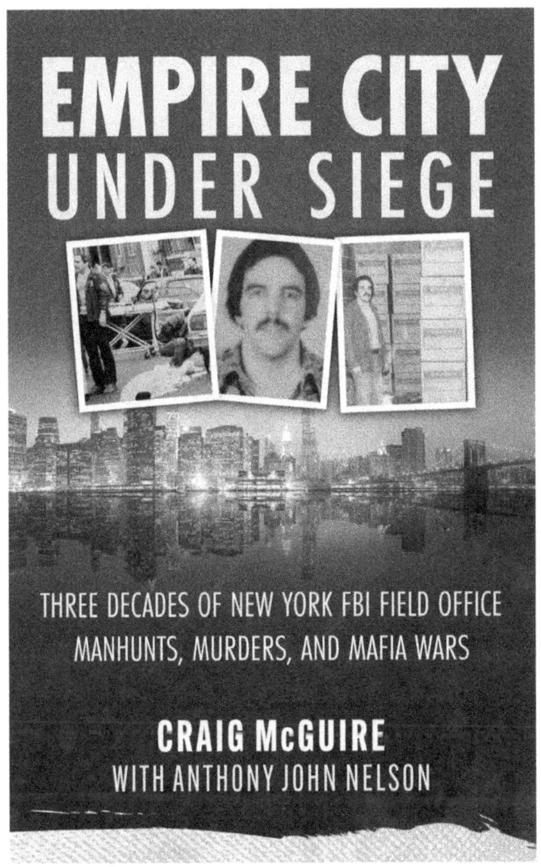

EMPIRE CITY UNDER SIEGE

https://wbp.bz/empirecity

ALSO PUBLISHED BY WILDBLUE PRESS

ALSO PUBLISHED BY WILDBLUE PRESS

THE REAL MR. BIG

https://wbp.bz/realmrbiga

ALSO PUBLISHED BY WILDBLUE PRESS

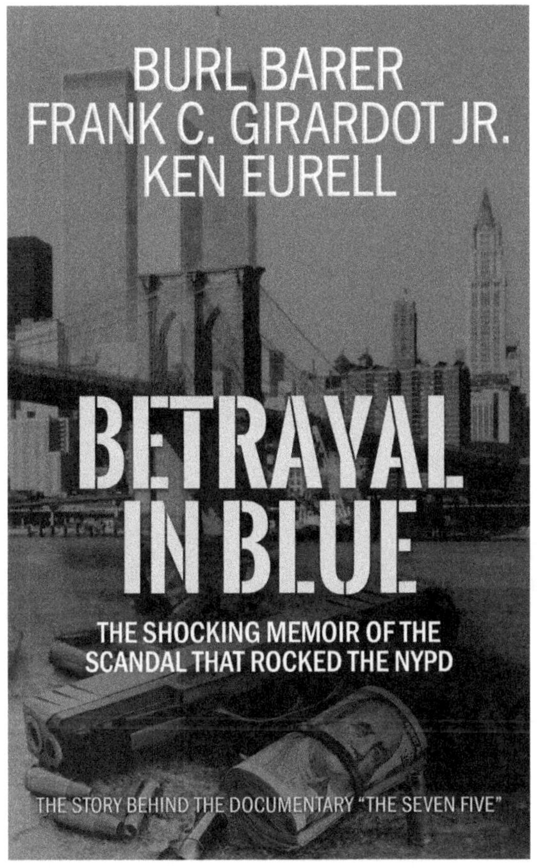

BETRAYAL IN BLUE

https://wbp.bz/biba

www.ingramcontent.com/pod-product-compliance
Lightning Source LLC
Chambersburg PA
CBHW051502030726
47592CB00006B/2065